WOMEN IN CHARGE

WOMEN
IN CHARGE

Dilemmas of Women
in Authority

Aileen Jacobson

105468

VNR VAN NOSTRAND REINHOLD COMPANY
New York

Printed in the United States of America
Designed by Sharen DuGoff Egana

Published by Van Nostrand Reinhold Company Inc.
115 Fifth Avenue
New York, New York 10003

Van Nostrand Reinhold Company Limited
Molly Millars Lane
Wokingham, Berkshire RG11 2PY, England

Van Nostrand Reinhold
480 La Trobe Street
Melbourne, Victoria 3000, Australia

Macmillan of Canada
Division of Canada Publishing Corporation
164 Commander Boulevard
Agincourt, Ontario M1S 3C7, Canada

16 15 14 13 12 11 10 9 8 7 6 5 4 3 2

*Acknowledgments of permission to reprint extracts
from published works will be found on pp. 227–229.*

Library of Congress Cataloging in Publication Data

Jacobson, Aileen.
  Women in charge.

  Bibliography: p.
  Includes index.
  1. Women executives.   I. Title.
HD38.2.J33   1985   658.4′09′088042   84–19584
ISBN 0–442–24587–4

Contents

Introduction

Boss Lady. I chuckled inwardly, thinking it would be a catchy title for a book about women as authority figures. But why did it seem so ludicrous?

The phrase conjured images of a woman on horseback, ordering around the tough cowboys on a ranch she had inherited from her husband, or of a woman in a hard hat, shouting instructions to burly construction workers, or even of a woman executive in a man-tailored suit, smoking a small cigar and heading a board meeting of men smoking larger cigars.

After all these years of heightened consciousness, liberated striving, and open mindedness about women on the job, *boss lady* still seems a contradiction in terms. A lady is not a boss. And no one would think to specify *gentleman* or *man* or *male* when mentioning the word *boss,* because after all, aren't all bosses men?

And so we continue to hear references to female managers, female bosses, and female executives, because the underlying, unconscious assumption is that the natural fulfillers of these roles are still men. Women are, even today, not immediately and naturally thought of as appropriate people to become bosses. And women are just as likely as men to harbor this unconscious prejudice.

The problem is complicated, and more than a matter of semantics. Women are not trained to think of themselves as bosses, nor are they usually conditioned, from childhood onward, to develop the skills and attitudes that are needed to become an effective boss—a woman in charge.

In these days of upward mobility for women, even the woman who never dreamed she would have to develop management skills is discovering that she will need them as she moves up the career ladder. The woman who enters a large corporation with an M.B.A. or other business degree usually expects to become a manager; that is the aim of a business career. But the woman who becomes a nurse, a doctor, a lawyer, an editor, a journalist, a teacher, a factory worker, or a secretary rarely thinks that she will ever need managerial skills.

Many of these women are finding, however, that as they enter their thirties and forties and the main growth stages of their careers, they are seeking or unexpectedly being thrust into managerial positions. They are becoming nursing supervisors or factory superintendents. They are becoming heads of professional offices. They may have a secretary. They may supervise younger workers. They may have to hire and fire.

Men usually slide into these roles with many fewer problems than women. Somehow, they find that they have always anticipated being in such positions and discover they already have many of the tools necessary to handle them. For women, these roles often come as a complete surprise, a result they had not bargained for, had not prepared for—even when they had been bold enough to enter the labor field on a footing they hoped would be equal to that of men. Especially for the woman who has worked her way up from a menial job—the type that men are rarely required to take—the role of ordering someone else to do a task she knows firsthand to be boring or degrading can be uncomfortable.

I was once responsible for leading a team of reporters and found myself experiencing some of these doubts. I was required to divide the coverage of our beat among members of the team. I also needed to collect from them their schedules for the following week, which I then was to combine into a lengthy note to be sent to editors. Not too difficult, really. But why did I sometimes feel that a nagging edge crept into my voice when I reminded the team members of their responsibilities? And why, when some did not fulfill their duties, did I try to cover up for them? Why was I lenient when some were late with their schedules, even when it meant *I* had to stay late? Worst of all, why did I giggle helplessly when one of my team members referred to me jokingly as the "beat matron"?

Clearly, I was afraid of becoming a boss lady. I did not want to be thought of as a nag or a harsh schoolmistress. I tried joking when I should have been serious. Above all, I feared being labeled with those female stereotypes I abhor. Is there such a thing as a *male* nag or a *male* shrew? No. There are male bosses who are hated but respected. There are kind bosses and ineffectual bosses who are men. But a nagging boss? A scatterbrained boss? A boss with a heart of gold? That boss is likely to be female.

Being in charge is more than a matter of title. It requires a stock of tools and a range of attitudes that do not always come as easily to women as to men—although they can be acquired.

This book aims to describe the problems that women have as authority figures, and by examining the histories of women who have had greater or lesser success in dealing with their own circumstances, offers suggestions for solving some of those problems. Those who have had to struggle more than they wished may be able to offer the reader as much as those who succeeded more easily. Hindsight is a great teacher.

I sought women from a wide variety of fields—including teaching, nursing, the creative arts—many of whom have devised innovative ways to integrate their special qualities as women with the demands of being a person in authority. Many have had to find a balance between work and family that is never required of men. This book is not aimed solely at the management woman in a large corporation. It is for all women, and includes views of professional management consultants, psychologists, and other experts with special insights into women's roles. I do not expect to supply a final answer to the question of how women can become good bosses and become comfortable with authority. But I do believe that the following pages provide guideposts to help women increase their competence and confidence when they are in charge.

1
Women and Authority: Why Women Have Difficulties

You are attending a meeting, and everyone ignores you. You bend over at the water fountain, and someone slaps your behind. You do a great job on your latest project, but your boss does not come by to congratulate you or offer to buy you a drink. You are walking down the hall of the corporation that has just made you a vice president, and a new executive asks you to bring him coffee. And the next morning, the babysitter does not show up.

You may think that these are your individual problems, but they are not. They are the dilemmas that many women in positions of authority now face. Some have found solutions, but most are still working on it. The women's movement has made significant inroads in the past ten years, but it has not been able to alter some basic patterns in our society, which perhaps may never fundamentally change. These patterns emerge from the quite different ways boys and girls are raised, influenced by different expectations from their parents, teachers, and peers about such matters as how fiercely they will compete, how readily they may cry or show their emotions, and even how loudly they may raise their voices.

These early childhood expectations—some of which may be related to biology and some to our culture—have profound effects on how women handle authority later in life. Their management skills, their attitudes toward power, and their whole approach to career planning are bound to be different from men's. Not only do others—supervisors, supervisees, and co-workers—treat women differently from men, women often treat themselves differently.

Sometimes these differences can be to a woman's advantage. If, for example, she is more likely to take her family life into account when planning a career, that may well make her a happier person in the long run. If, in turn, she is more likely to take a sympathetic team approach to management, she may well end up as a more effective boss than a man who has been conditioned to be rigid and power-hungry. But in many cases, the different ways a woman might approach the realm of authority will lead to problems in the workplace, and for that reason this chapter will be devoted to examining some of the dilemmas that women in charge often face. Although many of the topics will be highlighted in subsequent chapters, I will concentrate here on a broad overview of the difficulties experts have isolated and, in researching this book, I have observed.

The Aggression Image

Joelyn Iannone had prepared herself carefully for the meeting with the architects. The career education and training department that she heads at Grumman Aerospace was to move into a new building. She had brought along floor plans, lists of requirements—and a co-worker, a man. The architects directed all their questions to him.

"He didn't redirect the questions to me. He answered them," says Iannone, explaining that people had been introduced at the meeting by name but not by title. The same thing was happening to another female colleague at the meeting—except that her male co-worker was sometimes answering incorrectly. "I decided to jump in," Iannone relates now, recalling her thoughts just before she acted. "What you had to do was assert yourself, but you weren't coming across assertively, you were coming across aggressively. They were reading it that way. But you had to do it, you had to do it. There was misinformation being given out."

A man would never have had to face the dilemma of what to do, Iannone says; had he spoken up, he would have been seen as "adding to the information," not as aggressively butting in. "It was as though I didn't exist. So I sat there thinking to myself, 'When do you jump in?' I didn't want anyone to be uncomfortable. I had to do it in a professional way. I said, 'Can I just say this for a minute? There are two classrooms on the floor plans here, and I'd like to explain why.' And then, as I talked more and more, they realized, Oh, dumb Dora isn't just sitting there, she does know something."

Iannone was careful not to say to her male co-worker—who seemed unaware of the dynamics of the situation—"Hey, if you don't mind, I'd like to do the talking."

"I think they got the message, but I had to be very careful to keep my cool, though I was feeling a lot of anger inside. That's what women have to go through. I don't believe men have to go through all that."

Iannone was right to tread so gingerly. Women's assertive styles are still often interpreted as being overly aggressive. "To take just one example," says psychiatrist and psychoanalyst Jean Baker Miller, now director of the Stone Center for Developmental Services and Studies at Wellesley College, "a woman trying to be herself, merely being direct, honest, or even just stating anything clearly, still runs the risk of being called 'a man.' "

A February 1979 *New York Times* article recorded the comments of female leaders on whether the woman who deviates from the genteel, passive image is in trouble. Most answered affirmatively.

"There has to be much more measurement of a woman's personality—suppression, to a certain extent," said Carol Bellamy, president of the New York City Council. Bellamy is a strong leader who does not suppress her personality too much, but then she is also seen as aggressive by some and perhaps could not be as successful politically outside rough-and-tumble New York.

Millicent Fenwick, former member of Congress from New Jersey, contributed one of the most useful comments to the *Times:* "Women haven't yet developed the habit of limited aggression, which men have perfected: the good-humored, effective ways they've developed with such skill." Women who do not want to copy men may still do well to observe successful men closely.

For their roles as wives and mothers, women have been conditioned to be "supportive, nurturing, low-visibility people, content to be relegated to the background," said the late Madeleine Gardner, who was director of women's programs at the Adelphi University School of Business Administration. In an oblique way, this results in many women at the workplace being perceived as "too bossy, lording it over other women"—and with some justice. "We're too focused on process, how to get things done. Instead, we should be seeking results." Women tend to stultify those who work for them: "By natural inclination, we gravitate to powerless staff positions—personnel, research and development, training—where we continue to be supportive, persuasive, in the background, and carrying no direct responsibility for the success or failure of the company.

"Consequently, we revert to the behavior of the powerless, which really knows no sex. It is often seen in men holding powerless positions as well. We jealously protect our territory, establish ourselves as indispensable on the job, and become rigid and authoritarian." This type of behavior, said Gardner, was noted by management consultant Rosabeth Moss Kanter, who adds that the behavior militates against promotions, for both men and women.

But learning to be appropriately assertive does not necessarily ensure promotion to top management, according to Anne Harlan and Carol L. Weiss, who conducted a 1981 study for the Wellesley College Center for Research on Women entitled *Moving Up: Women in Managerial Careers.* They found that middle managers often promoted older, less aggressive women who were minimally threatening to them. The young, aggressive female dynamos—the ones with a shot at promotion to higher levels—would never even be given a chance.

The view of an aggressive woman not being quite "right" is deeply ingrained in our society. In 1970, Dr. Inge K. Broverman and others asked seventy-nine psychotherapists to describe a healthy man, a healthy woman, and a healthy human being. Their study is now considered a classic. Broverman and her colleagues found that the healthy man was described as aggressive, adventurous, independent, and objective, among other qualities. The healthy woman, on the other hand, was described as submissive, dependent, shy, and emotional. The healthy adult, sex unspecified, came out with characteristics almost exactly like those of the healthy man. Forty-six men and thirty-three female therapists contributed to the study, and their answers did not vary by sex.

This view—which I suspect is still common among leaders in many fields—places the woman in a double bind. If she wants to be considered a healthy woman, she sacrifices her right to be a healthy human being. She must choose between the lady and the tiger in herself, and either choice can be deadly to her soul.

Such expectations must change, of course, if women are to be successful in the workplace. Most women would opt for the more positive traits ascribed to men, but it is important to remember that a little emotion and compassion, the "softer" traits traditionally ascribed to women, are good for both sexes. Most women do not want to become like the most rigid men in the business world; they would prefer to humanize the workplace.

The Missing Casual Pat on the Back

Michael Maccoby, in *The Gamesman,* his highly regarded 1976 book on the behavior of business executives, mentions in a footnote one of women's biggest problems as managers. (That he mentions it in a footnote—one of only three direct references to women managers in the book—is in itself a comment on the odds women face.) Maccoby's researchers found that young female engineers at a technical company were receiving low ratings from their supervisors, which of course would stymie their attempts to become managers. The reason, the researchers found, was that many of the women needed more encouragement from male supervisors in order to perform better and, consequently, receive higher ratings. But the men were overly shy about seeming too intimate with the young women. "They were unable to pat them on the back in the spontaneous, supportive way they did with the young men they managed, and this reserve also limited their ability to give needed criticism." The problem exists in reverse, too: female managers often find it difficult to bestow the casual pat on the backs of their male subordinates.

Sometimes, of course, the missing element is more substantial than a casual clap on the back; it can consist of the basic groundwork support that any competent manager needs in order to survive. Maccoby, who is a practicing psychoanalyst and director of the Harvard Program on Technology, Public Policy, and Human Development at the John F. Kennedy School of Government, discusses this problem in his 1981 book, *The Leader.* Here he profiles a female manager, one of six leaders chosen to be studied in detail. No longer does he deal with women in a footnote, and while that in itself constitutes some sort of progress, the case study reveals a different if familiar story. Its subject, Elsa Porter, an assistant secretary of commerce during the Carter administration, reports to Maccoby that she found total lack of support early in her career. In one early government job she held, as manager of public inquiries for the Agency for International Development (AID), in which she explained foreign aid to the public, the two men on her staff refused to work for a woman, and her boss did not back her up. She left for another job, at the Department of Health, Education, and Welfare, where she reports working for a man who would not speak to her. An old-fashioned, courtly gentleman, he blushed when she entered the room. Both these experiences angered her, and so she helped to found a network of women managers in government. Nevertheless, Porter reports, most men at the top are still afraid of women and unable to work with them as equals; they either patronize women or discriminate against them.

Psychologist Hannah Lerman of Los Angeles, cofounder of the Feminist Therapy Institute, a national group, explained to me her feelings about not being part of the "fraternity" that was giving support to fellow professionals. Until the early 1970s, she said, "I tried to act in a manner which seemed appropriate as a member of the psychological profession. Although I thought that my behavior successfully approximated the type of behavior I saw in fellow (I do mean male) psychologists, full recognition of my efforts and full acceptance into the professional fraternity was never quite forthcoming. It was only after I had stumbled onto the feminist viewpoint and began to understand its concepts that I truly comprehended my dilemma.

"Certainly, I had not previously understood that the profession was indeed a fraternity and that what I had been striving for was practically impossible. Like many other women in relation to so many other aspects of our society, I had been feeling that my failure to achieve peer equality and full professional recognition meant that there was something wrong with me and that the 'something' in this case was an incomplete understanding of what was expected of me."

Lerman recalls that as a graduate student, one of few women in her class, she repeatedly had to insist that she did not want to work exclusively with children when she got her degree. "I remember late-night drunken convention arguments with at least one professor about whether women should be trained as psychologists at all, with his argument being the one I've heard so many times since—that women would get married, have children, and [would] not pay the profession back by working for the training." In those days even Lerman herself did not realize to what extent she was a prisoner of traditional notions: "I remember ironing my husband's shirt prior to a party instead of studying, because he had to study."

Missing Criticism

In addition to support and reinforcement, many women also miss getting the kind of constructive criticism that can help a career. Some male supervisors avoid telling a female employee what is wrong so she can correct it, and in this way—often quite unconsciously—never give her an opportunity to progress. Such men may be acting out of some mistaken sense of chivalry or may be afraid the woman will react emotionally to criticism. More likely, they have difficulty communicating with women at all.

In their 1981 study, *Moving Up,* Carol L. Weiss and Anne Harlan found such a pattern in a group of one hundred male and female managers at two firms. Male executives tended to ignore a woman's mistakes, sometimes because they feared she would cry or would not be able to bounce back the way they expected a man would.

Hava Pell, a female rabbi with a small congregation in Pennsylvania, found out the hard way that people have difficulty confronting a woman—until their dissatisfaction grows to such an extent that they ask her to leave. When half the board members of her synagogue suggested to her informally that she not renew her contract (a request she decided not to challenge, even though she thinks the congregation would have asked her to stay), she asked them what her being a woman had to do with their request. "They said, 'Nothing,' but they added, 'We felt, when you made a mistake, that we couldn't tell you. We were afraid we would hurt your feelings.' I always told them what I thought was wrong, though I turned out sounding like a nagging mom. But they let things fester. They couldn't say to me, 'You're messing things up.' " Pell, at thirty-two, was in her first job at the Pennsylvania congregation, and she thinks her difficulties were compounded by her own inexperience. She should have insisted on talking things out as soon as she saw the first glimmerings of unrest from members of the synagogue's board of directors, who were essentially her bosses.

She feels her problems stemmed from overcommitment. Though she had no secretarial help, she nevertheless was expected to send out mailings, raise funds, give speeches, arrange the chairs and prayer books for services, and still perform all the duties of a rabbi, such as visiting the sick and officiating at bar and bat mitzvahs and funerals. Not surprisingly, she often got the mailings out late, and that was what the board members objected to.

No man would have taken the job on such terms, she believes, and no man would have continued to overextend himself. "Because of the way I projected, they thought I was totally self-supporting and self-nurturing, that I didn't need any help." Since the break, some people have been openly angry with her. "That has been much more satisfying. There's been growth. . . . I should have been insisting that problems be discussed on a regular basis, once I heard that there were complaints." Like many women, though, she had not been taught how to handle power or business relationships, even though she had been emancipated enough to choose becoming a rabbi in the first place, and even though she comes across as a person of warmth, strength, and firmly held opinions. "But I as a female person was not raised to be powerful in a language that works in the world." And that was compounded by a board that did not know how to talk to her. "It was a lousy marriage," she says.

Her main criterion for a new job is that there be someone there from whom she can learn, someone who will be honest with her.

The Sexual Overtone

Almost any working woman is familiar with the awkwardness that sexual overtones can bring to a situation. It is important to recognize that the problem is monumental, yet sometimes so subtle that a woman hardly knows if a sexual innuendo is indeed operating in a given situation. It is difficult for most women to decide what to do when men use sex to make life uncomfortable for them, or when men allow others to do so.

At a New York State Assembly hearing devoted to a discussion of proposed legislation that would have made sexual harassment in the workplace just cause for leaving a job and qualifying for unemployment insurance compensation, a woman testified who had been the only female salesperson at a large company. Because of her energy and hard work, she had won several awards for high-volume sales. Her success did not save her, however, from the harassment of one of her co-workers. First he made advances toward her. Then, when rebuffed, he began making sexual jokes at her expense to her customers and to heads of other departments within the firm—jokes that included suggesting she would provide services beyond selling her product.

"At all of our business meetings, G. would embarrass me by smelling and touching me and making lewd comments. Once, in front of the group, I chastised and embarrassed him, hoping he would stop, but it didn't help. Everyone, including the district manager, passed it off as a joke and said, 'Well, that's just G.'"

Then G. became her district manager and threatened to fire her if she did not have sex with him. When she complained to the regional manager, he would not help. Instead, after several more months—during which she more than tripled her sales over the previous year—this regional manager, at the district manager's suggestion, did fire her. He took away her company car, put her in a taxi, and sent her home, without notice. In addition, she was told she would get no recommendations.

"G. did exactly what he had said [he would]. I refused him sexually, I lost my job, and my career is ruined." Naturally, she feared that if she used her real name at the hearing or brought legal action, she would never again get a job in her industry. She vented her anger by appearing, anonymously but publicly, at the hearing.

It is interesting to observe that afterward several other women at the hearing—all avowed feminists—mentioned to me informally that this woman may have undermined her effectiveness as a witness because she had testified dressed in what they saw as a provocatively tight-fitting suit. Perhaps she had provoked sexual abuse by her manner of dressing, these women apologized with embarrassment, knowing all too well how they echoed the stereotypical attack on the rape victim: "She was asking for it." I argued that the woman was neatly dressed and merely wore the female version of a natty salesman's outfit. In fact, her suit fit no more tightly than that of her husband, who had accompanied her to the hearing. No one would have accused him of being provocative or of "asking for it." These women with whom I spoke, representatives of various women's organizations, conceded that, while I might be correct in theory, I was not so correct in practical terms, and that their campaign to pass legislation to prevent or at least punish sexual harassment would have been better served by someone who presented a more conservative image.

Acknowledging the sincerity of their position, I still felt that the witness had presented a strong case. Had she not been extremely lithe, attractive, and vibrant—attributes that no doubt helped her be a top salesperson—no one would have suggested her complicity in the situation. I also thought that, if the feminist leaders could not overcome their own stereotyped attitudes, it was unlikely that someone like G. ever would, laws or no laws. As it turned out, the legislation did not materialize, even though the hearing sponsors did not blame the sexy saleswoman, whom they thought brave to speak up.

The problem of sexual harassment may never be resolved, because there is still so much shame attached to it. Many women still believe that any incident of it must somehow have been brought on by themselves. It takes a truly strong minded person to acknowledge and react to it. And even then, the reaction may well entail leaving the job. It can be a no-win situation.

That is what Charol Shakeshaft found back in 1972. She was in her early twenties, fresh from a childhood in Iowa and film studies in Nebraska, and had found her first job in New York City with a large company. "I was told [that] either I would have sex with my immediate supervisor or they would demote me," she relates now from her office at the college where she is a professor. "They told me this was a big world and I was much too idealistic; if I wanted to get ahead I had to play by the rules, and these were the rules. I didn't want to play by the rules, so I quit. But I still think of myself as being harassed out of a job."

This vivacious and charismatic teacher and speaker displayed back then the same tenacity and presence of mind she demonstrates now. She did not just quit; she went to see a lawyer. "At that time, we hadn't defined sexual harassment yet. Only a year or two after that, some states came out with laws, and it had a name. I only knew it was wrong." She was told the company had done nothing illegal, but her former employers apparently knew they were at fault; they awarded her several thousand dollars in severance pay. She soon got another job and left the film industry.

The Quiet Syndrome

A female manager I interviewed noted that none of the three women at a recent meeting of about twenty managers participated in the banter and the continuous commentary on each other's reports that the men engaged in to impress the company president. She noted it proudly, saying that women were above such obvious and juvenile antics. But a male manager to whom I related the story was appalled at the way these docile women were throwing away an opportunity to display their verbal skills before their boss, an opportunity their male co-workers would grab. A lot of office politics is carried on at meetings, and women miss out by often being only silent bystanders.

Women's silence in mixed groups is not news to any attuned observer. In college classes, in lecture audiences, in social discussions, women tend to raise their hands or their voices less, to ask fewer questions and offer fewer observations. Often they do it unconsciously, perhaps heeding the old recording in their heads admonishing them to "act like a lady." Acting like a lady often means acting like a child, being seen but not heard. Or it may mean being a good listener, the old advice to teenage girls on how to catch a man.

One study of undergraduate women found that 40 percent had occasionally "played dumb" on dates. One woman answered, "I am engaged to a southern boy who doesn't think too much of the woman's intellect. In spite of myself, I play up to his theories. . . . I allow him to explain things to me in great detail and to treat me as a child in financial matters." Another woman reported being happy to have transferred to a women's college so she could continue to get good grades without ruining her chances of getting dates by being known as a "brain."

I found this study of particular interest because it was based on data collected in 1942 and 1943, and yet the responses, of course, could have been made much more recently. The kind of programming young women receive about how to behave in relation to men has not changed that much, although perhaps today women would not be as ready to admit their self-deprecatory attitudes. On a more scientific level, the interviews in this study help to explain the dilemmas of women who are in their sixties today. The sociologist who conducted the study (reprinted in 1972 in *Readings on the Psychology of Women,* edited by Judith M. Bardwick), Mirra Kamarovsky, postulated that these women faced serious contradictions between two roles, which she termed the "feminine" and the "modern" (not too different from the Broverman study characterizations of the submissive, healthy female and aggressive, independent, healthy adult).

One student, for example, reported that her mother would write to her one week admonishing her to "subordinate everything to your studies. You must have a good record to secure a job." But the next week, her letter would be filled with news of local weddings. "It is high time, she feels, that I give some thought to it," the student said.

If a woman does speak up in a group or meeting, her remarks are often ignored or not valued as highly as a man's. Several women I interviewed noted instances of meetings at which women made suggestions that were ignored. A little later, at the same meeting or at another, a man would make virtually the same remark and be applauded for his imagination and intelligence. This kind of reaction —not at all uncommon—tends to stifle whatever impulse women have to volunteer a remark. Being ignored or belittled provokes anger, and once it has happened, there is very little a woman can do about it that does not make her look petty or foolish. The best defense is to plan for the next time, to develop a style of presentation that is so assertive it cannot be ignored.

The Identity Problem

In her 1975 study of institutional barriers that keep women out of the executive suite, Professor Cynthia Fuchs Epstein noted that female executives often must announce who they are to their colleagues and clients to avoid being mistaken for a secretary. "Imagine a male executive who could always expect to be mistaken for the salesman or the filing clerk, and would have to identify himself and hope he would be treated with respect."

Women are plagued, more than men, by physical characteristics not generally considered authoritative. For instance, they are more likely to have high voices or be short. Also, because of the dictates of our society, most women wear makeup and dress more elaborately than men, and jewelry, multicolored dresses, and high-heeled shoes are features that most people have not been accustomed to associate with people in power until very recently. These days, "dress for success" has become a cliché, but it is applied much more frequently to women than to men. Men do not have to worry much about how they dress, while women often must spend time and energy on it that they could more usefully spend on business matters.

Women are judged more by their general appearance than are

men. By seeking to be stylish—as many women do, including Gloria Steinem and other feminist leaders, who were influenced just as much by early conditioning as their less political sisters—women feed the syndrome.

Surely the answer cannot be that women will have to strip themselves of their feminine finery, learn to lower their voices an octave or two, and stretch themselves on the rack in order to be fully acceptable as persons in authority. Rather, the general perception of a powerful person must expand to include someone in high heels and a skirt, with long hair and a soprano voice.

Social and Family Life

Experts say that all ambitious people must detach themselves to a certain degree from family and social responsibilities. But a man (at least in the past) could usually find a wife to raise his children and take care of his home for him, to be part of his "support team." A career woman is unlikely to find a man who will do the same for her, and so she must, therefore, make difficult choices. In addition, she may have to reconcile her commanding, confident office role with a polite, deferring, traditionally female role at home.

Nevertheless, women who try to integrate their roles as workers, wives, and mothers are likely to be the happiest people, according to research conducted by Faye Crosby, an associate professor of psychology at Yale University, who published her findings in a 1982 book, *Relative Deprivation and Working Women*. In her study of four hundred residents of a Boston suburb, she found that the people most content with their jobs were married and had children. Housewives who did not work outside the home were less happy than working women, but single, childless people were least happy in general.

"It's protective to have multiple roles or identities," Crosby, the mother of two boys, said in an interview. "It helps put things in perspective. One role is not all-consuming of your psychological energy." A single person might dwell on something wrong at work, she relates, while a parent can go home and gain satisfaction from her life there.

Although women still bear the major responsibility for child and home care, she says, they score about equally with men on the happiness scale. Surprised at this finding at first, Crosby reasons that, among professionals at least, men are starting to take a more active role in parenting. "Working fathers are more involved in raising children, so they are feeling some of the pressures and pleasures of child raising." When she asked working mothers what their biggest problem was in their home life, they answered that it was not having enough time, having to juggle all their duties. Nevertheless, these women maintained that this cost was far outweighed by the monetary and psychological benefits of working. In chapter 9 we will explore the ways some women have found to juggle career and family life, including creative approaches to raising children and to relocating to different cities.

But some women doubt whether they can have it all. "I think I'm a strong person, energetic and able to cope," offers Susan Davis, a vice president of the Harris Bank in Chicago and the mother of two young children. "But I find juggling home, family, and job too much sometimes. It doesn't seem reasonable to juggle so much. Hopefully, people like me will be the transition generation. This is not viable."

Myopia

In their 1966 book, *Human Behavior in Organizations,* Leonard R. Sayles and George Strauss point out that effective managers need to spend a great deal of their time planning, coordinating their activities with other departments, and engaging in other long-range projects. These activities do not always come naturally to women. The authors cite the case of female nurses, promoted to supervisory positions in hospitals, who put off the planning and goal-setting parts of their jobs. Instead of delegating responsibility, they followed their subordinates, picking up where they left off or finishing the job for them. This "close" supervisory style, the authors say, is not as productive as what they call the "general" style, the kind that focuses on delegating work so that the manager has more time to spend on making decisions about the future of his or her department. The close style is the one to which women are often prone.

Women are also often myopic about their long-term careers. Many start out in a "job" rather than in a career, and forsake the kind of career planning that men are accustomed to. Fortunately, this has been changing as members of the younger generation are learning in high school about M.B.A.s, about dressing for success, and about the importance of mentors. Chapters 2 and 8 will examine this problem more closely.

Fear of Success

Matina Horner's landmark 1969 study, "Fail: Bright Women," revealed that women fear success as much as they fear failure. Women often undermine their own causes, and, as bosses, sometimes make mistakes when they should know better—perhaps because of unconscious guilt or a belief that it is not feminine to be in authority.

Horner, now president of Radcliffe College, presented hypothetical situations in questionnaires distributed to men and women and compared their responses. She reports the bizarre response of a young woman, whom she calls Monica, who answered typically. The questionnaire asked the female subjects to finish this little story: "After first-term finals, Anne finds herself at the top of her medical school class." Monica, an honors student with visions of a flourishing career, continued thus: "Anne starts proclaiming her surprise and joy. Her fellow classmates are so disgusted with her behavior that they jump on her in a body and beat her. She is maimed for life."

In contrast, a young man named Phil, given the same test with "John" substituted for "Anne," tells a tale of success for John, who is "pleased with himself . . . and eventually graduates at the top of his class." In achievement tests later, Monica scored higher than Phil when each took the tests in a separate location. But, said Horner, Monica dissolved into "a bundle of nerves" and scored poorly when they competed face to face on the same kind of tests.

Other women in Horner's study pictured Anne as leaving medicine, as being hated, ugly, and dateless, or as deliberately dropping down in ranking so that she can marry the boy who ranks number one.

Horner has taken one step further the double-bind conundrum identified in other studies discussed here. Because women may equate "intellectual achievement with loss of femininity," they worry not only about failure but also about success. Her conclusions are still valid, says psychologist Jacqueline Fleming, an adjunct professor at Barnard College and a consulting psychologist for the United Negro College Fund. Fleming wrote in the December 1982 issue of

Radcliffe Quarterly of a real-life Anne who fell ill just as she was on the verge of accepting a high-powered job. Although she desperately wanted it, partly because it would give her the opportunity to show her husband that she is as capable as he, she decided she could not take it in her condition. Doctors were unable to diagnose her illness.

"But you say you are successful and so the theory couldn't apply to you. Yet, like Anne, you may be a prime target for falling ill when you least expect it," wrote Fleming. "You say that you've always been ambitious and that if you fear anything it's failure. Success is what you seek. But the intensity of your drives wax and wane according to seemingly unexplainable moods. You never really seem to get where you want to be—a place where you can relax and enjoy it all. . . . You are free enough from fear to be able to fight for what you want, but not enough to resist resenting the struggle. It is this approach-avoidance aspect to the desire for success that typifies the fear-of-success woman."

Fear of Risk

When they were a little over one year old, thirty-two boys and thirty-two girls were studied by psychologists Susan Goldberg and Michael Lewis, who first presented their findings in 1969 and later published them as part of a 1972 book, *Readings on the Psychology of Women,* edited by Judith M. Bardwick.

"Boys and girls showed striking differences in their behavior toward their mothers," the researchers concluded. "First, upon being removed from their mothers' laps, girls were reluctant to leave their mothers. When [the children] were placed on the floor by their mothers, significantly more girls than boys returned immediately—in less than five seconds. . . . Once the children left their mothers, girls made significantly more returns, both physical and visual. . . . At the end of fifteen minutes of free play, a barrier of mesh on a wood frame was placed in such a way as to divide the room in half. The mother placed the child on one side and remained on the opposite side along with the toys. . . . Sex differences were again prominent, with girls crying and motioning for help consistently more than boys. . . . Boys, on the other hand, appeared to make a more active attempt to get around the barrier."

Even at this early age, girls seemed to fear taking risks more than boys did. It is significant to note, however, that when these same children had been observed at age six months, "mothers touched, talked to, and handled their daughters more than their sons." Seven months later, then, the girls touched and talked to their mothers more than the boys did.

What the researchers could not determine was whether the mothers' responses to their children at the earlier age were based on sex-role expectations or on behavior patterns in the children. They hypothesized that, in the first year or two, parents reinforce behavior they consider sex-role appropriate. These kinds of behavior are rewarded, and eventually the child learns to internalize them. Later, the child learns the explicit rules governing sex-role appropriate behavior.

Whether such sex-role-defined behavior is innate or learned, it is small wonder that management experts recognize in women a greater aversion to risk-taking than they see in men. The ability to take risks is, however, an important trait for any person in authority. It is needed for quick decision-making and for those leaps of imagination that often propel people from middle into top management. It is also important for entrepreneurs.

Luckily, many women have been able to overcome the fear of risk, as profiles in this book demonstrate. The ability was also found in those women studied by Margaret Hennig and Anne Jardim for their book, *The Managerial Woman* (1977). The two management consultants, both of whom hold doctorates from Harvard Business School, found that the most successful of the women they interviewed were also the most flexible and the most comfortable with taking risks in a traditionally "masculine" way. Each of the successful women in the book had been an only child, a first child, or a specially treated child. Each had had a close relationship with her father and been treated more like a son than a daughter. Consequently, these women had been taught early on to take risks as men do. "To see risk as a consequence of judgment based on experience rather than as an issue burdened by the near certainty of personal loss has traditionally been a man's heritage," write Hennig and Jardim.

One of the successful women they interviewed recalled this event: "I remember wanting to climb a very tall tree when I was about five. My dad said it was too tall for me but I could try if I insisted. My mother said that I would fall. My dad said that if I fell I would learn a good lesson about where my limits were but that if I made it I'd learn not to always let others set limitations for me. I climbed that tall tree straight to the top and I never forgot the lesson." Hennig and Jardim point out that it is "a rare father who thought of teaching his daughter his own response to risk and an equally rare mother who, as these apparently did, would have permitted it."

The Way Ahead

The dilemmas discussed thus far can be seen as roadblocks for women, but they can also be seen as challenges—challenges that women can meet in a uniquely female and strong way.

"Historically, men have worked together and women have worked together—but in work the sexes stayed apart," writes management expert Peter F. Drucker in *The Changing World of the Executive* (1982). "What we are doing now in all areas thus represents an unprecedented social experiment—surely one of the most interesting ones in social history. We are committed to it—but how such experiments work out one does not really know for quite some time —generations rather than decades." Having men and women together in the workplace causes problems. Having at least some of those women in charge presents even greater difficulties, to which both men and women must learn to adjust. Interviews for this book have revealed that women in positions of authority are not adjusting by simply trying to become like men. They are finding their own ways, which is a path applauded by many knowledgeable theorists.

"The problem has been that women have been made to feel that many of their valuable qualities were not only unimportant but even defects," says Dr. Jean Baker Miller, author of the 1976 book *Toward a New Psychology of Women,* and a woman of great warmth and strength herself. "Women themselves have been encouraged to ignore some of their own best inclinations and even to condemn themselves for them.... Just because most women are much less frantically afraid of weakness, they can more accurately assess a situation and devise appropriate paths away from weakness.... Admitting to the weaknesses that do exist ... is the first step in devising truly effective action toward greater strength."

Another important way for women to progress, she adds, is to find or form a supportive community of other women, as several of the women interviewed for this book have done.

As women change, so will men, says Alexandra Symonds, an associate clinical professor of psychiatry at New York University School of Medicine and a training psychoanalyst with the Karen Horney Clinic. "Many [women] are trying to be more directly expansive and less clinging. As women develop more and more in this direction, then men will feel the change. They, too, will have more freedom of choice—will not fear their tender feelings and will feel comfortable in expressing their needs for closeness and dependency. It is happening, and I feel it is a change in the right direction."

The change Symonds describes assumes a view of feminism that is close to the Swedish phrase for the women's movement: "sex-role revolution." The term has a special strength, because it does not limit the description of the transformations now taking place in the worlds of work and home. These transformations are affecting men and women alike in ways that are causing difficulties now but that, ultimately, will be beneficial. They will mean a better world for everyone, as Bernice Sandler, director of the Project on the Status and Education of Women for the Association of American Colleges, points out. Boys will grow up under less pressure to excel in athletics and other aggressive endeavors, and one standard of moral behavior will apply to all. "If it's good to be compassionate, it's good for both sexes," says Sandler. Management consultant Alice G. Sargent foresees an equally integrated future for men and women, in which the "androgynous manager"—one who combines the best traits traditionally ascribed to each sex—will be the most successful.

2

Making the Step into Management

Thirty women, all graduates of Radcliffe, recently sat around drinking wine, eating cheese and crackers, and comparing notes on their careers. They were mostly in business or law and had come together for some networking—hoping to make new contacts or at least new friends. As each told her life history, one dominant theme began to emerge. No matter how successful each was—a partner in a top law firm, a venture-capital specialist with her own business—nearly every woman there had come to her position by a roundabout route. Several had taken time out for children. Some had majored in medieval English literature or some other esoteric subject, had put in time as a secretary, and then gone back to law or business school. A few had started out in academia— perhaps because that had seemed an acceptable career for a young lady of learning—and later had switched to a "tougher" job in the "real world." How different their career patterns were, one person remarked, from those of their male classmates at Harvard.

Their stories followed patterns similar to those of many of the women interviewed for this book. For women, career paths into positions of power are usually very different from those taken by men. Some women do not decide until late in life that they want a management position. Some do not decide until the job is actually offered to them. Some decide, for reasons of family or personality, that they do not want to be in charge at all or that they want to stop their climb at a level where life is satisfactory to them.

A position of authority is not for everyone, and sometimes the wisest answer, when offered such a position, is no. That, however, should not necessarily be as quick and automatic a response as it sometimes is for women. Younger women may think they do not want administrative work, that they want to stay in the "creative" lower echelons, only to find that, as they grow older, their perspectives change. Unlike men, they have not been trained to think of a long-term career or of advancing in status as well as salary.

For men more than for women, a major reason to advance is usually to support a family. But both men and women find that, as they age, they grow weary of the same job and want the new challenges and greater control over their firm's product or service that advancement provides. Or they may wish to take the ultimate management step: to go into business for themselves.

Because their goals are likely to shift, it is important for young women, even those who think they will never be interested in high-level management, not to cut themselves off from changes they may want to make later in life. They should at least have the necessary groundwork of a good education. It is also important for older women to start thinking of themselves as possible supervisors, even if they have been secretaries or file clerks for long stretches of their professional lives. Court decisions are forcing some companies to promote women, and once there is a precedent, new opportunities open up. In addition, housewives reentering the job market should consider management positions instead of seeking only menial jobs.

Women often sabotage themselves, one management consultant told the authors of *Upward Mobility* (1981), a career advancement guide by the staff of Catalyst, an organization dedicated to helping career women get ahead. Barbara Boyle, cofounder of Boyle/Kirkman Associates, told Catalyst that women do not know how to sell themselves on the job market or how to bargain for higher salaries and raises; they set too low a price on themselves, they lack confidence, and they allow their concern for security to blind them to career opportunities. Boyle said she never thought of long-range career plans during her own first dozen working years, but that a woman today, because of the demands of the economy and increased competition brought on by the coming of age of the baby-boom generation, cannot afford to be so blasé.

Women are reluctant to make their career aspirations known,

adds Dr. Margaret Hennig, coauthor of *The Managerial Woman* (1977). She calls it the "waiting to be chosen syndrome." When women do not ask for a raise, the boss assumes she is satisfied, says Hennig. The same would apply, of course, to asking for a new position or title. Her advice is simple: when you want something in the business world, ask for it—preferably right after a particularly spectacular achievement.

The Catalyst team also points out other things to keep in mind:

• Your status will not improve until your salary does. A new title is not enough, and if you are offered one without the other, start fighting for both right away. A recent study of a thousand working women by University of Michigan psychologists Jean Manis and Hazel Markus found that the amount of money they earned boosted their self-esteem more than any other single factor.

• Watch out for the old trick of shunting women into jobs with different titles and lower pay than men have, in which they do the same kind of work that men do for more money.

• Try to get into an executive training program rather than working your way up through the secretarial ladder, as some firms would prefer their women employees to do.

Another important asset for women who want to enter the world of management is a professional degree. For several years, the M.B.A. seemed the magic key. Now there appears to be a glut of M.B.A.s (though it still does not hurt to have one), and a technical degree, by itself or in addition to an M.B.A., can be helpful. It may help a woman prove something that men never need to prove. "Even if a guy never opened a math or physics book in college, we naturally assume that he understands when we debate the merits of electronic components," a senior executive of a major consumer products firm told *Business Week* in 1980. "With a woman, we just naturally assume she does not—unless she has a degree to prove it."

With women interviewed for this book, however, career plans and academic degrees were not the major factors in the success of those who had made their step into management. Rather, the ingredients of their success included a combination of life accidents and a certain amount of grit and spirit that caused their reactions to those accidents to be the appropriate ones for success.

Three profiles follow here, of women who made their steps into management in various ways typical for many women—reluctantly, accidentally, later in life, or by an unorthodox route. Each woman had to make her own decision and her own adjustment, and each required an act of courage to make it.

Kathleen M. Brown is the assistant corporate secretary of the Long Island Lighting Company. She is the utility's only woman officer. Until 1969, she was not a corporate secretary but an office secretary—the kind that types, files, and sometimes makes coffee.

Brown came of college age in 1943, during World War II, with her two brothers in the service and her family on a tight budget. She wanted to become a teacher, but although she had won a partial scholarship to a local college, it was not enough; she accepted instead a full scholarship to a secretarial school.

Perhaps she could have worked her way through college, she says now. "But at the time I thought, Why not go out and see what the world is like? So I worked in New York as a steno for a while. I never thought of getting a degree that would lead to a management position. At that time, women didn't go into business that way." Her secretarial school was called a business school, but it was not handing out M.B.A.s. "Women who became attorneys or accountants or engineers were considered strange then."

Brown worked in New York for six years as secretary to the editor of a trade magazine. When he would not give her a two-dollar raise on her thirty-seven-dollar-a-week salary, she quit and went to LILCO. There, starting out with the title "Steno Grade 4," she got her raise. Brown worked in various departments and had a taste of management when she was put into a position in which two other secretaries reported to her. "I gave them work and kept track of them."

She liked the responsibility, and was crushed when that department was abolished and she was put back into the steno pool. Because of her skills and seniority, Brown became the unofficial assistant manager of the pool, substituting when the supervisor was out. "It meant coordinating other work and required organization skills. It meant getting along with people, sometimes trying to get someone to do a job she didn't want to do." But Brown had neither the title nor the salary of a supervisor.

While still in the pool she took a test to become what they called a certified professional secretary, and when a secretarial job opened in the legal department, she applied for and got it. After a while, she was asked to become secretary to the secretary of the corporation. When he got promoted, Brown assumed she would be transferred up with him. That was the way she had expected to rise as a secretary —along with her boss. But when he moved up to vice president, he did not take her with him. Brown was crushed. She never dreamed that she would rise in the corporate structure on her own. "I felt very hurt. I felt he didn't want me. But he spoke to me afterward and said, 'You mean you don't know why you can't go? You know that office too well. You're more valuable to the company in the [corporation] secretary's office.' "

From many bosses, those could have been empty words, but this boss proved his sincerity soon. First, he upgraded her title and salary, and then, when the corporate assistant secretary retired, the man who was chairman of the board at the time called her in. "He told me he wanted me to become assistant secretary of the corporation. I was shocked. You know, the mouth dropped open. Shock," says Brown, a healthy-looking woman who coaches volleyball and basketball as a hobby and who has a casual, hearty way about her. She is as open and friendly as her roomy office, a comfortable place that is more orderly than its slightly disheveled surface indicates.

Despite her amazement, it never occurred to her to turn the job down. When her unprecedented promotion was announced, her coworkers were thrilled. "The phones didn't stop ringing."

The women's movement, which was just emerging in its current incarnation in 1969, did not cause her promotion. What probably did, Brown thinks, was the man who was general counsel and corporate secretary while she worked in the office. "He had confidence in me. He allowed me to do as much as I wanted within my capabilities. He said that even if I made a wrong decision, he would always back me." Furthermore, this boss was always willing to give her credit for running the office well, which kept her name before the chairman.

As assistant corporate secretary, Brown keeps the corporate records and coordinates her company's relationship with regulatory agencies, seeing that the appropriate departments are notified of questions and that the answers make their way back to the regulators.

For Kay Brown, accepting the job title was the easiest part of her step into management. The hard part came later, when she had to revise her manner of relating to those who were formerly her bosses, now her peers, and to her former peers, now subordinates. In addition, she had a different role to play in the outside world, where she now represented her company and was asked to appear at functions where a female executive—or any unmarried woman, for that matter—was an anomaly. For example, one co-worker friend still treated her as a fellow secretary. She would casually call Brown on the phone and tell her not to leave for lunch if there were checks to be signed, a liberty she would not have taken with a man. Others in the office pointed out to the co-worker that she ought to be treating Kay Brown with more respect. When she brought up that point with Brown, she was told, "I don't mind, but I wouldn't want you to do it while someone is around." These days, that co-worker and other secretaries, with whom Brown still socializes outside work, call her Kay in private but Miss Brown in the office if other people are within earshot. "I think that's important for outsiders, though I don't flaunt my position."

In fact, she says, she has been complimented by secretaries from other departments for getting paperwork through to them on time. "I know I'm holding them up if I don't [get the work to them on time]. I'm more considerate than some other executives because I know I could be holding up a whole department." Rather than having difficulty delegating authority, as some women executives do, Brown has no problem at all trusting her support workers. "I have great confidence in secretaries and in the woman who heads the corporate record office. I would just as soon have them do the work. I have great rapport [with] and great respect for secretaries."

Outside the company, she says, people she knows, such as members of her church, are aware of her position. When someone new does not know, she does not make an issue of it. Usually her co-workers—such as those she bowls or plays golf with—introduce her proudly as a woman executive, so there is rarely confusion. Once, a new man on the LILCO bowling team asked her about her "classification," a term that applies to union-level jobs. The women around her "burst out laughing" and set him straight.

When Brown first started attending company functions, she made sure she had an escort. More recently, she has started to come alone. "I think it took them—the men here—a while to recognize that I was coming by myself. At first, I made a bigger effort to find an escort. Then I figured, why bother?" The first time she showed up by herself, "I felt everyone was falling all over me. They were trying to be nice." Now they have accepted her, an independent woman. "It's changing among younger people now, but in my time it wasn't so."

There are a few areas in which she has not been as assertive, perhaps, as a man might have been. For example, she does not have her own secretary, even though her predecessor did. She shares one, and she often does the clerical work herself. She has mentioned the need for more staff but has not pressed it. Also, Brown is the only corporate executive without a company car, a fact that has raised the ire of some younger women in the company, although she has never made an issue of it. The man who had the job before her had turned down the amenity, so she was never offered it. She might have liked the perk, she says, although she is reimbursed for using her own car on company business.

Another area in which Brown makes few waves is semantics. When a speaker continued to refer to the "gentlemen" in the group while giving a report, someone finally pointed out that a lady was present, too. She replied by saying, "Don't worry, I'm one of the guys." But Brown feels that, by working closely with men and not embarrassing them in public, she does more for herself and for other women in the company than she would if she were a strident feminist.

She has saved her assertiveness, she says, for the substantive issues. "One of the biggest things for me when I first got this job is that I was thrilled that I was able to stand up in a discussion and argue with an attorney. I told him he was not answering the question that had been posed, and he stood here for a good ten minutes discussing it with me, asking me, a former secretary, what my opinion was." It was more difficult, at first, to speak up in meetings, and it took her a few years to adjust completely.

Just about the hardest part was calling her former bosses by their first names, something she had almost to force herself to do. "I felt I owed it to the job. It was not just my cockiness. I was put into this job to bring myself to act as an officer."

That she has not advanced since her initial promotion is a disappointment to the company rather than to herself. Brown, who is single, has chosen to stay where she is so that she can have more time for her outside activities, including time with her brothers and sister and their families, with her church activities, and with the sports teams for youngsters that she coaches. She cared for sick parents for a while, too. "I recognized that moving up would take more time than I wanted to give from my overall life." This, too, is a phenomenon common to many women, who think more than men might of their lives as a whole. For most men, the only goal is getting ahead; pulling back to have more time with their families is not an alternative. In addition, says Brown, although she has domestic help once a week at home, she still must attend to the household details more than most men would. "I'm sure they don't think about those things. Their wives do."

One interesting point Brown makes about stepping up is that starting out as a secretary can still be a good tactic. If a secretary does not find the work satisfying in itself—which Brown thinks is quite possible—and she does not succeed in being promoted, at least she has seen what a particular field she is interested in is really like. Instead of rushing into advertising or accounting or legal work, a secretary has an opportunity to look around. "Men are at a disadvantage, having to go into a field directly. I'm surprised, with the salaries paid today, that more men aren't going into secretarial work." It worked for Kay Brown as a stepping-stone into a fulfilling career—which she also chose to limit for reasons that seem sane and sensible, even if they are considered stereotypically female.

It may be that Brown suffers from the fear-of-success syndrome that Matina Horner identified. She has stopped herself, as she admits, from going as far as she might have. Certainly her views are not in line with those of many younger women who are now trying to climb the corporate ladder, who would find her attitudes not only old-fashioned but occasionally antifeminist. Those younger women, or older women with different personalities and backgrounds, would have fought harder for their own secretaries, company cars, and additional promotions and salary raises. Kay Brown's adjustments in making the step into management, brave for her, are very much a product of her generation and background. Nevertheless, she provides an example of what may be one of women's strong points—the ability to limit their rise if it does not fit in with their enjoyment of life as a whole. While perhaps not everyone would share her choices,

Kay Brown is pleased with her decisions and feels they have been right for her.

Not every woman, of course, has a management position offered to her without soliciting it, as Kay Brown did. Most women, like most men, must work and maneuver hard within a firm, change firms, or start one of their own. Evelyn Echols, president and owner of International Travel Training Courses, Inc., of Chicago, created her own firm.

Now sixty-eight, Echols started out handling executive travel in an advertising agency; she later worked in a travel agency in New York, before starting one of her own in that city. When she moved to Chicago with her husband twenty years ago, she opened her present business, which trains travel industry personnel and has offices in four cities. In addition, she has expanded into training hotel employees. Among the teachers in her schools are training staff from American Express, American Airlines, United Airlines, Princess Cruises, and Hertz.

"As a woman, well, you never made as much money," she says. But even though she opted to open her own business, she thinks a woman now can work her way up "as fast as a man, or quicker, at least in travel and the hotel industry, where three-quarters of the executives are women—and in advertising, too." The pay inequities, she says, should even out in the next few years. "When I went into a company, I always advanced. I never thought about it. Now, I think women will get where they want to go, or they should change companies. There are plenty of companies that offer great advantages for women." Banking and broadcasting, she adds, are two other fields where women are being promoted rapidly.

Echols was able to start her own business because, she says, she has a supportive husband—an invaluable commodity for any career woman. Her husband, an advertising consultant, helped her build up capital and contributed his skills in advertising and marketing, subjects he now teaches at the University of Chicago. "Without a supportive husband, I doubt I would have had the courage to start my own business." In addition, she says, if she had had children, she would have stopped working for a while to raise them. Again, as she demonstrates, women think about their career climbs differently than men do.

She started out with a courageous move. Born in LaSalle, Illinois, the daughter of a farmer and a housewife, she went to New York right after high school to look for a job in the worst of the Depression. "It was quite unusual for a woman to do so then. I had no definite aspirations. I was only to stay in New York a short period, but I kept on extending it. It was very difficult to get a job. I just walked the pavements. I started out modeling for John Powers, then I went to an advertising agency."

She attributes her success to being "a very hard worker and very well organized. Also, I'm very service oriented. If I promise people they will get an education, they will. I'm conscientious. I get up at 6:00 A.M., work at a steady pace, and I can handle an enormous amount of work." Nowadays, she gets into her office at 8:00 A.M. and works straight through until 3:00 P.M. or 4:00 P.M., when she starts working on the many charity projects she is involved in. Her ability to work hard stems partly from her farm background, she says, and partly from her start during the Depression. "You didn't last if you didn't work hard, because hundreds of people wanted your job."

Her step into travel training, which has put her in charge of a much larger business than her travel agency was, came about almost by chance. A judge at a Chicago social gathering challenged her to prove to him that something could be done to rehabilitate young women in reform schools. So, as a volunteer project, she taught the travel business to girls from a local reform school. Her public service instinct led her to go a step further; she also found them jobs. As the courses continued, her program soon evolved into a certified travel agents' school, the first in the country. She had already recognized, in her earlier professional experience, that there was a need for such training. Agencies either had to train their own people or steal them from other companies, so they were happy to hire trained personnel. Her school has placed well over 90 percent of its more than ten thousand graduates, she says. A good idea that comes at the right time and is executed efficiently is always a good stepping-stone to management success. In Echols's case, it was not luck, though; it was personal experience mixed with business savvy.

Echols says, "If a woman has a good idea, everyone will be anxious to hear it." Part of her independent nature, she feels, may be attributed to her being an only child until she was twelve. After that, three brothers and sisters came along. She is a chic, good-looking woman—the modeling background is easy to see—who dresses in designer clothing. "I don't want to dress like a man, or be a man." In some ways, she differs from many younger women starting careers now. For instance, she thinks many women who felt they have had to fight their way up have become too aggressive. And in a major brochure for her firm, she identifies herself as Mrs. David H. Echols. But no one reading the brochure can miss that she is, proudly, founder, president, and chairman of the board of a successful company.

Having a yogurt lunch in the school cafeteria, the dean of Stern College for Women, which is part of Yeshiva University, is stopped on line by a student who needs her signature on a form. Later, faculty members come by to ask her questions, and her secretary interrupts her once to remind her of a meeting and again to call her to that meeting. She had not forgotten it; just then, she had been consulting her watch.

The life of a dean—in this case, the top officer of the college, which does not have its own president—is filled with administrative details and policy decisions. It is not the one that Karen Bacon envisioned for herself when she got her Ph.D. in microbiology. How did she come to this position of power? "Just happenstance, the story of so many women," says Bacon, a smile further enlivening her usually expressive and animated face. In navy skirt and print blouse, she looks as youthful as some of the students, although her short, curly black hair is beginning to be streaked with premature gray.

Actually, Karen Bacon was at first a reluctant woman in charge. Now she feels satisfied by her job, and the faculty members I spoke with think she has done it wonderfully, providing a strong guiding presence in a college that is attempting to maintain old traditions in a rapidly changing society.

Ambition, she says, has not been her driving force. "I haven't been aiming at achievement. It must be personal satisfaction for me."

In fact, she realizes that she has more power than she sometimes would like to admit to herself. She is the only administrator within the university who represents the women's college. "And so if there is any issue that is of interest to this college, they really must look to me for input or for approval." She does not have to use much of this power with other administrators, she says, because there has never been a showdown, but she does have power over the daily decisions, such as which courses, which teachers, and which students the college will have. "The faculty really discusses these subjects, but I give people direction. Even financially, if I said something had to be done here, that's it, it just has to be done. There's no one else who can contradict me. So it is a position of power."

Bacon was teaching biology at Yeshiva College, the men's school of the university, when she was asked to join the search committee for a new dean of Stern. After the committee met for many months, some of the members asked her to be a candidate. "I hesitated. I really wasn't very interested, but they kept on insisting. I never saw myself this way, but they said I could be the most powerful candidate they could put forward.... Somehow, the faculty saw in me this steel I didn't know I had. They wanted a stronger dean, and they felt I would be a stronger force.... The male deans didn't associate as much with the students, with their aspirations, with what the faculty was trying to accomplish for the students."

Her main reason for hesitating, Bacon says, was that she had never been trained for an administrative job. "I was trained as a scientist, and I haven't done any science since I came here. And I don't know if I will ever go back to doing science." She still teaches, but it is not the same. On the other hand, her attitude about science is one that she thinks can be generalized for other women, too: "I never felt about science that it was the only thing I could do, that my life and identity were tied up with being a scientist. I've often talked about this with my husband, who is a psychologist. He really cannot see himself doing anything else. Being a psychologist is part of his fiber. I enjoyed science very much, and it's exciting. It puts you on a high and a low. When experiments are working, you're sailing. Then everything fails and you can't figure it out, and you're in the dumps. So it's kind of an exciting life-style," she says with enthusiasm. "But I never felt it was the only thing I could do. The fact is, I enjoy photography, and if I had it to do all over again, I might have become a photographer, or I might have done this or that. But since I trained as a scientist, I never thought of doing anything else. I certainly never thought of myself as an administrator."

As a youngster, she had watched her mother, who worked with her father in the pharmacy they owned, take a leadership role in charity work. "She was constantly on the phone, organizing. There were lists, there were programs, there were speakers. And I saw all this management she was doing, and I thought, This is not for me." Indeed, Bacon does not do things in her mother's way. Her organizational style, she says, could be classified as crisis management. "There's very little stability from day to day, so one could not really develop a style or technique, except for crisis management, which in many ways I find the most exciting, quite frankly—even though I rant and rail that this is no way to run an organization. The truth is, crisis management is very exciting. It's almost like doing experiments again. You've got to do something fast, decide."

Bacon says she has no problems making decisions, but we discussed the difficulties that other women have. Henny Wenkart, a philosophy teacher at the college who was sitting in on the cafeteria interview, pointed out that women are constantly making quick decisions in a family situation, yet find it difficult to transfer that skill to the work world. I suggested that perhaps women are not as aware in the family that they are making decisions and therefore do not freeze when confronted by them as they do at times in the working world. Wenkart thought of another reason: "In a family, you know you have enough knowledge, you know what the dangers are. In a situation where you're dealing with other people, maybe you feel you never know enough." Added Bacon: "It's certainly true you never do know enough, and it may be that women are afraid to take that leap. . . . Or maybe they're a lot more thoughtful and realize the risks. This is something that always struck me as very true, that women, in evaluating a situation or making a choice, always consider what they have to lose. That is, If I decide this, I may lose X, Y, and Z. Men think more in terms of what they have to gain: If my decision is a good one, look what I'll accomplish."

(Bacon has noticed this, too, in the way some women and men choose marriage partners. A woman, she says, may accept a man because she is afraid "the next guy may be a real schlepp," whereas a man may hold out because "the next one may be Cheryl Tiegs.")

As for her own decision making, "I do worry about what I have to lose, but I don't make that the deciding factor. I'm cautious. One thing: I don't like for things to be static. Even in the home, I'm always moving furniture around. I like for things to be different; I can't stand dull."

An example of Bacon's flexibility has been her attitude toward the dress code at Stern, which she describes as "a continuing crisis."

Following years of laxity, some faculty and students began to call for stricter compliance with the code, which is based on Jewish law (though interpretation of the law is debatable). The code forbids students to wear sleeveless garments and slacks to class. But there has never been a dress code in the dorms, which makes for a contradiction. Bacon's approach so far has been to allow continued discussion and not to take action against students in slacks. "My sense is that a man [in her position] would come down harder, yes, but that he would get even less compliance."

With four years of this administrative job under her belt. Bacon discusses why she accepted it. "My husband kept on encouraging me, telling me I would be wonderful for this. And it was a challenge." She adds that she was hardly trading in a high-powered research job for the deanship. She had been teaching on the undergraduate level, with only some research involved.

Bacon came to Yeshiva University not to be in management but to make a career and family move that is familiar to many women. She and her husband had decided that Bloomington, where they both had positions at the University of Indiana, was not the place they wanted to continue raising their children. They had spent five enjoyable years in Indiana, but "as a family, we decided to come East." She took the position at Yeshiva because of her own good memories as an undergraduate at Stern. At that time, the faculty had encouraged her to go into biology, even though science is usually considered nontraditional for a woman. At a woman's college, she says, many students "really get a stronger sense of themselves, of what they can do. They try things they wouldn't try elsewhere. They say things, they open their minds. I mean, we all know—you've been in mixed audiences where the only questions seem to come from men. I think they can only lose if the faculty makes compromises, sets their sights lower, or has some preconceived notions about what women can and can't do. That's when I think it can be disastrous to be at a women's college." As an administrator, she is now trying to "invest more in faculty rejuvenation," to make sure its members do not fall into old-fashioned attitudes toward women. "We have to get . . . their juices flowing again."

Going to a women's college certainly worked well for Karen Bacon. She met her husband while at college, and they married the year she graduated. Being in science, she says, gave her flexibility while her three children were young. Her first was born while she was finishing her dissertation, and the other two while she was a research associate at Indiana. "I would often take them to the lab with me, when they were really babies. I could just leave them on a cot while I was doing research. And when they got older, I could put them to bed and then go back to the lab to work at night until three in the morning. I didn't have to be there when anyone else was there, so it gave me a lot of flexibility."

Bacon says that she does not want to project herself as a super-woman. Circumstances worked well for her—her husband was able and willing to work at home, where he could look after the children. Home and lab were close together, and the children, now thirteen, ten, and seven, were healthy and independent. She and her husband have encouraged that independence, and if she had had a sickly child, Bacon says, she probably would have stayed home. "But I also know that I would have done a very poor job of it, which would have been a disaster for me. I know I'm not good at home full-time. It would have been the worst of all possible worlds. I would have stayed home to help somebody, and would have ruined them by staying there." Bacon discovered her adversity to staying at home during the three months she did it in Indiana. "I'm not a patient person. I couldn't stand that lazy day. I have to wash the dishes in two and a half minutes. And I have to do the next thing in three minutes. I couldn't see myself slowly getting to the park. I mean, we've got to run to the park, we've got to swing real hard, and then we've got to get out of there." Her speed, energy, and efficiency seem to be much better suited to science and, now, to running a college.

We spoke at length about planning careers, since Bacon's was relatively unplanned (compared to most men's, anyway). It started out felicitously, since she and her husband were able to decide jointly on which cities to study and work in. First, they both chose Los Angeles for graduate work, then Indiana, then New York. If, however, her ambitions had been greater or less flexible, their mutual pursuits might not have been compatible, she says. Both of them are flexible—she probably more so—and both discuss things with each other. "My husband basks in my accomplishments. In fact, he toots my horn." Both of them place high value on a strong family life, which is part of Jewish tradition, she says. "I think there's been some confusion about historical periods when women had to stay at home versus today, when the woman can still have her primary responsibility be the family but not have to stay at home. People underestimate the importance of the time-saving tools that are available to us." She is gratified to see many young couples today discussing how their career plans might interfere with family life.

If she were starting out today, says Bacon, who is thirty-eight, she would do more thinking about the future of her career, "not so much because I think it is necessary, but because today it almost seems foolish not to make some plans. It seems naive just to let things happen. So if my daughter were asking for advice, I wouldn't say to her, 'Listen, just play one day at a time; whatever happens, happens.' I mean, that just seems a little bit dumb. But if you ask whether I'm unhappy or frustrated with the way things turned out or whether I would have done things differently, the answer is no. It's just that I couldn't live it again today. The conditions are not the same."

As young women plan their careers more, family life is bound to change drastically, because many will postpone having children or not have them at all. However, she adds, she would probably advise having children very early, though not during college, so that there is a minimal delay in getting a career started. "Career planning will have a dramatic impact on the family," she says. "Almost anything is feasible, but it takes a tremendous toll. Because the truth is, women bear the major responsibility, no matter what the rhetoric is. My husband does the laundry, and it's nice to find fresh underwear that he's done, but I have the major responsibility for the children. I don't resent it, because I get a great deal of satisfaction from it. I think I resented the laundry, which is why he did it." Bacon's husband also started coming home earlier from work when she took the dean's job, which meant later hours for her. "We never really talked it through. He just got the sense that I wasn't home and it would be nice for somebody to be home."

An additional bit of advice Bacon offers about career planning is to find out more about a potential husband than she did, though it turned out all right for her. "He really doesn't care what we have for dinner. He's not fussy. It may seem trivial, but it would have turned into a tremendous conflict between us, just because I couldn't meet his expectations, and he wouldn't be meeting my expectations— mine being, Be flexible; let's not get excited about it."

Flexibility and calmness during crisis, the two virtues Bacon sees in her attitude toward home life, are the very ones that stood her in good stead in her decision to become a woman in charge and in her ability to manage with enthusiasm and skill. As Bacon's experience indicates, women's career paths, often so different from men's, can be highly satisfying and nicely attuned to their family and social lives.

The stories of Brown, Echols, and Bacon show that it is not necessary to have management training to make a smooth step into management. It is important, though, to be flexible and to grasp opportunity when it is offered. None of the three women aspired to management jobs at first, but all did excel at the jobs they were doing. Though their motivation was not the same as that of someone hoping for a promotion, their behavior was. They worked hard, displayed energy and commitment, and were willing to take on extra tasks, as, for instance, Bacon did by being on the search committee for a new dean. The paths these women took, as well as the advice of other experts presented below, can serve as guidelines for other women who are contemplating the step into management.

- Young women should not cut themselves off from future management positions, even if they do not believe they will be interested. They should gain a good education and learn early how to sell themselves and how to bargain for higher salaries and raises.
- Older women who have worked in menial positions or who are reentering the job market after spending time at home need not rule out a supervisory position. Extra education and some added skills in assertiveness will help. It is important for older women, who might be overlooked, to let their employers or prospective employers know of their aspirations.
- An advanced degree in a specialized area, such as engineering, is helpful, especially if it is combined with an M.B.A. Women, more than men, must prove that they are knowledgeable. Getting more education along the way, including management training, is another good idea.
- Taking risks, taking on extra responsibilities, and being innovative are effective ways for women to gain positions of authority. It is important to study each new responsibility closely and to learn new skills on the job with each step taken.

• Though many women have gained leadership positions without planning, this is not advisable, especially if a woman wants to have a family, too. If married, she and her husband need to discuss their future career plans and how each one will take advantage of all the career opportunities that will be encountered. All the married women interviewed for this book cited a supportive husband as crucial in the step toward management.

3

The Practical Problems

In most male-dominated fields, a woman just does not *look* the part of a manager. Often she is exceedingly short, compared to a man. Sometimes she has a high voice or feminine manner that she cannot (or will not) change. Moreover, a given mannerism or action will be interpreted differently for men and women. Consider, for example, the simple smile.

A smile is not just a smile, the song "As Time Goes By" notwithstanding. A woman who smiles too much may not climb the corporate ladder as fast as a smiling man, according to research conducted by Carl T. Camden, a Cleveland State University communications professor. "Smiling and other nonverbal behaviors are misinterpreted by male co-workers as signs of submissiveness," he says in a *Chicago Sun-Times* interview. Women smile far more often than men, but it often is not to their advantage. "In a male-to-male conversation, a smile by one of the men generally wards off interruption. But in male-to-woman conversation, a woman's smile invites interruption because men interpret her smile as a sign of submission."

Women who smile a lot are perceived as less effective managers, Camden adds. Furthermore, other actions also make women seem more submissive to men, such as tilting their heads while they speak. Women also tend to lean back when they are in a group, Camden has observed, and men interpret this as meaning they are not involved or interested. In other words, the difference between men and women goes beyond not having the same type of body. The two sexes also do not speak the same body language.

Beyond this, even the most savvy woman encounters practical problems only a few men must face. Women must fight their own social conditioning, the "old boy" network, and the natural disadvantages of being in a minority position. "We [women] are socialized to taking backup positions, to getting kicks out of what our husbands and children do. We are not accustomed to sticking our necks out. ...Women don't carry authority comfortably," said Madeleine Gardner, who was director of women's programs at the Adelphi University School of Business Administration.

Women have been trying to counteract the dearth of support at work and sometimes at home by forming their own networks—either general ones for businesswomen in a geographical location or more specific ones for women in a particular field, such as engineering or broadcasting. In Minneapolis, as in a few other cities, there is even a private membership club for women. In Minneapolis it is called the Blaisdell Place, named after the avenue on which the brick mansion that houses it sits. Its twelve hundred members enjoy a handsome lounge, several meeting areas, a gymnasium, and a first-class restaurant for entertaining clients and business acquaintances—as well as each other.

Perhaps not coincidentally, it was in Minnesota that one of the most blatant court battles over sex discrimination in a business club recently took place—and was resolved in the women's favor by the United States Supreme Court. It involved the Jaycees, a national organization that promotes leadership and management development among its nearly 300,000 members through local service programs. During the 1970s, the Jaycees actively recruited female members, but in 1981 the group voted to demote women to a restricted "associate" status.

"Women have been told directly by the Jaycees, 'You are second-class citizens, and we plan to keep it that way,' " says Judy Avner, staff attorney for the NOW Legal Defense and Education Fund, which had filed an *amicus curiae* brief in an action before the United States Court of Appeals, in which the Jaycees had challenged a ruling by the Minnesota Supreme Court that the Jaycees of that state either stop discriminating against women or discontinue their operations.

If any woman is foolish enough to think that the barriers of sex discrimination are down, this case alone ought to make her reconsider. Minnesota is hardly the only state where women have been excluded from influential private clubs. In 1980 the University Club in New York City voted by a two-to-one margin to exclude women, ostensibly so that its members could continue to swim in the nude. In 1983 a furor developed, again in New York City, over another prestigious all-male bastion, the Century Club, where men go to make important business contacts.

"If you have been mystified by the response" of members to the suggestion that they allow women in, wrote Barbara Lazear Ascher for the *New York Times* in February 1983, "it is only because you perceive Centurians as the grown-ups their titles imply. Do not see them as partners in law firms, writers who win literary awards, critics who have followings. See them as eight-year-olds guarding their tree house . . . that mysterious male haven between the leaves of trees, held up by branches and the fear of girls. . . . We understand that this is the playground. No more. No less. This is recess time when boys were liberated from overheated classrooms they were forced to share with girls, and from the humiliation they were forced to share with each other, that girls were better at reading and handwriting, manners and cleanliness."

Nevertheless, most women are not fighting court battles or taking on entire organizations in their struggle to gain or maintain authority. They are trying to establish themselves on private turf— within their own psyches, their families, and their workplace. That alone is no easy task, especially for the woman who starts out with the additional "liabilities" (from the point of view of the male establishment) of being smaller and higher-voiced or—a problem for both sexes—a member of a minority group.

Following are profiles of two women who have successfully overcome the physical characteristics that do not allow them to fit into this society's traditional mold of business leadership. One is a dynamic (and diminutive) professor, the other a determined black entrepreneur.

The first time I saw Charol Shakeshaft, at a women's network meeting, I wondered why a teenager was attending the event. Short, thin, and freckle-faced, with bright eyes and quick movements, she introduced herself to the group, and I somehow expected to hear her explain that she was a high school student. But the words she actually spoke and her very authoritative manner of speaking them soon dispelled this misconception. Here was a confident young woman in her thirties, an assistant professor of educational administration and director of the doctoral program at Hofstra University School of Education.

Thinking back on it, I should have been tipped off by her sartorial appearance, which was hardly that of a high schooler. At the time —and at every subsequent occasion I have seen her since—she wore clothing of impeccable tailoring and taste. Dressing well is one of her defenses, says Shakeshaft, as is the style she has developed of being extremely forthright and well informed when she speaks. A male colleague who admires her says she is effective and popular among students because of her high energy level and her drive. She makes many contacts and friends wherever she goes, he claims, because people remember her and she remembers them. In fact, the reason her colleague and I had gotten together was because Shakeshaft had suggested to him that he contact me to speak to a class he teaches—months after our brief encounter at the network meeting.

A former student, a school administrator much older than Shakeshaft, praises Shakeshaft for her hard work in organizing a graduate program that has helped many female administrators get ahead. Neither colleague is bothered by Shakeshaft's stature, or by her youthful looks or high voice—qualities that seem to diminish in importance as one gets to know her well. But Shakeshaft is keenly aware of the image she presents, and she believes that her physical characteristics are detrimental, at least in the business world as it is now constructed.

"Height is very important," she says over lunch in her office, a typical academic cubbyhole crammed with books and papers. "I directed the dissertation research of a graduate student, Carl Bonuso, who did his thesis on what he called the 'leadership shell.'" Bonuso sent out identical resumés for school administration positions with different pictures, and received replies from 580 school superintendents. Each photo was a group shot with a dot over the head of the supposed job candidate. He had chosen particular types of people to pinpoint, ranging from tall and thin to short and fat. Half the imaginary candidates were male and half female.

"First, he found no differences in the ways superintendents rated resumés of males and females. In the past [in other studies], there had been great differences, and males were always rated higher. But the difference in height had a great effect. Tall people of average weight were rated significantly higher than short, fat people, equally for men and women. [Bonuso] controlled for facial characteristics and attractiveness. All you could tell from the photos were the height and weight of the people. He had them turned sideways, and he touched up the photos so they all had the same hair color and blurred faces. I think there would probably have been a racial difference, but unfortunately his research was done on the majority racial group only, so we don't know.

"People of average weight did better than fat people, and tall did better than short. Tall, fat did better than short, average weight. Tall always helped, and it helped equally for males and females. It goes back to that idea we have of image, and our image of a leader is someone tall. And women, by and large, aren't as tall as men. The factor of height is very important, and we fail to realize how much people have a concept of who their leaders are and what they look like. So for women, the issue of being short is a very important one in terms of presence and what people think of you as a leader."

A high voice is another significant factor, she says. "You have much more trouble establishing authority, because, again, you have the idea that an authoritative person has a low and deep voice. I think this will change, especially as we get more women in the media talking on radio and television. I hear changes already in male voices, particularly on the radio, and they are no longer uniformly low. Unfortunately, the women who are chosen for TV and radio fit the traditional male image in having low-range voices. I think if we start to treat people as individuals, and we understand that women's voices are higher, the trend toward fitting women into the traditional male image will diminish."

Shakeshaft says she often receives complaints about her voice when she gives speeches and lectures. "You should have a lower voice," some of her students have told her. "Not that they say it isn't pleasing, but they say it doesn't sound like an authority." After giving a speech, she says, "People will say, 'You were wonderful, but you really should do something about your voice. You need to have a much lower voice.' Then I'll say, 'Well, I wouldn't mind a lower voice, but I'm a woman and women have higher voices.' There's a lot of not wanting to accept me as I am. People want me to conform to a male leadership image." One reason that a leadership image is important, says Shakeshaft, is that, even when women gain a position of authority, they do not necessarily gain the same kind of power that a man with an identical job title might have.

"Authority is one type of power. Authority is legitimate power: you're the professor, the administrator, the principal, the head of whatever it is. That's one way people have power, through formal authority positions. That doesn't mean you necessarily can get things done. There are other kinds of power you need. Women have been appointed to more and more positions of formal authority, legitimate power positions, but sometimes we don't realize that we have to garner other kinds of power in order to make our positions stick. And sometimes we're given that formal authority without the informal power that goes along with it. So I see that as an issue for women."

Two news items come to mind that support Shakeshaft's contention. When Sherry Lansing resigned in early 1983 as president of 20th Century Fox to become a partner in an independent production company, industry analysts speculated that she had left her job as the first woman to head a major film studio because she did not have enough decision-making power there. She gave credence to that view by saying in an interview about her new venture, "The important thing is we will be making movies we believe in. I'm going to be able to be totally involved in the creative process."

At just about the same time, Karen N. Gerard resigned from her position as New York City deputy mayor for finance and economic development. In a departure interview, she pointed out, "The new deputy mayor has a broader charge than I did." She suggested he might be able to do the kind of economic planning she could not. She felt frustrated, she said, because many areas of economic development had been out of her control. Her successor was given fiscal and budgetary responsibilities that she did not have. He was also given an office on the first floor of city hall. Hers had been in the basement.

"I have a very simple definition of power, one that I've borrowed from Rosabeth Moss Kanter," says Shakeshaft. "Power is the ability to get things done. There are many kinds of power that allow us to do that: legitimate power, personal power—some kind of charisma that makes people want to follow you and do what you say—or expert power. Women have traditionally used expert power; that is, they're technically oriented, in the sciences or whatever, and they can answer particular questions. But, for the most part, women haven't added other kinds of power to their repertoire. . . . On particular issues, women overprepare, and so we use expert power a great deal." Of course, for women to be in a field such as science is nontraditional, but even there women tend to restrict their use of power to technical expertise.

Kanter and others who have studied the phenomenon have found that people who say they do not want to work for a woman (or a minority person) really do not want to work for a boss they think has no power. Says Shakeshaft, "A lot of studies have shown that people want to work for people who have power, and women and minorities tend not to have as much power in an organization as do majority men. Therefore, people don't want to work for them *not* because they're women or minorities—though that's the reason they tend to give—but really because women and minority men are perceived as not having a large power base."

The area of women and power, Shakeshaft adds, has not been explored thoroughly by academics yet, but other experts have speculated that women have not learned the kind of bargaining and political skills needed to gain power. "I really believe that for the future, you'll have to be both politically astute and very capable." Women who enter the job market, she feels, are on the whole more competent than men, because they are "the cream of the crop. . . . School administration is a good example. All studies between males and females in teaching find either no differences or find females more competent. Now, I'm not big on male-female comparisons, because I think what that does is create the concept of war and pitting one sex against the other. But most of those studies were done not to show that women were better, but in an era when people wanted to show that men were better teachers and that women teachers ought to be replaced by men."

The studies were conducted, Shakeshaft says, during the 1960s and early 1970s, when the formal leaders in schools, the principals and administrators, were mostly men. But Shakeshaft points out that extremely competent men have tended not to get involved in education—they become doctors or lawyers, for example—while "extremely competent women have gone into schoolteaching because they didn't have other outlets open to them. So at least up until recently, what we've seen is not only a numbers imbalance—more men in formal leadership positions and more women in teaching—but a quality imbalance, [where] less capable people lead the schools and more capable people teach in them." Because of that imbalance, "it's even more shocking that women aren't chosen" for the leadership positions.

Now that things are changing a little, Shakeshaft says, men in her administration classes are upset. "They expected to get administrative jobs, and now women are perceived as taking them. That's the first reason they're upset. The second reason is that the women are extremely capable, so they just have more capable people to compete against." Until now, she says, most women have been "innocents," relying on capability alone to get ahead. Now they must add political astuteness—including more awareness of their image. Nevertheless, Shakeshaft feels that the lack of political ruthlessness that women display is not a bad thing. "I find women much more trusting and more believing in the values they foster."

In the education field, women are still making only small inroads. Only 10 percent of all secondary-school principals hired in New York State in 1981 were women, according to a study conducted by one of Shakeshaft's students. More women are moving into the lower levels—elementary-school principals, assistant principals in secondary schools, or department chairpersons. One reason for this situation, at a time when other fields are opening up to women, is that many bright women are no longer entering teaching. "I see a crisis coming up," Shakeshaft says. "We're going to have to do something if we're going to continue to have quality schools."

Shakeshaft thinks that another special quality women possess, which is also an asset, may be related to their size. That is their ability to communicate, which leads to an ability to defuse a potentially violent situation and to a closer sense of "community" compared to men's. Shakeshaft believes that perhaps one reason there has been more violence in schools in the past decade, since more male teachers have arrived, is that "men haven't learned conflict-reducing techniques." Women's smaller size forces them to conciliate and to attempt to reduce conflict rather than to heighten it, she believes. Whatever the root cause, however, communication and conciliation are now part of women's socialization.

But this ability can turn into a liability, she says, because women tend more than men to have an "open-door" policy—which may be good for their students and fellow teachers or administrators, but is not necessarily so good for their leadership image. "Men are seen as important, and therefore you don't waste their time. Women are seen as not important, and you do waste their time."

Shakeshaft has been sensitive to issues of power and authority —issues with which she herself has not yet entirely come to terms —since she was a child. "As I was growing up in Iowa, I told myself I would never be a teacher or a secretary. That was my reaction to what I thought of as traditional female jobs, and so I devalued those jobs and could see myself only in what I thought were traditional male fields."

An activist for women's issues from a very early age, Shakeshaft cannot pinpoint how her feelings started. "I'm not sure that my parents did anything directly. However, they did encourage all five of their children—boys and girls—to develop themselves completely. I always knew my parents expected me and my two sisters and two brothers to work outside the home. The boys in the family, as well as the girls, were taught and expected to do a full range of homemaking skills. Therefore, although no specific career expectations were communicated to me by my parents, it was clear to me I was expected to have a career.

"My father is a businessman, he owns a company, and my mother is a homemaker. I don't identify with my father, despite what I read about women in professions. Though I respect him and care for him, I have not tried to pattern myself in his image. I have no single role model —I have used traits from both of my parents, as well as many other people I have met in my life, to build the 'ideal' professional that I would like to be. With the exception of my father, all the other people in the composite are female."

Shakeshaft grew up in a farm community, and both parents were Republicans. "I believe where I grew up has a lot to do with who I am. I think there's something about a farm community or a frontier that allows for more variations in roles. A farmer can be a woman . . . I think it's only in the suburbs that conforming to the stereotypes becomes so important."

Trying to get into a man's field, she chose filmmaking, which she studied in college in Nebraska before getting a film job in New York. There, she became a victim of sexual harassment, as her story in chapter 1 details. When she quit after refusing to have sex with her supervisor, she was soon offered another job teaching at a school for gifted children in Brooklyn because she had worked with some of the students during her job in film. She considered this new teaching job to be temporary—just to tide her over until she found another film job. But once Shakeshaft started teaching, she got drawn in. "It seemed a lot more exciting than filmmaking, and a lot more creative. And it also seemed more worthwhile. I see education as the great socializer, and there are a lot of things about the way people are being socialized that I didn't agree with. The main problem was the idea of being socialized into traditional male and female roles. I also looked into the leadership of these schools and thought, 'I can do better than that.' "

Shakeshaft decided to get a doctorate in education so that she could fundamentally change the way a school was run. But while working toward the degree, in Texas, her ambitions opened up. "I thought I could have a bigger impact if I could change school administrators, rather than just be one. Instead of changing just one school, I could have an impact on lots of schools. That's why I became a trainer of school administrators." She teaches courses on the methodology of research, on organizational behavior and theory, as well as a popular one on women in administration. "My teaching is how I try to articulate my social beliefs."

Shakeshaft does not feel she has solved the power problem. "I often have trouble when I first start teaching a class. I team-teach with a man, and the students have less trouble seeing him as an authority than they do seeing me as an authority—in the beginning. Also, I have many more students interrupting me, seeing me in my office, and calling me at home to ask me questions."

She has discussed this with her colleague. "He seldom has students calling him at home, and he doesn't have students coming into his office as much. Yet he's an open, caring man, and has much more interest in the students than I do. He likes to spend time with students, to sit and talk with them. I don't. I do it, though, and I give them enormous energy, probably out of guilt. And yet I'm the one who has all the students, and he doesn't, and we were trying to figure out why. I think it's because women are seen as more accessible. That's my duty: to mother, to take care, to listen to their problems even though I don't want to hear them. My time is not [considered] valuable. I'm seen as an extension, so what does it matter if they call me on a weekend? There are just big differences, and I think it's because I'm female.

"I dress very carefully, particularly when I'm starting a new class. I wear high-authority outfits, gray and white or navy blue and white. I really have to strive to make myself that authority figure, so that it's clear in my mind and theirs. . . . In the end, things do change, but I find myself preparing to meet the assault."

Most of Shakeshaft's students are teachers with years of experience in the field who now want to move into administration, and so they tend to be older than she is. About half are women—an increase from when she first started teaching three years before. Hofstra has a good reputation with aspiring women administrators, largely because of Shakeshaft's course and because teachers at the university are known to make an effort to stress equality of the sexes in all courses.

When I mention that her position as head of the doctoral program sounds authoritative, Shakeshaft responds that she did not have to fight for it, though she claims that holding such a position can cause one to feel somewhat exploited. For example, for a while she found that she was not given release time from teaching for her administrative duties, while heads of the other doctoral programs at Hofstra got one course off. This has changed, and Shakeshaft now has more time and energy to devote to being an effective administrator. She sees the coordinator position as coming with a lot of informal power. "I can help students, and I can make sure women get a fair break. So, for larger, for what I call moral reasons, it's good. But for personal reasons it's bad, because it takes me away from my research, which is what counts for tenure promotion and national recognition. I have to decide whether I want to keep killing myself for social purposes. I'm trying to . . . both change the world and secure a place in a traditionally male field."

The person who held the job before her was also the department head, and did have time off. Now the job has been split. "I didn't apply for the department chair, though I was asked to, because I said I felt an untenured junior faculty member should not be department head." The school would be better off, Shakeshaft thought, with a department head who had power within the university—someone brought in from the outside with a reputation and prestige. If she were department head, Shakeshaft felt that her power would be based on "expert power" and her loyal following of students, but these, she considered, would not be enough. Indeed, Shakeshaft says she has had difficulties establishing her authority within her own department. Some professors, former school superintendents, "tend to look at me as a cute little girl, or are irritated with me. . . . I've also had a problem because I'm very outspoken, very to the point, and, male or female, that seems to bother some people. I don't know how much being female has to do with it. I think I assault people on many levels, partly because I'm female, partly because I seem to be much more liberal or radical than they are." Shakeshaft considers herself to be a middle of the roader, but others see her as leftist.

Shakeshaft sees her sometimes distant relations with department members as diminishing her authority. "Probably the biggest problem is not having the close relationships to get information, and that goes back to the power issue, because information is power." It is at the club or the golf course that much information gets passed on, Shakeshaft says, and women simply do not get invited to these places. "Often men will ignore me, since I don't fit their image of a leader or authority. Rather than spending a lot of time molding myself into that image, I spend my time working with men and women to change their expectations of what a leader is. If being admitted into the club means making myself in the image of the male club-members, then I don't want to belong. That's not the world I want to be in. For many women, it is important to be accepted in the male world. Here at Hofstra, I make an effort at compromise. I mostly draw upon expert power, and here they will listen."

Shakeshaft's students include more women than men, and someone in the department called some of them her disciples. "That's not really true," she says, "but if you're committed to something, people tend to follow you with more fervor than if you don't seem to stand for anything. But I have drawn a lot of students to Hofstra and have tripled the enrollment of the doctoral program."

Charol Shakeshaft has not solved all the practical problems of how her appearance affects how she is perceived. She has changed what she can through the way she dresses and behaves, but she does not take voice lessons or attempt to wear makeup that would make her look older, because she does not think she should have to. When she is not able to make someone listen to her, she does not spend much time worrying about the problem. Instead, she spends her time building the kinds of power that will overcome the physical handicaps. She spends her time becoming more knowledgeable in her field, becoming a better teacher so that her students will respect her, and fighting injustices so that society will change its perceptions of who should hold authority.

Angelyn Ruth Shields also does not fit the usual mold of the woman in charge, but that is because she is black, heavyset, and from an economically disadvantaged background. She could easily have become an unwed mother on welfare, she says, had it not been for some early advice and her own drive and ambition. Instead, she has moved from being a data-processing supervisor to owning her own store, an elegant lingerie and hosiery boutique in a downtown Atlanta shopping plaza. Her attitudes and her methods of overcoming potential obstacles to her advancement have worked effectively for her.

If you enter Sutton Place at the Peachtree Plaza—as many office workers, tourists, and convention-goers do—you see immediately the care that has been taken in displaying lace-trimmed nightgowns and custom-made silk robes. Behind the counter you are likely to find Shields herself, asking, with the friendliness indigenous to southern establishments and with her own broad smile and graciousness, if she can help you.

Shields opened the store in 1981 with her sister, Juanita McDonald, but now she runs it alone. She started the store with $15,000 won in a malpractice lawsuit, but she had been dreaming of an independent business for a long time—and had been honing her management skills while employed at various jobs as a supervisor of keypunch operators, with as many as 125 people working under her supervision at one time.

For a woman who grew up in low-income housing projects in New York City ghetto neighborhoods, hers is a huge accomplishment. "I have a very strong personality. I've not had any problems asking for what I wanted," she says. "I'm a little courageous. I take chances."

Shields was taught by her mother, a domestic worker who supported her two children by herself, to be responsible and to work hard. When, at fifteen, Shields had a baby unexpectedly and out of wedlock, the experience only made her feel more responsible and more determined. "I never wanted to be poor. I like nice things. If you want nice things, you're either born with them or you go get them. I wasn't born with them, so my choice was to go get them. I'm capable, and I work hard. I've always worked hard. . . . I had a baby, but I didn't want five more. I made a mistake; I had a kid before I was ready for it. But it made me work that much harder."

Shields wanted to be a nurse, but was never able to pass the entrance examinations—probably a result of her poor school preparation. During high school, however, she worked as an aide at Lutheran Medical Center, where a kind head nurse gave her two important pointers: the first was an introduction to birth control pills ("I had no idea what to do to avoid being pregnant again"); the second was advice not to continue working at the hospital without a nursing degree, because she would not progress very far, but to get into the then-blossoming field of data processing instead. Shields credits this early mentor with having played a vital role in getting her started on the road to success.

While taking a night course in data processing, she completed high school with the rest of her class. The helpful nurse gave her time off from her hospital duties to look for work. Just as she was about to give up, she found a keypunching job. She was fired two months later for not being fast enough. "It was a blessing, because the next day I found a job with Hayden Stone, the brokerage company." Shields asked for seventy dollars a week and was offered seventy-five dollars, because the man who hired her was impressed with her. It is quite possible that her outgoing, confident manner was a factor.

Physically, she is a large woman—not the tall, slim type that rated first in Shakeshaft's student's study, but the type that rated second, tall and heavier. Shields keeps herself immaculately groomed. In her quest to dress fashionably and well, which she believes is important for business success and general self-image, she has even taken pattern-making courses at Fashion Institute of Technology so that she can make some of her own clothes. She is not one to be discouraged from looking as well tailored as a thinner woman.

"The most wonderful compliment you can give yourself is to always be presentable," Shields says. "It's discouraging for many women, because the media has depicted the skinny woman as right. But people were not meant to be a certain size. Each of us should be happy as we are. Am I inferior because I'm twenty pounds more than 'the charts, or not as pretty because my hair is not as long? If we concentrated on inner beauty, we'd all be better off."

Her size sometimes intimidates black men with whom she has business contacts, because, even though she thinks they should be keeping their minds on business, they are also evaluating her on a social level. "Men are more interested in the size of a woman's body than the size of her brain," she says. White businessmen usually respond to her mainly on a professional level. Women, on the other hand, react positively to her size. "They often look at me as a mother figure, a soft, loving figure. They're comfortable with me."

Because of this reaction, Shields often ends up counseling women who come to buy stockings or lingerie from her and to confide their frustrations about their figures. She tells them that they should be happy with themselves the way they are. Her own glowing appearance, she believes, leads women to find solace in that counsel. In addition, she believes that she provides a good role model for other black women. "It's positive for other black women to see my strength."

The broker's favorable impression of her at that second job was justified: "Within six months I was the assistant supervisor. Within a year and a half, I was the supervisor." Shields decided to try to supervise, because she did not care for sitting in one spot and keypunching all day long. Also, without a college degree, it was her only means for moving up. She started preparing right away: "I learned all the jobs that were there, and I did them well. I get along real well with people. I did my best at everything that I did. Whenever the supervisor needed me, I was there. And I let them know that I wanted it."

She was the first black to be hired in a department of thirty-five. The supervisor, she discovered, was looking for a new assistant. She and another woman, who had worked there for two years, were the only two who had interest in the job. "Not having the experience of knowing the politics that you play in business, I went to the supervisor and I told her I wanted the job." As it turns out, this naiveté led her to just the thing management experts say employees should do: ask for what they want. "I told her, 'I don't know any other way of saying it, any other way of bringing attention to myself except to let you know that I want the job.' And she gave it to me right on the spot."

The other woman, who had been there longer, was resentful,

says Shields. "It was a strange situation. As the only black there, I had gotten along well with everyone up to that point. Then, I would walk into the ladies' room and they would all be quiet. I don't think the others resented me as a black woman. I think it was just resentment that the other woman passed on to them."

The unsuccessful supervisory candidate also would not follow Shields's directions. "I asked her why she was resentful, and she said she felt she deserved the job. I told her if she deserved it, she would have had it way before I did. She took it for granted that because she had been there longer, she deserved the position." Talking about it did not solve the problem, however. "One day, she didn't do what I asked her, and the supervisor stepped in and took my part. The supervisor backed me, and the girl realized I would have the support of management, so she straightened out." It was an on-floor confrontation, in front of everyone. "The only other thing I had thought of doing was to completely ignore her. I didn't want it to become a racial situation, and I knew it could have become a racial situation. I had no problems with anyone else."

Using instinct rather than school-taught supervisory skills, Shields followed a course that fits the advice offered to black female managers by model-entrepreneur Naomi Sims in her 1982 book, *All About Success for the Black Woman*. In it, Sims advises black women encountering prejudice never to demand special treatment, never to make hasty judgments about why people are not getting along with each other, and never to be afraid to speak up if someone appears to be getting out of line. "Nip it in the bud. Make it very clear to everyone in the office that you do not appreciate that kind of familiarity or humor. If you let things slide, it will escalate."

But Sims also advises caution, a route that Shields followed: "If you approach your job in a predominantly white organization convinced that you will be subjected to prejudice, you will prove yourself right the first hour of the first day, as soon as a person fails to return your greeting.... If you expect to be offended, you will be; and you will give offense by projecting an obviously defensive attitude. ... I have seen intelligent young Black women walk into neutral situations tight-lipped and with blazing eyes, clearly expecting a battle and by so doing encouraging one. No one likes to be prejudged. Wait until you have solid evidence of prejudice before you make a federal case."

Richard Clarke, owner of a New York executive recruitment firm that specializes in minority placements, says that supervisors will always have people grumbling about them, and disappointed job seekers will always find something disparaging to say about the person who got the position they wanted. The only difference, when the supervisor or job winner is black, is that the grumblers will probably pick on race, the most obvious element, as their focus. "If both women had been white," he says, commenting on Shields's situation, "the other woman would have said that she sleeps around, or that she's fat, or that she has stringy hair. Her resentment could be manifest in many shapes and forms."

If someone does make a racial remark, Clarke says, the most advisable thing for a black supervisor to do is not to react in public, but to call the person later and ask to meet for coffee or a drink. Then she could explain, he advises, that the person had made an offensive comment, which the black person is sure the white person did not intend, and explain why it is offensive. "You've co-opted that person. You've laid a heavy guilt trip on him or her, and then you can move on."

Although Clarke believes that prejudice is pervasive in our society and that black people like himself suffer "daily inequities"— such as, in his case, being mistaken for an elevator operator despite his expensive three-piece suit—he thinks the real obstacles to black advancement do not start until a black person gets closer to the top of the pyramid. "At the middle-management level, you have innocuous social contact, networking-type contact," he says. "But closer to the top, your job carries over into the social environment." There, the black person has difficulty competing. "They have the greens of the country club. We have the concrete of the city, which is an unyielding foundation for success. It doesn't have the spring of the country club greens, or the connecting links for an exchange of ideas."

Shields never reached that country club level in an organization. But, having gained a supervisory position, she had no problems telling people what to do. "In fact, I'm attempting now to tone down my supervisory approach to people. When you have two to three people [as she does in her store], you work together. But when you have thirty, forty, or one hundred twenty-five, you never have that personal contact. You're always the general issuing orders. What I'm doing now is redeveloping my approach toward my staff, not to issue orders. It always comes out when I'm in a working situation with somebody that I assume a lot of authority and responsibility."

Part of that sense of authority, she thinks, was fostered early, when she and her sister traveled alone as children from New York to Georgia to visit their grandparents. She was seven when the visits began. "I was younger, but I was always the big one, and I always had the responsibility. The money was always pinned in my pocket, and I had to keep up with the lunches. I had to make sure we got off at the right stop, because my sister went to sleep." And then, having her own child so young added to that sense of responsibility.

During the time she worked at Hayden Stone, from 1965 to 1971, Shields married. She moved with her husband to Los Angeles, where she supervised four keypunchers at Motown Records. After getting divorced, she returned to New York. Answering an ad for a data-processing supervisor that specified "minorities wanted," she got that job. Meanwhile, though, "I realized that being a supervisor was as far as I could go." She had been discussing with her sister, off and on, opening a hosiery store. When she won the malpractice suit, she decided it was a good time, and moved down to Atlanta to join her sister.

Being black, she says, did not hinder her and her sister in dealing with suppliers or any of the other business people they needed to contact in setting up the store. They decided to include lingerie because "you have to sell a lot of stockings to pay the rent," and because downtown Atlanta had no other source for fine, private-label lingerie. Many of the garments she sells are made especially for her store.

Part of her ease in opening a store without encountering racial prejudice, Shields says, is due to its location in Atlanta, a city with a large black population and a reputation for encouraging black enterprise. One black woman works as an administrative assistant for the shopping center management, and two other black women own stores in the downtown mall, the Peachtree Center. Although Shields is acquainted with them, her friendships with some white store owners are closer. She feels that, because of her own personality, she has not encountered prejudice in any major way.

"I was always conscious that I might be seen as a single, black woman in a situation. But for that to come into play, it has to be part of my personality, and it's not. I deal with people as people. I have been exposed to all types, and I have no problems with communication. I don't own a black lingerie shop. I cater to women, not to black or white women. It's not part of my frame of mind, not part of my thought pattern." Her mother taught her to have friends of both races, she says, and not to differentiate between them.

Recently Shields discussed the subject of race with a white manicurist who works in the shopping complex. "She told me that people always referred to me by name, not by saying, 'that black woman' or 'the black girl who owns the lingerie shop.' The color situation is just not there."

Shields's situation is not the common one, according to Naomi Sims, who writes that this is still "a white man's world" and that black women must tread a tricky line to succeed amid massive prejudice in the workplace. But, she adds, "There are no easy answers. No two Black women share exactly the same perspective because no two Black women share the same life experience. Some tell me that they have never experienced any real prejudice in their lives and others that every working day is riddled with subtle put-downs."

Richard Clarke, however, is blunt about his view of Shields's philosophy: "Anyone who is black and says she is treated the same way as white people has her head buried in the sand. . . . There's an old black joke that goes, 'Mirror, mirror on the wall, who's the fairest of them all?' The answer is, 'Snow White, and you better damn not forget it.' "

California human resources consultant Julie O'Mara, who has worked with several black women, says that Shields's position as an entrepreneur protects her from some of the barbs that top black managers face. "As an entrepreneur, she comes from a position of power," says O'Mara. "There is a lot more pressure within an organization." Black women in organizations, she advises, should get as many allies as they can, among blacks and whites, and build a strong support group. The pressures on black women executives include their position as "two-fers" in affirmative action programs. "So if you are a black woman, there is usually more pressure put on you by the organization to be a superb performer, because a lot of them want to promote black women. When you're in a visible place in an organization, it always gives you more stress." In addition, black women must deal with the double issues of racism and sexism.

O'Mara thinks that if a woman encounters prejudice for either reason, "It is quite all right at times to show anger. But you need to be really calculating in your display of emotions in an organization. Sometimes it's useful to let your feelings be known, sometimes not. My advice is always to be in control of your emotions, to only show them if it is to your strategic advantage. For example, if someone is exhibiting offensive behavior, you want it very clear it needs to stop. ... I'm not in favor of ranting and raving, but if you are always unemotional, people don't know where you stand."

Though Shields says that there is no general prejudice surrounding her workplace, she does recall one small brush with resentment that manifested a racist tinge. When she and her sister first opened their store, they were in an out-of-the-way location in the basement. When the management gave her a better spot, on street level next to a large newsstand with a lot of foot traffic—because her store was doing well and always looked nice—she began to hear some "catty remarks" and sensed a little resentment from a few fellow store owners.

"Maybe it's jealousy, but it would be based on race, not sex." Women seem to resent her more than men, she says. "But it's just a small barrier. Once they talk to me, I can win them over." Because people in the South are accustomed to living and often working in segregated situations, it sometimes takes a little longer to get a smooth relationship going in her new location. She has never confronted anyone directly with charges of racism, she says, but by making her colleagues see her as a human being, she eliminates the few problems that have come up. Her approach, she says, may not work for everyone or in every case.

The one point Shields is sensitive about has to do with hiring a white saleswoman. "I have a lot of people tell me I would do a lot better with a white woman. I feel I've worked hard at this, and I'm not going to give the credit to someone else. And I believe that I am sharp enough and smart enough to deal with anybody that comes through the door. I'm not saying I would never hire a white person. I'm getting ready for a fashion show, and I will hire white models." A little later, she softens her stance, which seemed to have some ambivalence behind it, and says she would hire a white saleswoman if it was someone she knew very well. Although Shields says she does not notice color, she is aware that about 85 to 90 percent of her customers are white, since the mall is near several convention-center hotels and downtown office buildings.

While in her store, one observes both white and black customers looking and buying, equally comfortable with her presence—although they may mistake her for hired help. Shields says that such errors do not disturb her, as long as customers treat her with respect, which most do. She generally does not correct people, and she does not argue with those rare shoppers who are offensive.

As I left, Shields introduced me to a customer who knew she was an owner and for whom her race must strike a positive note—a member of the popular black singing group, the Shirelles. Shields stood proudly as the singer praised her store. Being black and powerful, Angie Shields has found, has many rewards.

Charol Shakeshaft and Angie Shields have both found effective ways to overcome or circumvent the physical attributes that may cause others to discount them as less than powerful or authoritative figures. Neither has allowed these practical blocks—not conforming to the common image of the tall, slim, white leader—to stop her from achieving her goals. Each is well aware of the impact that her physical presence makes on some people, and has found ways to compensate. The experiences of Shakeshaft, Shields, and others provide some lessons:

• Dressing well is probably more important for small, big, or young-looking women than it is for others. It is helpful always to be well groomed and appropriately dressed, to present an image of a successful person who cares about herself.

• Women who feel at a disadvantage in projecting authority for any physical reason might get an edge by honing their "expert power," as Shakeshaft did with her wide research knowledge and as Shields did by getting to know all facets of her first data-processing job before asking for a promotion.

• Women who do not fit what the majority of people have come to look upon as the norm need to exude an extra-large sense of self-confidence. Personal charisma helps, but if they are not born with it, they can at least develop authoritative styles. They need such styles more than do tall, slim, white males.

• Women in charge should not allow themselves to be distracted from pursuing their goals by innuendos or even direct criticisms about things they cannot change, such as a high voice or a weight problem. If they do want to speak up about intolerable behavior or comments, they should do so while in full control of their emotions. This is a tricky area, because handling the situation badly could make matters worse. Women must decide on a case-by-case basis whether it is to their advantage to respond.

• Becoming part of a networking group, either at work or outside it, can be particularly important for women who face practical obstacles beyond the major one of being female. Black women may find special strength in professional groups organized particularly for them. Having a wide, informal support group at work, with people of all ages, sexes, and races, is another way to get the boosts women need to advance in their career.

• Women should remember that merely their persevering presence as women in authority will eventually erode the old stereotypes.

4

Supervising Men and Women

When Marilyn Foodim started out as an administrator in a high school, she insisted that all the women—teachers and secretaries alike—be addressed as "Ms." But many of the secretaries—women who had returned to work after raising families and who were proud to be married—resented the title, which appeared on name plates on their desks. One woman even inserted her own r. After two years, Foodim decided her order was not a good management tool and abandoned it. Now, at her new job, she tells secretaries they can use whatever title they like, and she herself has gone back to being Mrs. Foodim. "It's less trouble. It doesn't get in the way."

Foodim has had different experiences supervising men. In one case, she delegated to a male colleague a job that had to be done over the weekend—and apologized profusely, adding that she was too busy that weekend to do it herself. When she got home, her business-executive husband criticized her for that approach. "Marilyn," he said, "that's a woman thing. You're supposed to delegate to him. You don't have to apologize to him."

On another occasion, Foodim was arranging teaching schedules when a male teacher walked into her office and asked to take a look at them. "Do you mind?" he asked, as he started looking over her shoulder. She did mind but did not say so—not until he started asking questions and requesting changes for himself. Then she told him, "I can't talk to you about this now." But she still felt guilty, even though she knew she was right and should have, in fact, cut him off the moment he had intruded into her office. "I don't talk to people

63

that way, because I'm a woman and I feel uncomfortable. I feel he won't love me. I just shouldn't care what he thinks of me, but I do. And it bothers me that I care. Intellectually, I know. But emotionally, as a woman, I want everyone to think, Isn't she wonderful, isn't she bright, isn't she capable." But Foodim had learned one lesson from her earlier experience supervising a man: she did not apologize, and never intends to unless she is wrong.

These episodes in Marilyn Foodim's managerial life underscore some of the special problems that female supervisors have. Some say that male and female managers have similar problems, while others say that women in charge sometimes actually have an advantage, a special touch—more compassion, more flexibility. Those views will be discussed here, too.

In fact, the problems and the advantages that women managers may have are often sides of the same coin. The compassion that leads to worker loyalty in one case may lead to laxness and less productivity in another. It depends on the situation and the people involved.

Psychiatrist and psychoanalyst Jean Baker Miller believes that women face a variety of fears when they confront power in their work lives. Because of many women's backgrounds in "caretaking" and "nurturing," they define power in different ways from men. Women who raise children, for example, are trying to foster someone else's power at the same time as they are using their own influence. Thus, women "would be most comfortable in a world in which we feel we are not limiting, but are enhancing the power of other people while simultaneously increasing our own," she writes in *Women and Power,* a Work in Progress paper published by Wellesley College's Stone Center for Developmental Services and Study, of which she is director.

When women do want more power, such as jobs in which they would be directing others, Miller says, they often feel that they are being selfish, a conception of themselves that many cannot bear. Men rarely display such a fear, she says. Other women feel they are being "destructively aggressive" if they become powerful, and some feel they become a "nonwoman." Though Miller thinks women should overcome their fears of power, she also thinks that it is not a bad idea for them to continue to define their use of power in their own way: to enhance, rather than diminish, the power of others. Marilyn

Foodim, as we shall see, incorporates this approach by trying to help others move into management positions.

Many women find no differences between supervising men and supervising women, while others find that the approaches differ. But it is not necessarily easier for a woman to supervise other women, as Foodim found out when she tried to impose her "Ms." rule.

The balance to aim for is between competence and compassion, says Washington, D.C., management consultant Alice G. Sargent, author of *The Androgynous Manager* (1981). Sargent suggests that men and women break out of sex-role stereotyping by learning a blend of the best management behavior and skills traditionally associated with the other sex. Thus, men would become better managers by learning to be more sensitive to others, more aware of the relationships between people, more responsive to others, and better able to express their emotions. Women would become better managers by learning more about solving problems analytically, by dealing with conflict, making decisions, and by being independent and competitive.

As a manager, it is also important to think of your employees in androgynous terms, Sargent says in an interview. More men—a growing minority, especially among younger men—are likely these days to want to think of their families while building their careers. They may not want to be tied to the single-minded career paths, including long hours and frequent transfers, that men had to expect in years gone by. And many women, of course, want additional responsibilities and decision-making powers.

The idea, says Sargent, is to build a team, to use fully the resources of both men and women, and to treat all employees fairly. Women and men can learn skills from each other, and the special qualities that women bring to the workplace, such as nurturance and expressiveness, should be encouraged. An androgynous manager is able to extend compassion as well as to expect good performance, Sargent says. For example, an employee who has just gone through a divorce should be free to ask for and receive a few months' grace period, after which he or she can make a commitment to return to a normal working pattern—just as the manager would be likely to grant such a reprieve to an employee recovering from a heart attack. "A lot of people don't believe it, but the way to increase productivity is to be effective in your relationships with people," she says.

Sometimes a different job requires a different kind of supervising skill. For example, Angelyn Shields, the Atlanta lingerie-store owner whose story was told in chapter 3, believes now in a strong team approach. Her idea of a good employee is one who does not need to be told what to do at every step. But in Shields's former job, as a data-processing supervisor, she used a different approach because she was overseeing large numbers of women.

"What I'm doing now is redeveloping my approach toward my staff, not to issue orders," Shields says, though when she was supervising 125 people at once, she had to be a "general issuing orders." She still catches herself occasionally ordering an employee—including her daughter, who works with her now—"to clean off the counter, check the dressing room when a customer is finished, stay off the telephone." But, she adds, "I don't want to do that. I would really like to work with people who have this as a thought in their own mind, who are conscientious enough to clean off the counter when it needs to be cleaned, take out the trash when it needs to be taken out. Someone who understands we're here to cater to the customers, who help pay the rent."

Shields learned another lesson about an aspect of supervision when she and her sister first opened their store together: "We were equal partners, and you can't work like that. You have to have a boss." The two worked well together when they were gathering information and supplies to open the store. Once the business was started, though, they argued over matters such as bookkeeping and record keeping. Part of it was sibling rivalry, Shields feels, but the situation could have been avoided if they had followed Small Business Administration advice to define their roles clearly before they started. "But when you're in with your sister or someone close, you say, You do your part and I'll do mine." The result of their disagreements? Her sister is no longer actively involved in running the store. Although it is certainly possible for men to make the same kind of miscalculation, this seems a pitfall that women, with a traditionally less structured approach to business, seem more prone to.

Since many women are now starting their own businesses, and often with partners, Shields's warning is especially timely: it is just as important to define duties and to establish who will be in charge of what with a partner as it is when you hire an employee. It is important to aim for a spirit of teamwork—something that many women do well—but not to let it go so far as having a team with no captain.

The two stories that follow, those of Marilyn Foodim and Katherine Heaviside, illustrate the pitfalls and triumphs of being a good supervisor of men and of women. Both demonstrate that a woman's background has a powerful impact on how she treats the men and women who work for and with her.

Marilyn Foodim wears her hair short and curly to frame her large eyeglasses. Her manner is both assertive and overtly concerned for others. At fifty-one, she is an assistant high school principal, an administrative position that took her a long time to attain but that she hopes will not be the last rung on the ladder.

"I started out as a teacher a long time ago, in 1953. I'm basically an English teacher, but I also taught social studies and typing." Like many women her age, she stopped teaching when she had children and did not return until they were in high school sixteen years later, in 1971. "I had no notion of administration at that time. I found teaching very fulfilling. Then I got involved in the feminist movement. One of my goals was to see more women in administration, so that young women in secondary schools would have role models."

Then, in a different school system, she became actively engaged in the women's movement after some feminists visited the school and were badly received by the class they spoke to. One of her female students was disturbed by the reaction, and with Foodim's help formed a women's consciousness-raising club, of which Foodim was faculty adviser. From there, she joined the National Organization for Women and devoted more time and energy to the movement, working on her NOW chapter's education committee and accepting speaking engagements. The classroom incident with the visiting feminists had changed her. "I had read Betty Friedan's book *[The Feminine Mystique]* in 1963, but it didn't really sink in. It took me a long time. I was home. I was scared, and I didn't know it. I was afraid to let go because of the women's syndrome: You stay home, so how do you know you can succeed?"

Foodim got back into the working world by substitute teaching, but every time she was offered a full-time position, even though her family supported her, "I always found an excuse not to. I now understand why, and I tell other women that they have to understand that we're all afraid because we've all been at home, sheltered, not expected to do very much. Homemaking isn't counted for much, although you do many, many things."

Her sheltered background also made her unable to negotiate successfully in the work world at first. She volunteered to become assistant adviser to the school newspaper, but was doing the work during her lunch hour. "Then the assistant principal said, 'You don't have to do that; it can be part of your program.' And I was thrilled, but I never even asked for that. A man wouldn't do that, give up his lunch hour."

She still was not getting paid, however, as teachers were supposed to for advising student activities outside their regular workload. That situation did not change until union leaders insisted that she ask for payment. Foodim feared she would have to give up working on the paper. "The adviser wouldn't share his money with me; he said he needed it. I felt I really didn't need it. We were comfortable." But the fact that her husband, president of a small electronics firm, could provide for her was, she realizes now, beside the point. She was finally convinced that she had to fight for a salary, on principle. And she got it.

Foodim was still working hard in feminist activities, but did not have aspirations for her own advancement. In the early 1970s, she was active in the movement to eliminate sexism from textbooks, giving speeches on the subject to various teachers' professional organizations and to library associations. Then another NOW member conducted a study showing that there were very few women in administrative jobs in any of the school systems in her area. As a result, several teachers formed a local branch of a national organization called the Council of Administrative Women in Education. "Most of us were not administrators, and some of us were aspiring. At this point, in 1975, I was still not interested in administration. I didn't think about it. I thought it was an important political thing to do, but it still was not for me."

Foodim did not get the kind of encouragement that male teachers might have received. "The interesting thing is, no one ever saw me as an administrator. No one ever came over and said, 'Gee, Marilyn, you'd be a good administrator,' which they do for men—lesser men, who don't have the skills that I have. I was always giving workshops and in-service courses and putting things together."

It was not until a year or two later, when she was discussing career moves with a friend, that she decided that perhaps administration might be for her, after all. She and the friend, a reading specialist, were discussing getting additional certification in their fields. "I said, 'No, Gloria, if our husbands should move, who would hire us? We're too old, too expensive. Nobody needs a reading specialist or an English teacher like us.' " Gloria's husband, a professor at Columbia's medical school, was in fact looking for a deanship or department chair position, so the possibility that she might move was real. It would be far better for her friend, Foodim argued, to get a degree in administration, which would broaden her prospects for employment.

"I convinced her, so we both went to C. W. Post evenings and summers and got a P.D., professional diploma." Gloria did eventually move away with her husband and is now a school administrator in Georgia. Foodim was not just tagging along. "I saw myself more and more as a leader. I knew I was a leader. I had been a leader in volunteer work and had even gotten invited to the White House for it. I could put conferences together. I realized, 'My God, Marilyn, jerk, sure you can be an administrator!' Do you know how long it took me? It was not until 1978 that I figured that out." That was the year she started at Post, in the twenty-fifth year of her marriage, with her two daughters already young adults.

It took a year and a half to get her degree. At the time, about a quarter of those in the program were women. Now, she says, it is more than half.

"I got my first job [as an administrator] partly because I had met the principal of the high school at a course, and he thought I was capable, I guess." The man, then still a guidance counselor, had also heard her debate the merits of Title IX, the federal program that mandates equal treatment for boys and girls in academics and sports programs. He was impressed and told her so afterward.

"I always tell women—and men—that if you want an administrative job, you must get around, you must be seen. You never know who might hire you." She was hired as administrative assistant at that principal's high school, in the same system she works for now. Recently, she was promoted to assistant principal, the highest position any woman had then reached on the secondary level in that system.

Foodim had applied for other administrative jobs before she got the high school job. In one case, she believes she was turned down as an assistant principal in a junior high because the principal felt threatened by her, though he might have accepted a younger woman. As it turned out, a young man with lesser qualifications got the job. Friends asked if she would sue, but she decided not to. She is glad now that she did not get a job that would have led to strife.

At age forty-eight, Foodim got her first administrative position. "I must tell you a terrible thing I did—and this is a woman thing, a scared woman thing. At the end of the second interview, [the principal] said, 'You're my candidate. I'm going to offer you the job.' And I said, 'My God, I didn't really think you would offer me the job. I have to think about it.' Would you believe that?" As Foodim says, "No man would do that. He would say, 'How wonderful, thank you.' Every once in a while, I'll catch myself in a woman thing, even though I'm pretty assertive. Some people call me aggressive. But thank goodness I'm getting more so, because I think I'm fair, and I think I'm nice to people who are nice to me. I'm learning not to be walked on. But there are these women things all the time."

The incident in which she apologized for rightfully delegating work, briefly recounted at the beginning of this chapter, can be considered a recurrence of her "woman thing" problem, she says. At a principals' meeting she had been given the task of starting a "snow chain," for calling teachers to tell them not to come in on days when schools are closed because of heavy snow. She had been told either to do it herself or delegate it. She delegated it to the new administrative assistant, as she should have. Calling teachers on snowy days had always been the administrative assistant's job, and he accepted it gracefully. It was the lengthy apology with which she accompanied the request that she now sees as unnecessary and that undermined the sense of authority she was trying to establish.

In the more recent incident, when a teacher interrupted her schedule making, she feels she did not act soon enough to stop him, though she did cut him short before he had wasted too much of her time. Her dilemma about how accessible she should be to her colleagues is one that is common to many female managers.

Women's problems with accessibility, compared to men's, was studied by Natasha Josefowitz, a management professor at San Diego State University's College of Business Administration. She found, in work published in the *Harvard Business Review* in 1980 and two years later in *Ms.*, that female managers were twice as accessible to their employees as male managers. "Almost no men complained of being *too* available, while most women did," she wrote. "Almost all women admitted to difficulty [in] saying no."

Being accessible, Josefowitz says, has many benefits. It strengthens employee morale and loyalty. It keeps up a flow of information between boss and employees, and it enables the manager to know more about each employee's strengths and weaknesses and how to motivate the employee. But there are also costs, particularly if the manager is too accessible: she may not have enough time to plan for the future or get other tasks done. Too much accessibility may impede her rise upward because she is overloaded with work and does not have time to be creative or get to know her superiors and colleagues. It may also discourage independence in employees.

Josefowitz's advice is to set priorities and to start each day with a list of "must do" tasks. "The trick is to organize your day so that the people working for you know that you usually will be available to them at certain times," she writes. She also advises women to use their secretaries or assistants to screen calls and visitors or, if they have no assistants, to put up signs, such as "Do not disturb unless important" or "Please come in." Learning how to end a conversation or meeting—by setting a timetable for a meeting or asking that the meeting be continued later because of a deadline the manager has to meet—is also important.

When she got her first administrative job, Foodim had trouble establishing her credibility not only with colleagues and teachers— they had to follow the principal's lead—but with students. "I would walk through the halls and go to a youngster, and the youngster would not believe I was an administrator. There had never been a woman administrator before. So what was I, a monitor or a substitute teacher or a new teacher they hadn't met? But not an administrator —that was laughable." Because they had once had a woman dean, the students called her dean throughout the years she was there. "I would try to stop them, because the status is not the same. I wanted the children to know there was a woman administrator. After me, there was another woman, and for her there was no problem. I paved the way." In the same way, another woman had paved the way for Foodim at her new high school. There, the students could accept her as an administrator. "And so I know, I have evidence, I lived through it, that unless the children *see* a woman in the role, they cannot conceive of it."

Her relationship with colleagues in the first high school, Foodim says, was excellent. They accepted her easily—except when she tried to reform their sexist language, such as referring to women as girls. "I just gave up. I think some of them learned, but I felt it was a losing battle, and I had more important battles to fight." Now she tries to be more low-key.

Foodim's past struggles with her "woman things" are no longer apparent in her management style, say several colleagues I interviewed. "She gives the feeling that everything is under control, even when things are very hectic," reports a teacher. "I've never observed her not in control."

Ronald Giancola, the school's administrative assistant, thinks Foodim is very good at delegating responsibility. "If she has a problem, she's done her homework on it, and now she has a finished product. The image she projects is an assertive one. She is thorough and does not feel any need to be humble about the quality of her work.

"You don't hear criticisms about her being a woman, but about her being a taskmaster, of having high standards and applying them to others," he continues. In one case, she spoke to a teacher who had left his classroom unattended to do something that could have waited. Giancola thinks her behavior was appropriate, because a serious problem could have erupted among unsupervised youngsters even in a short period of time.

Foodim always consults with "other members of the administrative team," Giancola says, and is good at the team approach. For a recent "sports night," an evening of interclass competition that required the enforcement of many rules and regulations for the participating students, she met with teachers and students first, then with other administrators. Very thorough in structuring the program, she also gained cooperation from all parties by including them in the planning, he says.

One of Foodim's supervising methods involves trying to be a mentor. "When I see a teacher who I think could be an administrator, I seek her out. I seek out women. I try to help them. Women who are secretaries, women in any walk of life—and men, too. Any deserving people." In this way, her background of having risen to power late in life, after fear and self-doubts kept her back, has had a great impact in the way she treats those under her, and particularly other women.

One teacher at the high school sees Foodim's helping ways as one of her strongest assets as an administrator. "What I like about Marilyn is that she encourages me not to typecast myself as a woman in education. She encourages me either to go higher [into administration] or to venture outside the field." Whenever she goes to Foodim's office to discuss an educational problem, Foodim always ends up by asking her, "How are you, and what are your plans?"

This teacher, in danger of being "excessed" because of budget cuts, has been offered by Foodim specific advice on how to repackage her resumé so that she can use her skills outside the field of education. "Marilyn presents herself as a role model for other women, and I see that as positive. She's mentioned women who have encountered obstacles, reorganized themselves, and gone into other fields. She's told me not to be afraid to knock on doors, to hang in there, to expect frustrations.... You always leave her office with a better feeling, and that's unusual." In the case of this teacher, Foodim's accessibility—which is encouraged in this particular school—has paid off with employee loyalty.

Foodim uses herself as a role model and example very consciously. "I have met women who are afraid of breaking out of what they are doing, and I tell them, 'I was afraid, and look at me.' I tell them, 'I was afraid to go back to teaching,' and they find that hard to believe, because they see me as such a strong woman. And I am."

Marilyn Foodim has definitely changed in the past few years, and it has made her a better boss. "I'm much more assertive, and I have less of a need to be loved. You can't be loved as an administrator. I still want the kids, even the kids that I discipline, to love me.... Not love, I want them to respect me as a person. I want them to understand that if they're punished, it's because they did something, that there's an effect, that I'm not doing something to them. And I think part of this stems from being a woman. I don't know if it's positive, negative, or neutral. But a need to be liked is learned, to perceive other people's needs, to make them want to see our point of view."

Education professor Charol Shakeshaft has said to me that studies show that some traditional women's traits, such as being nurturing, really make women better administrators, though perhaps not in the male mode. Women may, for instance, be better able to form a sense of community in the school or to form a team among their colleagues. Foodim agrees.

"Yes, in terms of working with kids I do have some traits that are good, and the best male administrators have that component in their personalities, too. And I'm lucky enough to work with quite a few of them. In our district, many of the men are nurturing. I'm tougher than some of the men. But this is not typical."

One thing that Foodim has softened on is the matter of sexist language, ever since she failed to get the secretaries at her first school to use Ms. She says, "I admitted to my boss after two years that it didn't serve me well. That Ms. made people question, 'Is she married, is she single, why does she use that awful word? Is she a feminist, is she a communist, is she a lesbian?' So when I went to West [the new school], I threw out my nameplate and sold out."

It is considerably less trouble to use Mrs., she says. "I want to move forward, and that [Ms.] doesn't serve me well." Younger women seem to be able to get away with it better, she adds. As for the secretaries in the new job: "I now tell them they can be called Miss or Mrs. or Ms.—I don't care which."

Her aspiration now is to become a principal. "I think principal is the hardest job. It's very prestigious, and it would say something to all the young women in the school." There have been several female principals of high schools on Long Island, she says, but many of them are single women who have "dedicated their lives. Men don't have to do that. Men can be married and have families, and live normal lives. They don't have to be monks."

Foodim has been able to have a family and aspire to being principal by approaching the tasks consecutively. She belongs to a transitional generation, which has not seen women moving into positions of authority until late in their professional lives. She grew up —as many of us have—in a milieu different from today's, one in which traditional sex-role values reigned.

"My parents were immigrants, from Rumania. They came here with very little education. My father worked in a sweatshop, my mother was a homemaker. We lived in Brooklyn. I have a brother who is six and a half years older than I, and they were aspiring for him, that he would go to college. For me, they hoped that I would become a secretary. In fact, I took the commercial course in high school. But a teacher—she was my faculty adviser—saved me. She felt I could do more demanding things. She urged me to take enough courses so I could get into college." Foodim's average was high, and she got into Brooklyn College. "My parents allowed me to do it because by then my brother was married and out of the house, and the war had come along, and my father was doing a little better financially. And I was a strong kid, and I said, 'This is what I'm going to do.'" She worked after school and during summers to pay her way.

She had not wanted to be a teacher, but took education courses to mollify, or "fool," her parents. "And then, when I went into student teaching, I realized, Hey, this is fun." She began with junior high teaching and was good enough to get special classes of bright kids assigned to her in her second year. Her teaching experiences were not finally satisfying to her, however, so she was happy when she got pregnant and could stay home, which is what most women did then. "Though I wasn't happy for long. I was kind of bored." Back in 1955, she says, people did not think about that kind of boredom. She and her husband had just bought a nice house, and he was doing well enough so that she did not have to work. "It was the American dream."

When it is suggested to Foodim that many women going back to work in their forties manage to move up quickly because of their added maturity and life experience, Foodim agrees. That, "and knowing people. I know a vast number of people in lots of fields. I can call people if I need a favor. Just having lived, feeling comfortable with yourself, helps. I feel good about myself."

Her two daughters are growing up in the new age. One is at Cornell Medical School—and her boyfriend is a secretary. The other daughter studies psychology at City College of New York. Foodim thinks she may have confused them as they were growing up. "I did a turnaround." She also sent them a double message, because she told them when they were younger, "Oh, when you grow up you're going to be a mommy," while she herself had ambivalent feelings about full-time motherhood. "After two months, I didn't know what to do with myself. I was bored. My husband bought me a dog. There were times when I would kick the washing machine. It was rough for me. But I felt guilty about not being this wonderful Mother Earth."

Now she does not feel guilty anymore. Times have changed, and times—for women like Marilyn Foodim—are better now.

When I visited Katherine Heaviside in her office one morning, she was the only one there. Heaviside, who owns her own public relations firm, Epoch 5, allows her account executives and administrative assistants to work flexible hours, also known as "flex-time." The result that morning was an obvious dearth of workers. The boss herself had to answer phones, accept deliveries, and receive visitors until the first colleague arrived. Since then, she says, she has solved her problem, although not as one might imagine. She has not abolished flex-time. Instead, she has relinquished the job of trying to schedule working hours for the seven people, some part-time and some full-time, who work for her. They now work out a schedule among themselves.

"Because I'm accommodating to many people's schedules, I had a problem at first. I was the one who had the least flexible schedule. My hours were eight-thirty to five-thirty or six. I was the first one in, and I was closing up. Now I no longer have that problem, because we all schedule in. There always has to be two people in the office at least, so the responsibility falls to everyone to ensure that I'm backed up by at least one other person. They actually do it themselves, and that has taken the burden off me."

Although morale is high in her office—as I discovered by interviewing her employees—Heaviside did not institute flex-time for altruistic reasons only. She thinks it is good business. "People tell me I'm very accommodating about their schedules, and as a result, every one of them puts in 150 percent effort, for the good of everybody. I never have to say, You have to be in there at nine o'clock."

Most of Heaviside's employees are women, and most have young children. She has been able to attract a high-powered work force to her suburban New York office because she offers part-time work and flexible hours to women who do not want to commute to New York City. She understands their needs, because she has three children of her own, aged nine, twelve, and fourteen. "It's my belief, because I know what it was like, that it's better to have somebody there totally, with a commitment to being there, than to have someone who has perhaps left a sick child sitting by himself in front of a television set because she feels she must go to work, and then is sitting at work a thousand miles away. To me it just makes sense. I would rather have people there working effectively and not making mistakes."

She remembers her own experience, while working for someone

else, of having to meet with a client during her son's first-grade play. "I know that meeting didn't go that great, because my emotional state was not good. Everyone suffered." Her account executives are not allowed to neglect clients, but they can schedule meetings when it is mutually convenient.

Heaviside is a good example of someone who has translated her own experiences as a woman into a special approach to supervising men and women. She has created a suburban office in which the personnel are intensely loyal—even though they could get higher salaries in the city—and where morale is "terrific. They say they've never worked at a place where people work for each other. If something comes up, they work around each other, they cover for each other. They'll call someone at home only if they don't know what's going on with the account." In this case, Heaviside's accessibility to her staff has resulted in some of the benefits that management professor Natasha Josefowitz described: better communication, high motivation, and great loyalty.

In Heaviside's office, whoever is available—not just one of the two administrative assistants—answers the telephone. That is one of the reasons for the rule that at least two people must be in the office at all times. Also, each account executive is responsible for all the work on accounts he or she handles, so if an assistant is not available, the account executive must do all the typing and copying and even take packages to the post office. Everyone, of course, makes his or her own coffee.

Another aspect of the office organization is a recently instituted group meeting, which allows everyone to find out about the direction of the company and to make suggestions. "If you can describe my kind of approach—it wouldn't work in a terribly large organization —I have more of a team approach to managing. When we have a problem, we talk about it—everybody."

Heaviside's approach as a supervisor seems to fit in with the power model described by Jean Baker Miller: she enhances other people's power while building her own. Everyone does have an assigned role. The account executives have their accounts, while the administrative assistants take care of the secretarial and organizational duties, although Heaviside encourages them to take on more tasks if they desire. She would train them to be account executives if they wanted, because she started as a secretary herself—unwillingly

—and wants to "open a door that had been closed to me, until I just banged at it and sort of forced the issue. I think it [being a secretary] is a good way to learn a business, and I also think people burn out at it. They just get tired. But it turns out that many people don't want the door opened to them."

Although neither of her two assistants has ruled out becoming an account executive, they have both grown in other directions. One does much of the bookkeeping and financial work, and the other sometimes writes announcements and has taken on the responsibilities of office manager, including arguing with the landlord about upkeep and other services.

Jacquelyn McCann, one of the assistants, says she was hesitant at first about working for a female boss. She had had a bad experience in a previous job, where that boss had "tried to oversee everything, and also put her hands into all parts of the pie. She was flighty. She would give a direction, and halfway through she would say, 'I didn't want you to do that.' She was not good at delegating." But Heaviside, she says, impressed her from the opening interview. "I became very confident, because of the way she presented herself. She was kind, but she knew what direction she was taking, what she wanted of someone working for her. Her whole image is very professional. I thought, This is someone I can learn from." In response to Heaviside's tone, McCann, who has extensive experience as a secretary, office manager, and production supervisor, reacted in a very confident way. She told Heaviside, "The best thing you could do is hire me. I would be a plus on your staff." Heaviside smiled, and later told her that that remark had won her the job.

Heaviside has encouraged her to oversee and correlate accounts and take on any responsibilities she wishes beyond typing and answering the telephone. "I've learned how to write press releases. I've learned to slow down in my speaking, to think carefully about what I'm going to say. Every word [Heaviside] uses is carefully chosen. On the client level, I've learned about the placement of ads, the deadlines for radio ads, and getting models for brochures."

In addition, says McCann, who thinks of opening her own business some day, she has found a model for how to behave as a successful female executive. "Katherine is very professional. She handles clients beautifully, and she's very articulate. I've seen many men who are intimidated by women in command. They're ill at ease about tiny things like pulling a chair out. She remains professional but feminine, not 'Look at me, I'm a big professional woman and you're a menial man.' She makes it easier for them to communicate. Men are receptive to her, because she's not bossy. That's true for the employees, too."

McCann thought there would be difficulties when Heaviside hired a male professor of public relations. Her own husband, McCann says, would probably feel "degraded" if he worked for a woman. But the professor has fit in nicely. "I thought he would be uncomfortable, but she handles him the same way she handles us. We're all treated equally.... She's authoritative, but she encourages everyone to show their strengths."

For all her understanding, Heaviside is not lax, says one of her account executives. "It's a comfortable place to work. She gets the job done through precise direction, but there's always an element of flexibility. She will write down her ideas in short notes and then sit down with you for ten minutes and be very specific." For example, explains the account executive, she handles an account for a professional guild that is involved in trying to get their trade, electrolysis, licensed in all states. When the guild told Heaviside they needed help in a licensing campaign in Texas, "we had a short meeting, and I was told to contact newspapers, senators, and others, and to relay this information in three days. It was a mountain of work, but I had the outlines of what needed to be done." After she had written a draft of a background paper, it went to the editorial person on the staff, then back to the account executive for a rewrite. "Katherine will look at a final product if it's controversial or may involve litigation." She does know how to delegate.

The same account executive compares her current job to a previous one with the public relations department of a bank, where she also worked for a woman: "I was given specific tasks, but I had no leeway in terms of thought processes. There was no element of creativity.... I think there's more respect in this office, more respect for the intelligence and the abilities of the workers." Then, when she worked for a man in another job, she says, "The feeling was that maybe you're not as experienced, maybe I should spoon feed this to you, I don't know if you have any gray matter. It took an effort to make my intelligence known, to offer ideas and to get them heard. No one is treated that way here." Even the interns who sometimes work in the office for college credit are considered to have valuable ideas. "We try to benefit from their input as well as give them information."

Some men find it difficult to work in her environment, says Heaviside. One in particular—who did not last very long—turned out to be "probably one of the world's great chauvinists." Example: the informal office policy has someone—whoever needs to use the ladies' room—pick up all the dirty coffee cups on people's desks at the end of the day and rinse them out. A female account executive did it for the new man the first day. A day or two later, when she returned to her desk with a washed cup, he pointed to his own cup, saying, "Excuse me, you forgot this." When she replied, "What?" he said, "It's your job, isn't it?" She simply stared at him. After several similar incidents, Heaviside fired him.

After a short stint as secretary in an engineering firm, Heaviside landed a job at a Manhattan public relations firm—as a secretary, of course. "This was in the early sixties. At the time, the only way to get a job in the field was to work as a secretary, and then take work home to prove to them that a woman could actually put together press releases. I was the first woman account executive there."

She had majored in English in college and had been steered by her parents into an interest in business—although not with an eye toward a career. Her father owned his own business, in wholesale meat, and her mother returned to work as a secretary when Heaviside, the oldest of three children, was sixteen. After graduating from college, Heaviside took a secretarial course at breakneck speed, finishing in one summer. "An interesting job was what you aimed at then. I just happened to get that job [in public relations]. I wanted a job where I could do some writing."

Heaviside did not tell the firm she wanted to move up, but "I didn't waste many weeks once I was there. I said, 'I have so much time on the train, why don't I take things home?' At first they weren't too happy. They said, 'Don't expect to get paid for this.' I said, 'No, I just want to do it.' Pretty soon, I showed I could do it. I was there not that long before someone got sick and left. It was not that hard for them to accept me because, even though I was the first female, I accepted the fact that I didn't do a lot of the same things. I didn't go out to lunch with the clients. I was kind of a housebound executive. I stayed in the office. A woman just didn't come calling on a client."

Later, Heaviside worked as an in-house public relations person for a few years and then, at twenty-five, stopped to have children. During that time, she wrote magazine articles and did consulting work. "I loved being home. It was a new challenge. I became a good cook and learned how to put up wallpaper. It was all new to me."

When her youngest child turned three, she worked briefly for a local public relations firm, then decided to start her own. "I started by bartering my services with a few small accounts." Her first commercial account was a shop that sold jogging shoes and other items for runners. It caught her attention because, a serious runner herself, she felt she might have an affinity for their product. She saw their sign on a building before they had opened, and just walked in.

"I decided that I needed clients to get clients." They offered Heaviside ninety dollars' worth of merchandise in exchange for whatever publicity she could get them. She spent about forty-five minutes interviewing the woman of the husband-wife team who owned the store, sitting in a nearby soda shop and feeling very frustrated about how she was going to get them publicity, when the woman casually mentioned that her husband had won the first New York City Marathon. Heaviside went to a newspaper with that angle—still not extremely confident, because the running craze was not yet that strong —and got both a sports columnist and a magazine writer interested. She was on her way.

"I never asked for more payment. I considered my payment the fact that I had a client." At about this time, she was asked to do publicity for a New York State women's conference and ended up writing an article about the conference for a national women's magazine, in which she interwove her own experiences as a runner. "I tried to weave in how feeling command of my body gave me confidence in other areas. . . . It got to be a story about how I redeveloped confidence in myself by this experience [of running], by setting out with goals I'd made and feeling physically fit." Out of that article came another client: the husband of one of the magazine's editors had a firm that needed public relations, and he hired her.

Heaviside worked out of her home at first, until her company grew too large. "I had a young woman working with me in my bedroom. I had photographers in, but I could never have clients in." She finally rented an office.

She has had no difficulties supervising the photographers, artists, and other creative men she sometimes hires for jobs, but every once in a while, she says, she will sense that there is a client—if he is not the one who hired her for the job—who does not want to speak to a woman. For professional expediency, she likes to keep at least one man on her staff. "Whether I agree or not, some of my clients have technical companies and want to talk about mechanical things to a man, even though Mrs. X might be more knowledgeable because she's been doing it [a mechanical repair] around the house for ten years. But he will feel better talking to a man, because he feels this fellow will know what a wrench is."

Heaviside, like Foodim, likes to be a mentor to those who work for her, particularly some of the college interns, whom she keeps in touch with long after they have left her employ. She feels "motherly," she says, toward some of them.

As for her attitude toward her employees: "I try to work with people who are better at certain things than I am." One account executive is a better editor, she says, another is better at visual presentations, and one of her assistants excels at finances.

Heaviside's approach has been a success with the staff. "None of us consider her The Boss," says one account executive. "She's just a very comfortable person to work for and with."

Earning that kind of approval from a staff member is a goal of any supervisor, male or female. But becoming a successful supervisor sometimes requires more effort for a woman than it does for a man, as Foodim's and Heaviside's stories demonstrate. Not only must a female supervisor overcome the reservations about having a female boss that some of the people who report to her may feel, she also must overcome her own conditioning. The woman manager herself sometimes resists the idea that she can be a calm, competent, and convincing supervisor of men and women. Further, she may feel that she will sound shrill or domineering if she asserts herself in totally appropriate ways, just because she is female. Or she may fear that becoming a good supervisor means giving up some of the "softer," nurturing attributes that she values.

But the perceptions of others and one's own personal conditioning can be changed, as is demonstrated by the experiences of the two women profiled here, one within a larger organization, the other in a small business in which the supervisor is also the owner and has complete control. Their stories point out some valuable lessons for all women who must direct other workers:

- It is necessary to overcome those "woman things"—such as apologizing for giving an order or being overly accessible to employees—that get in the way of being an effective supervisor.
- It is not necessary to give up the special compassion or understanding women might have as a result of their social conditioning or of being mothers—especially if they can turn it into an effective tool that promotes better communication and greater loyalty from those they supervise.
- Women must try to develop an air of confidence and authority, so that those who work for them will feel that they are always in control. People do not like to work for someone who seems weak or unsure of herself; they like to work with winners and people they feel they can learn from.
- Female managers must learn to delegate authority and then allow the person to whom they have delegated a task to do it undisturbed by meddling. This does not mean there cannot be established procedures for checking the work afterward, but giving a little leeway promotes creativity.
- A good manager treats everyone, including secretaries and interns, with respect. People generally rise to the expectations others have of them.
- Women who supervise should give specific directions and know what they want. As kind, understanding, and respectful as they try to be as bosses, they are still in charge and have the final responsibility to see that everything is done right.

5

In a Man's World

Sometimes women will find themselves in what is truly still a man's world: lumbering, contracting, or some aspect of the construction trade are examples. These women get a more intense dose of what many other women managers must face as well—trying to project authority in a setting that is still largely masculine.

While banking, retailing, and other white-collar professions are slowly letting women sneak into the corporate boardroom, the hard-hat, technical, and engineering fields are among those that remain the bailiwicks of men. Usually, this is not because the men in those professions are more chauvinistic than the executives of IBM or Citibank or a large corporate law firm; rather, it is because women, until very recently, have not even thought of entering those careers. Or, even if they did think of entering them, they often did not have the training, background, or guts actually to try. These male-dominated fields are, nevertheless, where the large salaries and healthy opportunities for aggressive entrepreneurship often reside. Younger women, who are gaining degrees in fields such as engineering in ever greater numbers, are beginning to realize this. When more mature women get in, it is usually through some fluke—but then, that is how most women seem to have fallen into their careers.

There is little question that these nontraditional fields for women are good sources for money and jobs, at least for the 1980s. Economist Pearl M. Kamer, who has analyzed United States census, labor department, and office of education statistics, concludes that except for nursing the job outlook in "traditional" women's professions, such as social work, teaching, and library science, is not bright. A Ph.D. in science or engineering can command a high salary, yet women are still not conditioned early enough in their lives to strive in these fields, she says. During the 1980s, Kamer predicts that the best-paying professions with the greatest number of openings will include accounting (61,000 new jobs a year), engineering (46,500 new jobs yearly), law (37,000 a year), medicine (19,000), and the life sciences (11,200). Even among clerical workers, a fast-growing but low-paying field, the woman with skills as a computer technician or word-processing operator stands a much better chance of gaining a high-paying job than a clerical worker without these skills—although still not as high as a computer systems analyst or an engineer.

Once inside these traditional male bastions, women have found that their experiences are not that much different in quality from those of managerial women in any corporation where the woman in charge is still an anomaly. They have problems finding restaurants or clubs in which to entertain clients where the check will be brought to them instead of the male client. They may find that new business contacts refuse to deal with them on the telephone, insisting that they must speak to the person in charge, who cannot possibly have such a high-pitched voice. Or they may find themselves complimented, as was one structural steel contractor in Kansas City, by having a man say about her, "She's the most businessmanlike woman I know." The difference is really only one of degree. The situation may be exacerbated when a woman works outside a large metropolitan area (where most men have learned not to *say* certain chauvinistic things even if they still think them).

The women I spoke to in male-dominated fields exhibit varying attitudes toward the occasional prejudice or difficulty they encounter. Some are angrier than others; some are amused; others barely pay attention to the problems. They are united, however, on the best way to ease their burdens, heavy or light. Their answer is expediency: plan ahead to avoid embarrassments where you can, and ignore the rest as much as possible. For the top executives I talked to, business comes first, no matter what their emotions might be. Not one of them thinks she ought to be fighting for the feminist cause at every doorway, coatrack, and restaurant table. Many management experts agree that a noncombative stance is often the best.

At a seminar on developing executive skills for female managers,

Chicago management consultant Marge Rossman recently was asked by a young woman who holds a supervisory job at a railroad what to do about the men working for her who say sexist things to her. "I don't respond, but I feel hostile," she told Rossman. Rossman in turn advised her indeed to reply, and to say something like this: "When you say that, I feel angry, hurt, and put down, and I don't want you to do that anymore." Avoid raising your voice, Rossman cautioned. "It should take no more than five such responses to discourage the remarks. Part of the reward people get for making sexist remarks is an emotional reaction. They'll stop when you're just no fun to harass."

Another woman working for the same railroad then asked Rossman, "But won't that approach work better in an office, where the men are more subtle?"

"No," answered Rossman. "It may even work better with railroad men. They tend to be more direct. You can say, 'I understand that you don't want women around, but I'm here and I'm going to stay.' There's no need to defend your right to be there. They don't want an intellectual explanation. They're speaking from their emotions."

Another managerial woman at the same seminar commented that, regardless of whether a woman acts in a way that is aggressive or appropriately assertive, she will "get labeled as pushy."

"Is that necessarily bad?" asked Rossman. "As soon as you stop acting like 'the good woman,' as soon as you don't fit the mold, you're going to get labeled something. Some men are able to see women only in three traditional roles: as mother, dependent, or sexual partner. . . . Let's be realistic. Just because we've seen the light and want nontraditional jobs, why should the men understand? They don't see any value in more competition in the workplace. They see no rewards." Even though they may not articulate it, men are often fearful of seeing more women in the marketplace competing for the positions they seek. Their frequent reaction is to label the new competitors as pushy or aggressive.

The course for women to take, Rossman concluded, is to become more assertive, to develop their enterprising, independent "male" side—without giving up the caring, nurturing "female" side they have been taught to develop as traditional women. Like others, Rossman believes in the proposition formulated by psychoanalyst Carl Jung, that we all have male and female characteristics (Jung called them the *animus* and *anima*), and that the ideal is an androgynous personality, with each element equally expressed.

Following are stories of three women in various parts of the country who deal nearly exclusively with men in their business environments. One started her business with her husband, another started it by herself, and the third took over the family firm—having been selected by her father over two older brothers.

Diane Johnson had her first date with her husband-to-be when she was fourteen. They went to the movies together in Pueblo, Colorado. Five years later, they were married, and Johnson stayed home with their three children for eighteen years. "I did what was expected of me in my younger years," she says in her soft, youthful-sounding voice. "But I was never a happy homemaker." She had worked only briefly, before her first child was born in 1954, as an X-ray technician. "I intended to go to college when the youngest child went to school, but I was twenty-nine then and afraid of the competition from eighteen-year-olds." Ten years later, she was no longer afraid. "I was terribly unhappy with my life, and I came to the conclusion that it was no good just to complain."

By that time, the women's movement had had its impact, too. "When I first read [Betty] Friedan, some of the things she said really applied to me. I had been raised, as other little girls of my age, to be popular, to have everyone approve of what I did. So a lot of us lived a kind of sham existence, and we thought we were crazy not to accept it. To have someone publish a book saying we were not crazy was good. I felt, here you are sitting in this town playing bridge once a week—though I love bridge—and I wanted to get a job." After some traveling around the country following her husband's jobs in a steel corporation, they had returned to Pueblo. Johnson was no longer interested in X-raying and so got a degree in accounting. At the same time, her husband had become disillusioned with his own job and was offered a new one in Houston. They decided that she would complete her degree in Pueblo while he went ahead to Houston. "We lived apart for fourteen months. It was a difficult time, but we saw each other once every month or six weeks. It was a conscious choice, rather than have one of us give up something that was precious to us."

The main incentive for her husband's decision to take the new job in Houston, in which he sold oil-field pipe, is that he was on a bonus plan instead of straight salary and was able to accumulate in two years enough money for them to start their own business. Today he is president, and she, at forty-nine, is executive vice president of Houston's Central Pipe and Supply Company, which they own fifty-fifty. "We're dependent on each other's skills. It's a true partnership."

"Most of my time is spent with men. I have few contacts with women in business," she says. "There are difficulties, but they're something I basically live with—except there'll be days when all sorts of little things happen. They seem immaterial, but they add up, and I'll get angry." Johnson cites an example of a recent telephone call the receptionist put through to her from a woman who greeted her voice by saying snootily, "I was holding for the owner of the business." Johnson's answer: "Well, you got her." That firm did not make a sale to Johnson's company. But the irritation did not stop, Johnson says. She received several pieces of mail the same day addressed "Dear Sir."

In general, she is treated well by clients and suppliers she already knows, and particularly by their suppliers in Japan, even though one man from Tokyo told her she was the only woman he had ever talked business with. Often, however, all the executives in the firm except her will receive an invitation to a cocktail party or other get-together. "Two companies always have the courtesy to send me a separate invitation. I tell them I appreciate it." When she attends conventions, too, she always registers separately, even if she has to pay extra. "It's the only way to get my company name on my badge. Otherwise, women get no company name as a matter of course." These problems, she points out, are not matters of "life and death. But they're irritating."

With maturity, Johnson says, she has learned to react with "expediency" rather than with anger, something she thinks her peers have learned, too. "How I react depends on the situation. It's very difficult never to be given the check at the country club at which I am the primary member." In fact, it was difficult to find a private club that would take on a woman at all. "I was the only officer [in our business] without a membership." Even the country club she does belong to ended up sending the membership card to her husband, though at least they put her name on it. Another upsetting practice she has encountered is that of giving a special "women's menu" with no prices stated. Johnson considers different menus for men and women an "insufferable insult. Women make economic decisions every day and are quite capable of facing the sometimes harsh realities of restaurant pricing." Finally, there is the tradition—encountered by Johnson twice, once in Houston and once in Vienna—of giving a woman customer a rose to carry out. "I don't want a rose in my hand. I'm not in a pageant. And if you leave it on the table, they're likely to chase you to the door."

Johnson has a great deal of confidence in her management and financial abilities. Her husband knows the product end of the business, but "I can learn almost anything that has to do with business and money," she says. "I'm very aware of the importance of advisers, so we have a banker, a C. P. A., an attorney, and an insurance professional to advise us. I don't mind asking questions."

As a manager, however, she thinks she does do some things differently from the way a man in her position would, "because I'm forced to. Some people consider me, because I'm the wife of the president, to be hanging around typing the letters or something, or hanging around being supervised. If his brother were here, he would be more accepted in many places as being a real live person instead of an addendum. I think I invite myself in to meetings more, if someone is visiting the office, than I would need to if I were a man. I just have the feeling that I might ask to join something more often, whereas a man would be told automatically. I have to be more aware of things, things I should be present at, and that I've probably not been told of in advance—not just in the office, but all over. I kind of have to explain my presence a lot. When I meet someone and give them a card, they say, 'Oh, you're involved in a business,' or 'Oh, do you work full time?' It's like you're always visible. Even though you don't want to be specifically visible, in many cases you are, if you're the only female in a room with ninety men. So it does change your behavior, though I don't know exactly how. You're not one of the guys."

Mainly for reasons of comfort, Johnson wears pantsuits most of the time; she finds them easier to wear when stepping into and out of the helicopter she and her husband own, which gets them between their sales office and a small pipe-finishing plant they also own. She works long days, perhaps sixty hours a seven-day week, and does a lot of worrying about the economy and their plans besides. "If I can't sleep because I have a problem, I come to the office. I came once at 3:30 A.M. last week. There's no sense in being at home if I can't sleep." Whereas her husband will sit in their breakfast room pondering a problem, "I do better if I accomplish something. I review, do a little internal auditing, write some letters, do some tax forms, whatever." Hers is a business, she says, in which customers usually order for delivery "right now," not three months from now. "I love it. We both love doing it, even though we do get tired."

Having their own business together was something she and her husband had dreamed and talked about for years, so finally having accomplished it means a lot to them. "There was no way either one of us could have done it without the other," she adds. "It has been good for us, because we have our separate spheres, but we talk a lot, and we have total trust in each other." Her husband sells the pipe, while she handles the "paper flow."

As nearly every married woman I interviewed pointed out, having a supportive husband is imperative to success in a career. "We believe in equity, that women are real persons," one of the reasons for their fifty-fifty share of the stock. Nevertheless, she is not sure whether, if she had not suggested splitting the stock, it would ever have occurred to him to do so. That is something a woman is more likely to pursue, Johnson says. "When you've lived your whole life not being able to get a charge card at Sears Roebuck without your husband's signature, you want to change things. I've decided I can't change the world by 10:00 A.M., but I can change my little corner of it."

Even though she uses the model of expediency in her business life, she has gotten more militant over the years in her private life— filing a complaint with the Federal Trade Commission, for example, when a department store would not use her first name, only her husband's, on a charge card, and having a running battle with the post office because it kept forwarding her mail to her son's new address after he moved out of their home. They automatically forwarded mail with a woman's name on it, it seemed. They never forwarded her husband's mail. She never found out why—perhaps they assumed she was the wife of the man whose mail was being forwarded.

In the case of the charge card, the department store's chairman of the board sent her two free tickets for their shoppers' lunchroom. In the case of the United States Post Office, she had to cancel her son's forwarding request and deliver his mail herself. "Those things take energy. They make me mad. But I don't want to waste energy on things that shouldn't be happening anyway."

If she would like to see the world of business change at all with the advent of women, it would be toward less intensity and more freedom and humor, something she tries to inject herself. "I try to do it with men in business, and they react quite well." What she really admires, however, is the "free and easy, but efficient" attitude of younger businesswomen. Perhaps this is due to more encouragement in the development of their abilities and personalities. Their expectations, she says, "are wider and unencumbered by so many years of restraints."

Mary Farrar of Kansas City founded her business by herself. It came about quite by accident—or, rather, by a fortuitous chain of events. Although she acted alone in the founding, Farrar, like Johnson, raised a family first and has a very supportive husband.

Farrar, who is forty-two, is the president of Systems Erectors, a structural steel contractor, which erects the steel structures or preengineered building systems for industrial buildings. Ten years ago, she knew nothing about the business and had never even thought of it. But then, when all her children were in school, a friend asked her if she wanted a part-time job—two days a week, ten o'clock to two o'clock, nothing ambitious. It just happened that the friend, for whom she had done some accounting and bookkeeping at home, knew a man just starting a structural steel contracting firm who needed some part-time help.

"I felt maybe it was something interesting to do," says Farrar. "I started with the office management, such as bookkeeping, payroll. It was a typical woman's job." But, because the business was just starting and was sometimes slow, she had time to learn about the "field side" of operations. She learned how to read blueprints and how to make estimates, because she developed an interest in those things. "I never sensed a lot of resistance. I'm sure there were instances when maybe my word wasn't good enough, maybe people double-checked, but it was never blatant. I was never aware of any time I was actually questioned or put on the carpet. There may have been a few times, in the early days, of condescension, but I came into [the business] so gradually."

The slow, unassuming way Farrar came into the field may be the key to her acceptance in it. While still working for that first boss, she became active in the local trade association. "I was just accepted as one of the fellows," she says. Another key, she thinks, is that she always remained very professional, never coy or flirtatious. It was through the trade association that she heard the comment, "She's the most businesslike woman I know," which amused her. Like Johnson, she has experienced some problems with entertaining men at lunch, but has not gotten upset. "When you take a man to lunch, it's uncomfortable for him, but I don't think you can do anything about that. I've gotten used to it. Men need an adjustment period, too. I just try to do it the same way they would. I ask for the check early."

Farrar learned so much about the field that she wanted part ownership in the firm. The owner, however—who has since gone out of business—did not want to sell to her. So she took a bold step; she started out on her own—with only $500 in capital. Her break came when a client was willing to meet her payroll on her first job. The weekly payroll, she says, is usually $10,000 to $50,000, but the contractor gets paid only every thirty days, so it would normally take a stake of $60,000 to $100,000 to make it through until payment time. Paying for supplies can be put off for thirty days, so the payroll is the major start-up cost.

The client who helped her was one she had met through the trade association. She had gradually let it be known there that she was unhappy not being a part owner. "He gave me an opportunity, though I was sorely undercapitalized and afraid. I don't know where I got the courage to do it."

Through all of this, her husband, Farrar says, "has been a hell of a guy." Jim Farrar is employed as a commercial air conditioning and heating installer, and his wife now makes more than he does. "It doesn't seem to be a problem. His feeling is, I supported you for twenty years, now it's fine if you do it." In fact, she says, he is proud of her and introduces her at trade conventions to more people than she would approach on her own.

After twenty-six years of marriage, the Farrars spend nearly all their spare time together, more so than other couples they know.

They had dated in high school, and she married him soon after graduation, opting out of a nursing program to which she had won a scholarship but in which she was only halfheartedly interested. "Then the babies came one right after the other," she says, until there were five, now ranging in age from twenty to twenty-five. (They have produced, in turn, three grandchildren.)

"I was content at home. I made the girls' clothes when they were little. I don't know how I can be so satisfied doing what I'm doing when I was so satisfied at home. I guess there's a time and place for everything, and I don't miss the home things. Everything just fell into place. I feel very fortunate I had the opportunity to do both. I feel *luck* is a good word. I did just fall into the learning experience the first place I worked."

Many management consultants who work with women point out that women often will assign their success to luck, whereas men would stress their own active role much more. In fact, Farrar's first employment, as she admitted, could have turned into just a dead-end job. She took the initiative herself to learn the field side, to become active in the trade association, and to put out feelers about getting started as an owner rather than to remain an employee. When I challenged her about her modesty, she agreed there was more to it than luck. "You have to have some kind of crazy drive. Most people wouldn't have bothered to learn how to estimate. It was both interest and a drive to learn something new and different. I wanted to know about the whole operation. I think a small company gives you an opportunity like that. It wouldn't be the same in a big construction company."

It may also be that having the confidence that derived from being a competent homemaker helped her, too. The women I have interviewed who returned to work after years at home have usually struck me as uncommonly calm, measured, and wise beyond the maturity that comes with their greater age compared to young women straight out of college. Counselors often advise returning women to try to translate the work they have done at home raising children and managing a household into business terms for a resumé. Unfortunately, it does not always lead to a good job, no matter how true the skills may be. There is no doubt that Farrar did have good luck—but then, so do most men who make it. It is how you react to the luck that counts.

"I've always had a drive to learn," says Farrar, who grew up in modest circumstances, the oldest of six children. Her father was a Santa Fe railroad conductor and her mother a housewife, who fifteen years ago returned to school and is now a teacher. "I've had it all my life. I always wanted to know more about things. If I was playing sports, I wanted to be the best. I wanted to win, not just play. I had a crazy drive. I wanted to have the cleanest house of anyone I knew; I wanted my kids' clothes the nicest and cleanest. I'm competitive."

As we speak of these things, Farrar says the discussion prompts her to consider things that she has rarely paid much attention to: she feels she does not fit the image of the introspective, self-analytic, and sometimes angry career woman so common in the media. But, then, she has not come up through corporate ranks or through an M.B.A. program, and it may just be that it is her down-to-earth manner, local roots, and traditional background that have made her so acceptable in the man's world of construction.

Much to her surprise, she has not had trouble supervising men on the job site. Because hers is a union shop, she must talk to the workmen through their foreman. "But if someone's wife had a baby, I stop and ask him about it."

When she visits the job site—something she does every day— she usually stays in her business clothes, because often she must go to a customer's office the same day. "I go through shoes very quickly, but I try to keep a moderate appearance." If there is mud around, she will wear the boots she keeps in the trunk of her Buick, along with the hard hat. "That's part of my uniform," she says.

Although Farrar has read some management books—and now passionately would like to earn a degree in engineering—she manages "by gut-level feeling. If it feels right, I do it."

She has raised her voice at a site only twice. "I don't believe that's the way to handle people. They're human beings the same as I am. If I blow up, it's directed at the problem, not at the person." Her problems tend more in the other direction, of not putting her foot down promptly enough, such as when it comes to firing someone. "I have a tendency to let it work on me, to let it keep coming back to me, that I've got to do this, this has to be." But men, she has observed often, "get into just as much trouble reacting too quickly." She thinks women managers are probably more prone to delay, which occasionally works out for the best. In her case, she says, a foreman has sometimes solved a problem himself when, for instance, she has delayed getting in touch with a manufacturer about a fabrication problem.

Some of the younger workers called her "mom-boss" when she first started, but she has not been called that in the past couple of years. "Now we've gotten used to each other, gotten to know each other." On the whole, she tries to work through personnel problems rather than fire people, which she thinks men are more inclined to do.

Despite her lack of engineering background, she thinks it a positive thing that she entered from the business rather than the field side of construction, because too many male owners have floundered by spending too much time at the job sites and not enough at the books, looking at cash flow and other important items. Though she has a bookkeeper, she does the long-range financial planning herself.

Her success in the trade association for metal building dealers has been enormous. She was president of the local chapter for two years and is active in the national group, where for many years she was the only woman. Recently, national officers asked her to help them identify and welcome other women in the field. After much search, she was able to find two more. Although she was against having anything like a "women's auxiliary"—because she "wanted to be on the same level as the fellows"—Farrar has found it comforting to know that there are other women out there with the same problems. She talks to them once a year at conventions about the very occasional worker who does not want to work for a woman or will do things the wrong way just because a woman told him or her what to do. "But the bottom line is we probably are just as interested as the men in making a buck and being successful."

And successful she has been. "It was always something that happened so naturally. My resumé looks so stupid. It doesn't make any sense at all. But that's the way it happened. I'm not apologizing for it. I'm happy with it."

It is not unusual for a man to pass on his business to his son, but it is unusual for him to pass it on to his daughter—especially if there are already two sons working in the firm and if the firm is a lumber business.

That is what happened, however, for Barbara Webb, who became president in January 1982 of Webco Lumber of Grants Pass, Oregon, when she was thirty-four. The firm had been founded by her father twenty-five years earlier, but had been floundering in recent years, unfortunately a common situation in the timber industry, which has been affected by the decline in housing construction.

The reason for Barbara Webb's ascendancy is fairly straightforward: she was the one who decided, and persuaded others in her family to agree, to take the step that saved the business. That step has turned things around, so that instead of closing sawmills, laying off workers, and facing a steep decline in profits, the business is now growing fast, adding workers, and even turning away orders.

The decision was to sell to Japan. In retrospect, turning to the export market seems a logical and simple step, but at the time it went against the usual practice of the United States timber industry. It meant cultivating long-term relationships patiently and being willing to change to Japanese standards and specifications. It also meant taking a big risk.

When the opportunity came for a group of lumber executives to visit Japan on a trade mission, Barbara's brother Ronald, the sales manager/secretary/treasurer of the company, questioned whether they could afford the five-thousand-dollar cost of the trip when they were having difficulty paying their bills. She recalls telling him at the time, "I don't think we can afford not to go." Within six weeks after the visit, two dozen Japanese firms sent representatives to check out the mill. The Japanese turned out to be tough customers, wanting their unfamiliar lengths and shapes cut precisely to size—more so than American customers—and sending emissaries to monitor the work, which slows it down and which American firms never do. Nonetheless, Barbara Webb continued to encourage the export trade, even converting a former headquarters building into a guesthouse, and that prompted the four directors of the company—her father, two brothers, and herself (though her father, she says, had the strongest voice)—to elect her president. "My two brothers are both older [thirty-seven and forty] and have trained longer in the lumber business. But there are no bad feelings. You can be trained for a position, but you need the personality. You need to be willing to have one-to-one confrontations with people, to have one-to-one competition. Some people don't mind doing it." And she is one of them. For example, Webb says, there were some personnel problems, "people who needed to be talked to or terminated." She dealt with those problems, although she did not personally fire the one employee, of seventy-five, who was permanently let go. "But if I had to, it would be no problem."

What was it that gave this young woman her grit, that allowed her to break away from a traditional woman's role and to take charge in a man's world? "For me, it was the crisis, the high-stress situation. It meant survival of the company, and it changed my attitude. A few years ago, I could have been described the other way [having the traditional women's problems with firing, making tough decisions, and taking risks]. But I felt I had to save the company." Before she came on board, her brothers had been making many of those personnel and business decisions. "But it was more difficult, more unpleasant for them than for me. It's just personality." As for what shaped her personality, she is not sure, except that she seems to take after her father.

"As I was growing up, I was spoiled rotten. I was treated well. I think my father expected more traditional things of me. He encouraged me to get a strong education, but we never talked about what I would do. I couldn't decide. I was always in conflict in high school between what I could achieve versus what was the traditional role of women. I knew I was capable of *this,* but women do *that.* I did that in college, too." There, she majored in psychology and was considering a career in counseling before it seemed that the firm needed her.

A concrete example of her role conflict was her decision to marry her high school sweetheart just after graduation and to have a child a few years later. "I was fulfilling the traditional role then. But I also went to college at that time." Her daughter, now eleven, often stays with her grandfather or a neighbor during the frequent twelve-hour days her mother spends at work. "She's a strong little girl. She's so capable. She can do whatever she wants." Webb remained married until she joined the family business in 1977. She was divorced in 1980.

"It was my own decision to join the firm. I was welcomed in because they needed the help." She started out doing bookkeeping, as her mother has, too, in the past five years. But she quickly moved into computer and administrative work, and now she is involved in production as well. Her brother Larry is vice president and manager of the sawmill.

But managing the company was not always easy, and she has learned and changed over the past few years. "I've lost a lot of sleep in the last year and a half," she says in her soft-spoken, low-key way. "I talk to people, I try to accumulate as much information as I can. The hardest part is making my best judgment, and I do that alone. I drive an hour to work and an hour home, and I do a lot of my problem solving then—as well as at 2:30 A.M. I make lots of lists, do lots of thinking, looking at each problem from different directions. I've mostly learned this myself. It's my own way of doing things. I keep to-do lists. I often make major decisions away from the office, when I'm driving or having dinner."

One thing Webb decided recently is that she should reorganize the company with more of a team approach toward management decisions. "The financial difficulties pulled me away, and now I'm trying to organize again," she says. "A lot of people were let go and then brought back, which isn't normal. I kind of like getting going again. But because of the newness in the international field and the new financing, it's difficult." She has learned to delegate more and more tasks, she says, to one of her brothers, to their accountant, or to whoever is most appropriate.

Like her female compatriots in highly male-concentrated fields, she does not allow daily sex-discrimination irritations to interfere with her work. "Some customers are surprised a little at first [to meet a woman in my field], but there's no problem once they start talking to me. If there's any condescension, it's not too evident." Japanese men, she finds, are more accepting than Americans, in general, and some of the most negative reactions come from women themselves. Often women are assigned to telephone her company with sales pitches from suppliers. "If they ask for the manager and the receptionist gives a woman's name, they'll hang up."

With a B.A. in psychology and an academic interest in how people get along with each other, she takes a calm, bemused view of her position in the world. "The more I'm in it, the more I feel that being a woman is an asset. Maybe because of my nontraditional role in the industry, people seem to listen more. They remember us. I think my personal philosophy is that women carry a softer club, so they're better managers in some ways. A long time ago I heard someone say that nothing is more gentle than real strength, and nothing is stronger than gentleness. I think it fits—though some women can be real abrasive. I'm more gentle. I believe in treating people the way I would want to be treated." But what about those tough decisions she made and those tough actions she took? I ask. "That's the club. Sometimes you've got to do it."

Being a woman in authority can be an asset, Webb maintains, "if I keep an open mind, if I'm not offended by the people who have a hard time dealing with me. I can't let it bother me. They were brought up that way, and eventually they'll change."

Keeping an open mind and being strong with gentleness can be effective paths for any woman in charge. The woman who works in a "man's world" may just find it more difficult to keep to that course, because she may be more likely than other women to find discrimination or insensitivity among her colleagues. The women interviewed here who work in fields dominated by men echo themes that all women in authority have voiced. They may feel some problems more intensely, but the differences in their concerns are merely ones of degree, not of substance. All women can profit from the special insights of those who are isolated from most other women in their professional lives.

- Women are strengthening and changing themselves rapidly, while the men they supervise, work with, or work for are struggling to keep up. But it is not worthwhile to waste energy worrying about them. They were brought up to look at women in different ways, and eventually they will change. It is better to work on one's own advancement than to fret about recalcitrant men.
- Women need to learn more than the bookkeeping aspects of their fields if they are to advance. They should also learn the nitty-gritty technicalities, such as specifications for products, how to estimate the cost of a job, and how the manufacturing process works.
- It may be easier for women to start their own company in a male-dominated field than to work their way up in someone else's company. They must know the field well, however, or have a partner who does.
- Although women should not reach a state of anxiety about sex discrimination, they should be vigilant about times when they might be excluded from professional discussions and should not hesitate to invite themselves in.

• It is important for women to become active in professional associations, but also to be wary of "women's auxiliaries," which might isolate them from the mainstream. Finding other women in the same field, however, may be comforting and helpful.

• Women may not have to conform completely to male manners, but they nevertheless should behave appropriately at all times. They can be as soft-spoken as they like, as long as they assert their authority, and they can dress as fashionably as they like, as long as the hard hat and boots are in the car, ready to use if needed.

• It is never too late to get started, and sometimes it may be easier for women to do one thing at a time: raise a family first and then start a business. Having that kind of order to their life does not appear to undermine the authority of women in business and probably enhances it. Few men can point to such a variety of achievements.

6

Hiring and Firing

Without the right "team," the most creative manager can fail. Putting together the right staff requires mastery of hiring and firing, but because women, more often than men, are brought up to be polite and sensitive, they often find the processes of hiring and firing very difficult. This aspect of authority can be crucial. Women who avoid or pass on to others either or both of these responsibilities abdicate some of their power—as well as control over their own future.

Most women interviewed for this book said they do not know if their problems with hiring or firing are worse than they would be for a man—or else they deny that there is any difference. It was possible to detect, however, a gentle approach among most women that is not shared by some men. The ways one hires, turns down rejected job applicants, and fires are closely connected to how one treats people in general. Women in general do value some qualities differently from men.

One of these qualities is compassion, which very often paralyzes women who must make personnel decisions. Successful executives manage to overcome the paralysis without losing their humanity, and many such examples will be given in this chapter. Caring about others can be a positive force for a manager.

Carol Gilligan in her 1982 book, *In a Different Voice*, argues that women's moral and psychological development is different from men's. Whereas men are taught to separate themselves from others and to become increasingly independent and autonomous, women continue to struggle throughout their lives to balance their commitment to themselves with their responsibility toward others. They see morality more as a matter of caring than of impartial justice.

"Sensitivity to the needs of others and the assumption of responsibility for taking care lead women to attend to voices other than their own and to include in their judgment other points of view.... Thus women not only define themselves in a context of human relationship but also judge themselves in terms of their ability to care," writes Gilligan, an associate professor of education at the Harvard Graduate School of Education. She bases her conclusions on three studies she conducted.

Although women may generally be more sensitive about the way they actually accomplish a firing, they share with men a common anxiety about the prospect. Turning down unsuccessful applicants does not cause the same kind of stress. "You always have difficulty firing someone. It's nerve-racking. It's difficult for a man or a woman," says Diane Johnson, whom we met in the last chapter as executive vice president of Houston's Central Pipe and Supply Company. She and her husband share the hiring and firing duties. Hiring is no problem for her, but firing is. "You do anything to avoid having to do it. It depends on how irritated you are with the situation, if it affects the morale of the other employees. You have to think of the good of the others then and fire the person. I try to make it as easy on the person as I can, to put it on a job basis rather than a personal basis."

True to what Gilligan and other experts say, the women I spoke with often mentioned taking into account the other person's feelings when firing someone.

Karen Bacon, dean of Stern College for Women, says that for her, firing someone—such as a faculty member who is not being reappointed—is the worst aspect of her job, even though the decision is never hers alone. "I see the individual's personal situation," she says. "I haven't fired people alone, but in concert with other administrators. It's very difficult, but once the decision is made, and hopefully it's the right decision and made thoughtfully, then I stop dwelling on it. Otherwise, I would debilitate myself, and then I wouldn't be very functional. So in a sense, you reach a certain point, and then you turn away from it and you just say, 'That's it.' I often wonder about physicians who have done all they can for a patient. Do they turn themselves off emotionally and say, 'That's it'? I have a brother who's a cardiologist, and sometimes when I listen to him, I get the feeling that with some patients he has to say, 'That's it.' "

Becoming good at hiring and firing is often a matter of experience, and most women tend to have less experience as managers than men do, says California human resources development consultant Julie O'Mara, president of the American Society for Training and Development. "An inexperienced manager might be awkward and put things off. But once they've done it a couple of times, they know it's something they can deal with." Experience, she thinks, is important in making the right hiring decisions, too. But women, she believes, make better "people decisions." Because of their socialization, she says, they instinctively have better ways of dealing with people, asking the right questions, and eliciting useful responses.

Pennsylvania management consultant Ellen Jacke expands on that idea. "Many times women have the edge because of their intuitive people-watching skills. They don't just read the words, they read the words and the music, too." However, she says, interviewing is a skill that can be acquired, and that, unless someone is trained, she is not likely to do a good job at it. "It's a two-way street. The prospective employee is also interviewing the company or the organization, and both parties have to be prepared for the interviewing process. It is the responsibility of both sides to know what they want, to be very clear on what they have to offer. The organization should be clear on what kinds of skills they want, what the job will look like as a whole, what the relationships with other people will be, what part of the jigsaw puzzle the employee will fit into."

The interviewer should learn to ask open questions that elicit responses more than yes or no, and that make the interviewees talk about themselves. Jacke says that "Tell me about yourself" is the classic question, but it can be followed by "What is there about this company that makes you think this is the kind of atmosphere where you would be an effective worker?" and "What kind of atmosphere do you need to have in order for you to blossom, to work most effectively?"

The answers, she says, would indicate whether the person has done his or her homework in researching the company and assessing his or her own skills. "They're not the normal questions, but if you learn to ask those types, you get more information." Some good questions to look out for from the interviewee, she says, include, "What's it like to work here? What is the culture of the company? Tell me stories about how it got started."

Jacke says that women probably are better at letting down

gently those who are not successful applicants, but that a woman's response may well be shaped by the cultural norms of her company. "I like to think women would do that [reject gently] more often, but in many situations, particularly nowadays when women are under the gun, where they go out of their way not to be perceived as soft, it's hard to make generalizations. A lot depends on what the top management does, what kinds of examples they've seen. They could look at [a situation] and say, 'How would I like to be treated?' or they can be hard-nosed. Hopefully we're getting away from extremes and going to the point where we can be human rather than male or female."

One woman who agrees with O'Mara and Jacke that training and experience are important is Carnie Ives Lincoln. For ten years, starting in 1963, Lincoln was in charge of hiring the administrative personnel—all women, which was the company's custom—for Connecticut General Life Insurance Company's branch offices. She traveled around the country interviewing about three hundred women a year for thirty jobs. She read approximately three thousand resumes a year. Those people she hired were trained by her for two years afterward, so she also had some experience with firing.

Her first experience with firing was disastrous, she says. "The first time I had to do it, I was terrified. I guess I thought she would attack me." The woman had not been doing her job. "If there was a way to do it more inefficiently, I don't know what it is. I did not have her work record documented. She started arguing with me, and I didn't have the documentation. I conducted the interview at one. It ended at two, and I let her stay in the office till five. She darn near destroyed the morale of the office in those three hours with her complaining. I also didn't know what her termination paycheck would be."

Terminating a person properly, says Lincoln, requires doing the opposite of everything she did the first time. "Have the performance documented, and also know what the company is willing to do, whether they just want me to hand the person a paycheck or place them in outplacement counseling. Also, I should have practiced the actual termination, particularly if I'm new at it. A person new at it should role play the whole termination, from beginning to end, with a member of their family. That way, they'll know if they've done all their homework."

It is also important, she says, to be sensitive to the feelings of the other person. She had to fire one woman in Michigan with whom she had often talked on the telephone about her poor performance. Each time, the woman had cried. "I flew in, bought some Kleenex at the airport, went to the office and told her, 'I've come to fire you. Now, you cry for as long as you want, and then we'll talk about it.'" The woman cried for half an hour and then came out to say she was relieved about being fired and had been hoping she would be. She wanted to return to her home in North Carolina, but her mother had insisted she take the Michigan job. She asked if her record could indicate she had left voluntarily, but she wanted to tell her mother she had been fired. Lincoln agreed.

Lincoln says she had only one rule about firings that differed from most men's at her company. The firm at that time had a double standard about men and women having sexual relationships outside marriage, she says. Women were fired, but men were not. But she always gave women a second chance. If a woman working for her was caught a second time, she did fire her—regretfully. Lincoln had no such regrets about firing for poor performance, once she got over her initial awkwardness.

On the hiring side, Lincoln found her style of interviewing and making decisions did not differ at all from an effective male manager's. In fact, she gained more experience than most male managers ever get. She had to teach herself how to interview, she says, and hit upon a style that she characterizes as very directive. She would tell the interviewee that the session would last half an hour and that, in the first part, she would ask the questions, while in the second part the interviewee could ask questions. "I could interview eight people a day, with a half hour to write up each one, and make a decision based on that. Back in those days, we didn't have the affirmative-action rules and regulations we have today, so I spent a lot of time making sure they would stay with me for two to four years. I asked about boyfriends and marriage plans, questions that would be illegal today. I was hard-nosed."

But what she has found, in later jobs in which she has trained supervisors, is that most women interviewers are not like her. "Women tend to be chatty, folksy even, maybe because they want to make people feel at ease. Men go after the information. They're more directive. I've taught both kinds of interviews, the directive and the nondirective, and men have generally liked the directive kind better." But both kinds can be effective, she adds.

In her ten years of hiring, says Lincoln, she made her share of mistakes. One was in hiring a woman who had been through a tragic divorce. Her husband had run away with their son's wife, and the son had tried to commit suicide soon thereafter. The woman had such a negative view of life that no supervisor wanted to work with her for very long. She bounced around in the company for seven years before being fired. "I liked to give women who were returning to the workforce a chance. I felt they had transferable skills." Usually such hires—which she believes a man in her position might not have made—worked out well.

Another factor that makes it more difficult for some women to fire is an inability to keep business and friendship separate. This is particularly difficult for women who have moved up from secretarial positions and find it difficult to sever friendships with their former peers, says clinical social worker Deborah Karnbad. Karnbad sees many managerial women through her private psychoanalytical practice and through a New York organization of which she is vice president called Help-Line for Working Women, which provides therapy and workshops in such areas as stress management. She cites the case, related to firing, of a woman who was assigned to head a committee at her firm. A former administrative assistant, the woman had been promoted to a supervisory position in which she oversaw certain projects, including the committee to organize a social event for her firm. But among the women on the committee were several she considered friends.

"She had to set aside her priorities for the needs of the committee. She wanted to release some of the women from the committee, becasue they weren't doing any work, but she didn't want to alienate them as friends," says Karnbad, adding that the same emotions would have come into play if the woman had had to fire them from the firm instead of just from the committee. She did release some of them and did, in fact, lose some friends. "Men are much clearer about their business relationships. If they do have friends at work, the friendships are more businesslike. But women's positions are changing so much; they're moving up and they find it more difficult to cut themselves off from their former co-workers. For men, it [cutting themselves off from former co-workers] seems to flow more easily."

Sometimes, says Karnbad, women agonize more than men do

about hiring and firing because they are more nervous than men about keeping their own jobs. "Women tend to be more frightened in the higher-echelon jobs than in lower ones, and their fear of losing the job is greater. So they don't like to rock the boat that much, and firing poses a lot of questions for them: How will it affect their job, how will others see them, are they making the right decision? The result is that women tend to think about it more, and they tend to give the man or woman they're thinking of firing a second or third chance. Many women are not comfortable with firing, especially with firing another woman." In some cases, she says, managerial women are not in touch with their own competitive natures and unwittingly end up firing someone who is competent because he or she poses a threat to them.

"I think in many ways women can be a lot tougher in hiring. They ask more questions," concludes Karnbad. "The women who make it to these positions tend to be more demanding because they're more demanding of themselves. It's been a tough fight for them."

A woman whose way of handling hirings and firings might be typical is Sandra Levenson, a second vice president at a major New York bank. She is compassionate but has also learned, through experience, to be efficient at both hiring and firing. She values her career highly and believes that having the best people around her helps her to do her best job. She spends much of her time—as any good manager should—trying to avoid firings by motivating lethargic workers to become top producers.

Just as in the area of supervising men and women, a female manager's particular background seems to influence the way she approaches a hiring or firing. Levenson, a single mother for most of her career, worked her way up the ladder from near the bottom rung and also was very dependent upon her job for the welfare of her children, now eighteen, twenty-one, and twenty-three. There was no second income to back her up.

"I got divorced when my children were very young, so a career was a necessity for me," says Levenson, who at forty-one is a very youthful-looking and lively person, with brown, frizzy hair and a penchant for stylish clothes. "It was a matter of fitting everything in —the children, the career, a social life, and coming home to cook."

She started with the bank twenty years ago, toward the end of her marriage. Before that she had been a public stenographer and typist, working out of her home. She had married at seventeen, just as she graduated from high school. She has not had any further schooling. Her experience has meant that, when it comes to hiring people, she is more likely than most executives to try to assess the person's drive and intelligence rather than to look merely at background and credentials. She has worked hard, however, to avoid the trap that Karnbad identified, of mixing business with friendship.

"At one point, I hired on a trial basis someone who was a close friend for many years from another part of the bank. He was out of a job [when his department was sold to another firm], so I gave him a chance, and he failed at that chance." Because he held the job in her department even a short time, he was able to get severance pay, time to look for another job while still working, and other benefits that he would not have received otherwise. Nevertheless, says Levenson, "he hasn't spoken to me since." A man in her position, she thinks, might have left him in the job. "The women managers I know don't leave someone who is not competent in a job. I know people say that women are more emotional, but the women at my level who I know are more work oriented. They temper what's best for the company with what is best for themselves."

Levenson does not think that she acted as she did because of fear about her job security, as Karnbad suggests might sometimes be the case. "I have a reputation for really caring about the people who work for me, so if I'm tough on anyone it's going to be on the managers." This man was a manager, and his bad work was affecting others, she says. She felt betrayed by the incident, because she had acted out of friendship but was not willing to tolerate incompetence. "I stuck my neck out for him, and he didn't produce, he didn't give it back. I did that at the beginning of my career, and I wouldn't do it again."

Management consultant Ellen Jacke thinks that, despite Levenson's assessment, a man probably would fire his friend, only without the guilt that Levenson felt. Women—as Carol Gilligan found in her studies—often have a difficult time separating their personal and business responsibilities. "They feel a conflict between the necessity to be task and output oriented and the need to like the people they're working with," says Jacke. Perhaps because of men's background in team sports, she says, a man is more likely to think, " 'I may like that person, but he's not performing.' He doesn't question the fact that it has to be done, though he doesn't enjoy it."

Levenson's caring manifests itself in instances when she does not fire or, if she must, in the benefits that she is able to get for those she does fire. There, too, Jacke believes Levenson's type of behavior is a positive example of one of a female manager's strong points. "Women tend to act more as a counselor," says Jacke. "They're able to empathize, to actively listen. With their relationship skills, they can ease the transition period. They're more supportive of the person, rather than telling him to clean out his desk."

Levenson learned some of the skills of working with people by being a mother. "You learn to understand people, to have an insight, when you raise children. You learn how to motivate by motivating your own children," she says. "I had to communicate closely with my kids, to listen to what they wanted." She also learned to be sensitive to how important livelihoods are to other people because she was so dependent on her own job to maintain her family.

In a recent situation, she says, she had three men working for her who had bad reputations as managers. "I organized the department differently, and I utilized them so they would excel with their talents. I was very proud of that. Now they're all highly thought of in the bank. People now say they're terrific, and they're being promoted." She allowed each man to make more decisions in his area of expertise, which led to each becoming more motivated, working harder, and taking more responsibility. The men recognized her role in their transformations and have thanked her, she says, and management was also aware of her strategy, which led to a promotion for her. "I do not believe that firing is a solution."

In another instance, she could not avoid firing two men, a manager and the supervisor who worked for him. A few days before she was to take over a particular department that she was already working in in order to familiarize herself with it, the two men had an open verbal brawl in front of their staff. She called both of them in and told them to go home and not return to work the next day, while she conducted an investigation. She discovered that the two had not been getting along for some time and had been upsetting the work flow, causing poor productivity and low morale among workers with their weak managerial approaches. Because of the public incident, she felt she could not salvage the situation.

"It was hard facing them, though. I discussed the issues, where I thought they went wrong. What was hard was that one had put in a lot of hours of hard work. I had never let anyone go prior to that who had technical value. He was a good technician, but he was bad with people." She did all she could for both of them, she says. "I think I'm always more compassionate about firings than men are. I sent both these men to personnel, which had agreed to help them write resumés. I also tried to have personnel find them jobs in a technical area within the company. And I told them I would give them recommendations for jobs outside the bank in technical areas, though not in management. I don't think a man would have done as much." In fact, she handled the firing as experience dictated to her: she took very few days to come to her decision, she had the full support of her own boss, and she had checked with personnel on the offers she made. It turned out that the morale of her department improved, even though her firing one of four managers just as she stepped in to take over the new department meant more work for the other three.

Levenson started out as a keypunch operator at night, but was soon promoted to a daytime job as a supervisor in the check processing section. From there she moved to a job as an administrative assistant and soon was assigned a higher-level job developing new systems. One can see from her rise a key to her feelings that people do not have to be fired if they can change to fit the right slots.

"Throughout my career I've had to change to fit in, to understand the informal organization, to build my own network of friends, to understand the dos and don'ts, to learn to take risks. It was something I had to grow into over time."

She began as a sixty-dollar-a-week trainee, with only her high school typing to qualify her. "But I seem to have a natural instinct for systems analysis. I had good recommendations from the check processing department. I had shown assertiveness in trying to improve the systems there. I became a senior systems analyst quickly because of my background in banking. A lot of senior men were looking for someone to talk to, and I learned a lot. There were a lot of older people who had been in check processing for many years, and they really took time to teach you. That doesn't happen so much anymore. If they saw you were assertive, they took time with you."

So even before Levenson knew about the term *mentor*, she had several and took full advantage of them. She does recognize, however, that the help may have had a sexist tinge, though it worked to her benefit. "They were helpful because they didn't find me threatening. I imagine if I were a man they might have felt in competition and wouldn't have been so helpful. Women today have that problem more, I think: they're perceived more as being competition." In fact, she did not really see herself as a competitor at first. The promotions started coming long before she had built a career plan.

Her own assertiveness, or motivation to succeed, came, she says, from within. "I had a need to grow, to succeed, and to put bread on the table. If I was ever shy, I don't remember it. I know I felt afraid at times, about getting promoted. But I was always so eager to learn. I had a thirst for knowledge. I was like a sponge. I absorbed everything."

The administrative assistant job she held in the check processing division was in the area of quality control. "I built it into something powerful, by assessing the real needs. I broadened the spectrum of the job. I was able to get myself into every aspect of operations and make recommendations."

From there she went into computer operations. "I'm a manager, not a programmer, though I'm up on the technical aspects. I helped to design some of the computer-oriented productions, such as helping computers 'talk' to each other—getting different types of computers connected cohesively—and office automation. I worked on a project to automate the back offices of branch banks." Levenson is a classic case of a woman who demands a lot of her workers because she has always demanded a lot of herself. Although she did not set out seeking a vice presidency, Levenson did set new goals for herself every time she was promoted. The turning point came about six years ago. "I was more attuned to what had happened, to gearing myself for management. Before that, things happened, and I was in the right place at the right time and always an effective person. But then I realized I could make things happen."

What she learned about managing and motivating made her a more acute interviewer when she hires, she says. "My technique is to get people to talk, so I can hear how they handle things. I make good decisions in hiring because I believe that people's insights are more important than their technical qualifications." Technical qualifications, after all, were not her strong suit as she advanced. "I take them on a tour of the shop, and I listen to their questions. If someone asks me about the morale of the office and the salary structure, then that is a good sign. If they get into motivational techniques and talk about the things they've done, then I know they can effect change and that they think of their people as people."

As she has progressed, she has also learned more about how to fire. Her first firing, when she was still a supervisor, was of a Chinese woman who worked the night shift in check processing and always brought in Chinese delicacies for her co-workers, so she was very popular. Levenson, too, liked her personally. "She was a sweet person, but I had to do it. She was not doing her job." Levenson put off the decision for a couple of months, she says, and gave the woman many warnings, but finally she just had to do it. The woman cried when she was told.

Soon after, Levenson had to fire other poor producers. "It was hard. But as I progressed, though it was never easy, I always tried to ensure that they understood the program well before it got to that point. The only way I could deal with it effectively was to give them measurements [progress reports] and specified goals. Then, when they fell down, I didn't feel bad. I might have gone overboard sometimes with second chances, but I had to see that I did everything I could."

Katherine Heaviside's experiences with hiring and firing are closely related to the way she runs her public relations office, which is described in detail in chapter 4. She uses flex-time to give her employees greater freedom, but she also expects them to take total responsibility for their jobs, which means that if the administrative assistants are busy or absent, the account executives must type, photocopy, mail, and take care of all the details for their own accounts.

Once she had a young man straight from college apply for a job as an account executive. "One of my questions is always, 'What do you like to do best?' I find that if I ask whether they like this or that, they always answer yes. This young fellow said, 'I look at myself as a big picture. I don't want to be bothered with the details. I want to be the guy that does the creative.'" She laughs as she recalls this interview. "I said, 'Michael, the guy that does the creative around here is me. The person I'm looking to hire is someone who will do the details.' And I stood up and I kind of walked him to the door and said, 'I don't think we'll be good for you.' I wished him the best of luck and said, 'I'm sure you'll find a firm that fits in with your broader picture.' I was chuckling to myself, thinking everyone who is just out of college pictures themselves handling the big account."

She believes it was more his youth than his sex that was responsible for his attitude, although one wonders if he would have been as straightforward with a male employer, and his faux pas about being the "guy" doing the creative work may well have indicated some real sexism about who should be in charge. Heaviside did not take offense, however, and—because she has had bad experiences with young people she has hired just out of college—she adds, "I think I will never hire someone again out of college. I'll wait until they have some humbleness, until some humbleness has set in," which is sure to happen after a job or two.

The gentle way in which she escorted the young man out of her office is typical of the way that Heaviside handles both hirings and firings. Some men, of course, use the same techniques, but the humaneness of her approach is typical for many women. She was doing the same things even when she was hiring for companies that she worked for, before she left to have children and then open her own firm.

Of her hiring, she says, "In each case I did something that I don't think most people do. I sent a letter to everyone who even sent me a resumé. The people who came in, I always got back to them. I always made them understand it was not a reflection on them. I said someone else had more experience or more experience with a particular kind of client that they didn't have, but certainly the fact that they came in for an interview was testimony to the fact that I thought them worthy, under the right circumstances. They just weren't the right person for the job." These communications, for the interviewees, were by telephone, not by letter. "I made sure they at least hung up the phone with a good feeling. It wasn't my favorite thing to do, but it was not too hard. I've learned that the worst thing you can do is to get a person in and then let them go."

The hardest time she had not hiring someone, she says, was when a woman with personal problems came for a job interview. "It was a little hard, but I knew from the moment the subject came up that I had to say no." First of all, the woman, whose credentials looked good on paper, was inappropriately dressed, an important factor in a public relations firm, since account executives must go out to meet with clients. "I think she was wearing a velour jumpsuit in purple and had long, messy hair. In general, she looked very unkempt." But the thing that made Heaviside feel sorry was the woman's tale. "She came in and sat down, and—I'm very attuned to vibrations—she was upset. She said she was nervous. I talked to her for a while to see if this was just an interview nervousness, and she said, 'I really need this job, because I'm going to go through a divorce in the next few months, and I need something to hang onto.' And I felt terrible, but I thought, I can't be a haven. My clients don't deserve to have someone who's going to be using the job as an emotional rock. They need the attention. They can't be giving solace. There was nothing I could do for her. Besides, the job wouldn't have done her any good anyway. It would have been too much pressure at that time in her life."

Heaviside uses the same compassion on the firing side. "I have learned that if you're going to make a decision, you have to do it right away. The worst thing you can do is spend more and more time hoping that things will get better." She has learned this the hard way. "In one case, someone wasn't producing. I thought at first it was because they were new. Then more weeks went by, and they weren't getting along with people. Suddenly, I realized I was letting it slip, and it was not good for the morale of the other people who were working. People working there should feel they're on a winning team. If they feel one person is not doing what he should, then it's very bad." She has some difficulty firing, she says, but so did her husband when he worked at a large engineering firm, so she suspects men have the same problems. "The first one is the hardest, and it's also hard when you know there's a real personal problem. But I think it's important when a person is being fired that they leave with their self-respect." She thinks she has been successful at it, because people she has fired have called her back to let her know how they are doing.

Her toughest firing, she says, was a young man who was "prepared to fight me on it. I had to be gently insistent. I told him I was sure he was going to do wonderfully at other places, but that this particular account didn't seem to fit with his abilities." He wanted to call the client to find out why they did not like him, and she had to persuade him that this was not appropriate. Actually, she says, it had been a mistake to hire him in the first place, and she had gone against her initial instincts because she had been impressed with his brilliant academic background, which included fine colleges, high test scores, and many awards. "I was just so bowled over by his background. Plus he was very eager to get the job. During the interview, he was so stiff it seemed he could hardly talk. And I attributed it to youth and nervousness. He had never worked before." But soon she discovered that he could not handle the work and that he fought any editing of his copy, besides which, he was a male chauvinist, which especially did not fit well into her office. Her mistake here was in waiting too long. Morale among the other workers dipped, and she ended up having to pay unemployment insurance for the young man. Moreover, because he was not able to hold another job for long enough to qualify for it with another employer, his unemployment compensation continued for a long time. She noticed from her payment deductions for him that he got a couple of other jobs, but lasted in each only about three or four weeks.

Her gentlest firing came with a female employee whose husband had lost his own job, soon after Heaviside had spoken with the woman about how she was not working out in her position. "She knew it wasn't a good fit, and she was a very nice person. We talked about whether there was anywhere else she could fit, but there wasn't. I had told her at first, 'Well, let's just finish it out, stay another two weeks.'" It was during those two weeks that Heaviside learned about the woman's newly unemployed husband. "I just kept her on until her husband found a job. It was another three months. But I never offered it in that way. I'm not sure how I did it. I didn't refer to her husband's unemployment, because I felt that would be difficult for her, to think she was getting charity. I just extended the schedule."

The successful managers interviewed here have demonstrated that it is possible for women to learn the skills of effective hiring and firing without giving up the values that they believe are important. Some good advice may be culled from the practices of these women and from other management experts:

• In hiring, interviewers should learn how to ask the right kinds of questions, open-ended questions that will get the prospective employee talking about himself or herself at length. Experience in interviewing helps, but taking a course or practicing with a friend or family member is also a good idea.

• Interviewers should know what they want, so they can explain the job clearly. They must be prepared for questions the interviewee may ask and listen carefully to them, because the questions can provide keys to the person's concerns and skills.

• It is helpful to try to tune in to the applicant's emotional state and to attempt to distinguish between interview nervousness and someone who really does not get along with others. This is particularly important if good interpersonal skills are required for the job. One should follow one's instincts.

• It is far more humane to take the time to let those who were not hired know that the job has been filled, and to let them down easily, than to leave them hanging. It may take a little more effort, but it could have practical results, since personnel policies become part of an employer's overall reputation. The better the reputation, the better will be the people attracted for future job openings.

• If an employee is not performing well, it is best to talk over problems promptly and give the person plenty of advance notice that his or her job is in jeopardy. If there is a temporary personal problem, the employer may be able to work out an interim solution until the person is settled again. If the person is a good worker, it may be worthwhile to give him or her a few chances—but not an unlimited number.

• Once a manager has made up her mind to fire someone, she should not dawdle. Delay will not make it any easier to fire the person when she finally does get around to it, and meanwhile the employee may be damaging company morale and draining resources that could better be used for other company matters.

• No matter how ripe for firing a person is, the manager should try to let him or her leave with dignity intact. Again, how one fires becomes part of one's reputation with possible future employees as well as with present ones. A manager should not be so gentle, however, that she allows the employee to talk her out of her decision or gain concessions that she had not planned on making.

• The manager must be prepared with all the facts when ready to fire someone—the work record should be documented, the firm's personnel policies researched, so that all questions about termination pay and help in finding a new job can be answered. Women who are inexperienced or nervous ought to consider rehearsing the entire session with another person beforehand.

7

Relating to a Secretary or Aide

Life can be so much easier with a good secretary. But many women find it difficult to deal comfortably with this most intimate of boss-subordinate relationships. "With professionals, I deal with a problem immediately. I always feel I'm on equal turf," says one competent female executive I interviewed. "But I can't with my secretary. I don't deal with a problem right away, and then I water it down. I'm kind. I'm almost apologizing for bringing her in. It's not stressful to talk to a professional, because I get no argument. But I go through all kinds of dramatics with my secretary, and I feel I might be taking advantage of her." Many men, of course, have similar problems.

On the other hand, because many women executives started out as secretaries, they often have special insights into the boss-secretary relationship. A surprisingly large number of female executives, in fact, started out in secretarial or clerical positions—34 percent, according to a 1982 Korn/Ferry International survey of 300 top women executives from America's largest firms. That 34 percent is equal to the number of women in the survey who started their careers in managerial jobs. Older women were more likely to have started in a clerical position: nearly half of those fifty-three years and older did, while only 23 percent of the executives aged thirty-seven and under did. Even 23 percent—nearly one-quarter—is high, though, compared to the number of male executives who have been secretaries. No one has even bothered to count them.

The problem that some former secretaries face is that they cannot find a secretary as good as they were. "I was ambitious, and I realize I'm putting my values on someone else," says one former secretary who has advanced into management. "But it still bothers me that someone expects a good salary and doesn't want to do her best. And, after all, when letters go out incorrectly [as they did when her secretary mixed up a mailing so that letters went out in envelopes addressed to the wrong people], it's my credibility that's on the line."

The secretarial field is changing, and there is a shortage of good secretaries. Many younger women who in another age would have had few choices are now getting M.B.A.s rather than secretarial school diplomas after college, and, as the statistics show, many older women who started as secretaries have moved on. The smaller number of good secretaries—those who can spell, type accurately, speak well on the telephone, and take on office responsibilities intelligently —makes it imperative for women who want to succeed to learn the best ways to deal with their secretaries.

For some women—probably the ones who have been only marginally successful themselves—the problem is an inability to use a secretary properly. Unused to having someone available who can take care of the details of a job, do the typing, screen the calls, and even prepare the research for a presentation, some women do not take full advantage of the benefits of having a secretary. That was one of the findings in management professor Natasha Josefowitz's 1980 study of 68 male and 102 female managers who were observed at work. The women, she reported in the *Harvard Business Review,* were less likely to use their secretaries to screen out potential interruptions in their work day. Josefowitz compared two "representative statements by managers interviewed" to illustrate her point. The typical women's reply was, "I try to answer the phone rather than have my secretary say, 'She's not available.' " Men, on the other hand, typically said, "My secretary's main responsibility is to limit my availability. She screens out requests for appointments."

Many women now working as secretaries have started a movement to gain more respect for their positions, partly in response to the film *9 to 5* and the secretaries' organization by that name that sprang from it. Seeing a secretary as an intelligent person and treating him or her respectfully are two items that many of the women I interviewed suggested—and women may be slightly more prone than men to do so, since they may feel more kinship with the woman who has chosen that profession.

A boss can make a great deal of difference in the way secretaries are treated and the way they respond. Brooklyn District Attorney Elizabeth Holtzman, a former member of Congress, told a New York University forum, "Women and Work" (printed in 1983 in *Working Woman* magazine), about actions she took when she became D. A. "When I started working, all secretaries and all women in clerical positions were referred to as girls, by everyone. Remarkably, that too has come to a halt . . . at least in my presence. I had to correct people only a couple of times, and it's amazing how I no longer hear that term. It's not even a question of changing attitudes—it's that they *have to do it.* And it makes a big difference."

Holtzman also advocated a program "for encouraging those women who work as secretaries to advance. . . . I remember that the woman who headed my congressional office in Brooklyn first came in looking for a job as a typist. She was capable enough to be given the highest responsibility in that office."

Sometimes, of course, a female boss will find herself in a ticklish situation with her secretary, who may have wanted to rise to the very job that the executive has taken over. The secretary would have resented having to teach the outlines of the job to a new man, too, but she usually resents it even more if a woman has taken the position that she wanted. That is the situation one woman executive I interviewed found herself in.

"I had no experience in the job, and the secretary who worked for me resented me. She was angry." Although she trained the executive for the job, she was openly belligerent. "After a couple of months, I sat her down and said. 'I will never deny that you know more than I do about this job. But if I had been a man, what would I have done? Wouldn't I have taken this job?' " Since that session, the two have been able to joke about their positions. "I don't think she would have been as outspoken with a man," the executive says. "She would have accepted that it was her job to bring him up to speed."

There is still some residual anger on the secretary's part, the executive says, but "I can't get angry, because I understand. Once she is ready to make a career change, I'll help her." The executive is trying to help her surreptitiously now, because she has observed the problems the woman has, including lack of a college degree and an image in the company of having a "negative attitude."

"She doesn't know how to dress or how to handle herself in a professional way. She isn't willing to stay late or come in early. In fact, at twenty past four, she's already packed up, and she's even walked out of meetings that weren't finished. I try to help her with these things, but very carefully, because if I let her know that I'm helping her, she would feel it was a put-down."

The following stories concern two women who are in good positions to advise others. One owns a placement service for executive secretaries and has a strong relationship with her own male receptionist/ secretary; the other is a former secretary who is now a vice president in a large company.

Ruth Manning, whose Manhattan firm specializes in placing executive secretaries and administrative assistants, has two men and two women working for her in her midtown office, including three placement counselors and a receptionist/secretary. The receptionist/secretary is male.

Manning says she treats her receptionist/secretary with the same respect that she accords the rest of her staff. "I give people a lot of flexibility," says Manning, who also founded *The Daily Plan-It,* a newsletter on events of special interest to working women. "I don't like to stand over them and say, 'Did you do this? Did you call him back?' They have to have their own sense of what has to be done. . . . I can't spend my day doing their job and my job. Then I don't have to pay them."

Allen Salod, Manning's receptionist and "guy Friday," as he defines his job, agrees with her assessment of how she supervises him. "Ruth is a great person to work for. She's very open to suggestions. There are no hard-and-fast rules. As long as I remain productive, I'm allowed to do whatever I want. I structure the job the way I feel it needs to be structured."

Among the responsibilities he has taken on is developing an advertisement for *Avenue Magazine,* which goes to top executives on Manhattan's East Side, who are good prospective clients for Manning's firm. Salod also took responsibility for many of the technical aspects of a recent move to a new office. Certain macho types— telephone, security systems, and copying-machine installers—preferred talking to a man, says Manning, even though they knew he was the receptionist and she was the boss. Once they were in, he was given the job of arranging the furniture, partly because he had once worked as guy Friday to an interior decorator. He is proud of his decorating accomplishment.

Salod thinks Manning would have treated a woman in his position the same way. He has worked for other women in guy Friday positions, he says, and all were good at giving him the leeway that makes his job more interesting, but some male bosses can be just as amenable. "I like to think it comes down to a personal basis, whether the person is able to delegate responsibility." Men, he says, "may tend to be a little harder and a little stricter, but that may come from their training and experience." Many women are better at treating an assistant with kindness, "maybe because they are women and they understand that there are feelings involved, and they have been stepped on, and they know how it feels; therefore, they will go out of their way to compensate and allow the other person to do what they want."

Manning's respect for her guy Friday and for the others who work for her does grow out of her own experiences, out of knowing how it feels to work in menial positions."Whenever you hear a success story, people always talk about how every door was closed to them, but they persevered," Manning says, and this was her experience, too, until she found success by opening her own business, Staff by Manning, five years ago.

Now she sits in an office on East Fifty-seventh Street, a swank part of Manhattan. Job applicants must pass her receptionist, a waiting area with couches, a table laden with trendy magazines and a jar full of candy, and three job placement counselors in their own offices or cubicles before they reach her. The walls of her office are covered with photos and other memorabilia, including an old picture of what look like the first female secretaries ever, in long dark dresses and upswept hairdos.

On her desk is a phone with several lines and an intercom. As we talk, Salod interrupts a few times, either quietly in person or on the intercom, with news of incoming calls. Her response is always quick: "Tell them I'll call back" or "I'll take it" or "Tell him we have someone lined up." The leeway that she gives Salod, expecting him to tend to his various responsibilities on his own while he still keeps a tight rein on calls and visitors, appears to work well. Salod has taken care of several of the phone calls himself, using his own judgment, he reports later.

"I call up more and more companies where men answer the phone," says Manning. "In the Victorian era, all secretaries were men. Nowadays, it's shifting back. There are no barriers anymore. More women than men want male secretaries. Men are a little insecure because of the sexual innuendo. Women don't prefer it, but they don't mind. Sometimes they do it just to be different, like having a male maid. People mention it to me, and I say, 'He's wonderful.' . . . People can't afford to fool around anymore. They want quality, and the sex doesn't matter. . . . A good secretary can make or break his or her boss."

Manning says that she expects a lot from employees because she expects a lot from herself—she is always the first in in the morning and the last to leave. "The biggest key to control is self-control," she said. "People will take their image from you." She also had a long history of being an employee, so she knows what it is like to report to someone else. Her best work was done when she was left alone by bosses to use her own imagination and ingenuity to shine in her job.

Not all female secretaries, she says, would respond well to the kind of management she offers. "A lot of women sit and wait for things to happen to them. Women can be extremely passive. You can't just sit and wait, because other people are busy. They're worried about their own careers. . . . Women tend to blame their lack of success more [than men do] on other people treating them badly." Sometimes this may be the case, she admits, but then the woman should get out of such a situation fast.

Many who come to her seeking high-paying positions with great responsibility—as office manager, perhaps, or top executive secretary—balk when she mentions hours longer than nine to five. Many also are reluctant to relocate or to plan on changing jobs in the future. "I had a woman who came in here saying, 'I want my next job to be my last.' I said, 'Are you planning to die next week?' They want to sit down and work and work and work, and have no one make waves. It must be the nesting instinct."

Manning also believes that attitude—how you present yourself —is more important than physical attributes. She came to her own authoritative manner despite looking very young. Although she has a nineteen-year-old son, she could pass for a woman in her twenties. Also slender and short (five feet, two inches), like Charol Shakeshaft, whose story is told in chapter 3, she makes up for that potential managerial handicap by wearing smart clothes, finished off by a short, sleek haircut and large glasses, and having what she calls an "attitude" of authority. Initial response to her youthful appearance and slight stature is usually dispelled after she begins to talk, she says. "I decided I didn't care anymore. This is it, this is me. After a while, after you chat, they forget the externals."

When I first met Manning at a "networking salon," I, too, had the misleading impression that I was meeting a young woman—stylishly dressed, on the way up, but just starting out. Soon, however, it became clear that she was indeed a woman in charge, as she began telling me about her business and about her publishing enterprise in a clear voice that carried over the din. Later, when she addressed the huge crowd—she was one of the event's sponsors, which was a useful way for her to make contacts—she displayed the same forceful and forthright manner. No mumbling or shuffling at the microphone for Ruth Manning. She spoke out loud and clear.

Manning makes sure her clients see her as authoritative, as well. "I have more clients who 'dear' you to death. They think because you're a woman, they can get away with murder, and they find out they can't. I can call up and ask for the money just like anybody else."

Manning's road to management was not an easy glide. Her father is a C.P.A. with his own business, and her mother a housewife. An older sister just received her Ph.D., and a younger one owns her own pottery business. "I was a survivor. I was always the kind [for whom] it was never enough. I always wanted the next level. I was always rebellious. I always wanted to get out, to be on my own."

While attending college, she worked for a man who supplied trained animals for television. When she graduated, she arranged promotions and trade shows for seven years on a free-lance basis, sometimes also doing movies, scripts, and public relations. It was an exciting life, but not an easy one. "You do a show for three days and then you look for work for three weeks."

She was married briefly—it lasted only a year and a half—and had a son. After her divorce, she decided she needed a steady job and went to an employment agency. The woman who interviewed her suggested she come to work at the agency. There were ten counselors there, and the man who owned the company put her in a back room and told everyone else to give her their dead files. She spent the first few days at the discouraging task of sending postcards to the dead-file job seekers saying, "We have a terrific job for you. Please call us." Surprisingly, they called. Even more surprisingly, she got many of them jobs. Her boss and the other counselors were impressed. When a desk opened in the front office (the woman who had interviewed her left), she moved up.

"This is a funny business. Either you've got it or you don't." She had it—that mixture of perseverance and matchmaking skills that makes for a successful placement counselor. She stayed in the job a year and a half, then worked for another agency before being recruited for a job starting a showroom for men's and boys' wear.

That job required organizational and managerial skills and provided a good background for running her own business. But it was a boring job, Manning says, and after a year she quit. She did not want to return to being a placement counselor, but when an acquaintance told her of an opening in her agency, Manning took the job reluctantly. She ended up staying several years.

Manning opened her own business because "there were things I wanted to do that they didn't let me do. I'm an idea person." Her idea was to specialize in placing top-level executive secretaries. She found an office, got her licenses, got a phone system installed and ads written—all on her own time while still employed elsewhere. "I left one place Friday and was in business the next Monday at nine. At ten after nine, the first applicant came in, and I was moving."

Manning says there is sometimes a difference in the way older and younger women handle their secretaries. "What I hear about the younger women today [from secretaries she has placed] is that they are difficult; they're cocky, very impressed with their own being. They haven't been seasoned, and they don't treat other people nicely. The older ones who have come up through the ranks, who have worked their tails off, know what it means to have done that." She knows what it is like.

Most people, male or female, do not make good enough use of a secretary, she says. "They tend not to want to give away things. A good secretary can say, 'I'll take care of that. You do your other things.' "

Some women, she says, "love the power" of being a boss so much that they mistreat their secretaries. " 'Would you get my coffee, and would you return my stockings to Saks, and'—oh yes, sometimes they're worse than men," she laughs. "They love to have someone who'll do that. Secretaries resent it, whether their bosses are men or women. I had one case, an executive who came out of her new office, Miss Hotshot, to ask her secretary, who was typing away, 'Do you make coffee?' Without breaking pace, the secretary said, 'No, but I'll be happy to show you how to do it.' We had a company once where the president said secretaries would no longer make coffee, the coffee wagon would come through. People went crazy. They were toppled off their thrones. But the president felt if he could get up himself to go to the wagon, so could the others."

The way people should use a secretary, Manning says, is as "another set of brains. The higher you are, the more conceptual you must be. Allow someone else to work on projects, to handle something you don't want to handle, to understand what's going on. The worst thing is to have an executive who says, 'Do this, do this, do this.' One secretary had a boss who was wonderful. He came out of a meeting and said, 'Let me explain what went on, so that you will understand what we're doing.' It's a different feeling, that they're a part of it. It makes them feel they have a part in the company, that it's a team effort, that we're all there to make the company do better, to make more profits. When everybody does their own thing and doesn't know what's happening, they come in at nine and leave at five, and that's it."

One woman who came to Manning's firm had been working for the same company for twenty-six years and did not know what the firm's gross sales were. "That's a head that isn't functioning. She just types the letters and stuffs the envelopes. You've got to bring people in, so that they care. Then a secretary will say, 'Let me take care of this for you. This has to be done. Why don't we do it this way? Let me call him for you. Let me do this, let me do that.' I say, 'Fine, do it.'"

A willing secretary, Manning says, maintains rapport with her boss's customers and clients and often has good ideas. In fact, she says, a good secretary wants to do more. One secretary recently complained to her that her boss, who inherited his company and is rapidly losing money, is not letting her do enough. "This secretary said, 'He pays me $30,000, and he lets me do nothing. He could have hired someone for $12,000.' She says she feels so stupid, sitting there doing absolutely nothing."

Though some women who have worked their way up through

the ranks are particularly nice to their secretaries, others "do a turn-around and become very haughty. They want to divorce themselves from that level. They want to be a big cheese." They are not likely to succeed, though, if they do not have the support of their secretaries.

Joan Muessen is a former secretary who has worked her way up, and she is particularly careful to make the best use of her secretary. "I explain things thoroughly. If a secretary knows the reason for a job, the pitfalls, and what the projected end is, she will respond better."

When Muessen, fifty, now vice president of personnel relations administration at McGraw-Hill, gives her secretary a project to work on, "I always tell her why, for whom, what the necessary pieces of information are, what we want as an end product and why." For example, she says, she might ask her secretary to compile statistics for an analysis of salaries. "If she knows how I want to put them together, then if she sees something out of the ordinary, out of the norm, she can alert me to it."

When Muessen started out, she says, "women were expected to be secretaries. It was a mind-set at that time." Her father was a business executive, and her mother a housewife. She majored in English at Skidmore College and thought of going into the fashion field. But when she did not get a training position at Bloomingdale's, she took a typing and shorthand course, which was "necessary to get a job" then, unless a woman was going into nursing or teaching.

Her first job was at a gas company, and when her boss there left for McGraw-Hill, she followed. She still works for him, although now she is a fellow executive. Her promotions started about ten years ago and continued at a rapid pace. Although she did not ask for them, she says she would have eventually.

First Muessen was made an administrative assistant, although that was still a secretarial job. Then she became personnel adminis-trator, where she stayed three years before becoming vice president of career planning. Her present job, she says, is a step up from the other vice presidency. She gained confidence as she went along and learned both from watching her boss and from remembering what she had observed of her father in her youth.

"I'm not sure what other people do, but I try to have a concern for my secretary's point of view, her work load. I try to have her understand where I'm coming from rather than to issue orders. I like to think that the two of us work together."

Muessen does not ask her secretary to make coffee or to run personal errands, "unless I'm in a bind and she offers." Although Muessen herself was sometimes asked to do personal things, she says, that was in a different era. "It didn't bother me at the time. It would bother me now.... The pendulum has swung in the other direction." However, when Muessen has a meeting in her office, her secretary always asks if she can bring coffee, which Muessen thinks is fine.

Since becoming an executive, Muessen has had several secretaries. She chose her present one after interviewing many candidates. "I looked for good skills, good verbal skills and, frankly, good appearance and how she handled herself in the interview, because I'm in an executive position."

Her secretary wants to get into personnel recruiting, says Muessen, "and I have encouraged her in that. I've encouraged her to finish getting her [B.A.] degree. She's gotten a good many credits [toward it]."

Muessen also offers advice for the woman or man who has difficulty confronting a secretary who does not do his or her job well. She knows the syndrome. "If a secretary has poor skills, I would first try to get the person some kind of remedial training, in typing, shorthand, or telephone technique. If she refuses, you have a performance problem. If she [accepts the training and] still fails, you also have a performance problem, but at least you've tried to help the person. It's important not to skirt the issue. I know people sometimes have a hard time confronting a secretary about too many typing errors or a strange shorthand translation. They don't demand a better piece of work, and they should."

If Muessen were starting out now, she would not become a secretary, although she thinks it is a fine occupation. "It can be a very rewarding job. There are all kinds of things a woman can do if she's good. She can take over an office and run it, and that can be very satisfying." Some women do not want to jump from secretarial work to management because they are getting a higher salary as an executive secretary than they would in a management training job, and they are not willing to take a step back, even temporarily.

If she had it to do over again—starting out today, with a different mind-set—"I would have more of an idea of what I wanted to do when I went to college. I think being a security analyst would be interesting, or maybe corporate planning. Or maybe I would get an

M.B.A. That's a hot ticket now." Or, she adds, she might be doing exactly what she is presently doing.

Beginning as a secretary is still a viable road to management— although a difficult one—and may make a woman more sensitive to the best ways to deal with her own secretary once she arrives in a position of power. But, as Ruth Manning points out, all people, whether ex-secretaries or not, have individual ways of dealing with a secretary or aide. Some are effective; others breed resentment. Much more than men, however, women are prone to feelings of guilt as they assign menial work and may not delegate enough, perhaps because they can more easily identify with the role of the secretary. Ruth Manning and Joan Muessen, because of their backgrounds, bring special sensitivity to their views on how a secretary or aide should be treated and how a boss can make maximum use of her assistant's talents:

• Bosses must show respect for the intelligence of their secretaries or aides and allow them freedom to take on added responsibilities. But bosses should not shrink from assigning such menial work as filing, typing, and photocopying, which are rightfully in the secretaries' domain and which will enable bosses to make the most efficient use of their own time.

• Bosses should not expect personal services that are not part of a secretary's professional role. Such expectations cause resentment that can undermine the relationship.

• Bosses should give their secretaries the sense that they are part of the boss's team, that they are both working together for the good of the company.

• Bosses giving directions should include the complete reasons for doing a project, so the secretary is sufficiently informed to do an intelligent job and to use her own judgment.

• If a secretary lacks skills, it is best to confront him or her promptly and suggest taking courses to improve.

• If a secretary aspires to a better position within the company, the boss ought to be helpful to this end. This will ensure good work while the secretary remains with the boss and provide a valuable ally after the secretary has moved ahead.

8

Ambition and Career Paths

Most women are just now catching on to the way men climb up the ladder: advance planning, thinking in terms of career moves, thinking ahead to other jobs—the stage at which fear of success sometimes sets in. Having made the initial step into management, a woman must now think of the next moves, which require considering more than how to supervise those in her charge. She must think now about office politics, about relating to her superiors and peers in new ways, and about her career as a whole, not just her present job or her current company. She might as well set her sights high, if she plans to devote herself wholeheartedly to her career. Why not try to shoot for the top job in your field, and actually make the career moves to get there?

Research has shown that women are often too narrow in their view of what a management job is about. They put all their energies into mastering the job at hand without preparing themselves for the next job or understanding the signals that show them that a path to a better job may be opening up. Women often concentrate on getting perfect work from their subordinates—even doing it or correcting it themselves—rather than working toward long-range goals of building a better system or a better environment for the workers. The long-range goals, if presented properly at meetings or in memos, are frequently the more effective tools for promoting the woman to higher-level jobs.

Management professor Natasha Josefowitz has described in her 1980 book, *Paths to Power: A Woman's Guide from First Job to Top*

Executive, three beginning phases in a woman's career development. First comes preparation, which includes assessing skills, preparing a resumé, and finding a job. Next comes what she calls moving in, which requires understanding the norms of the company you are working for and deciding how much you want to conform to them. Norms include such items as how people dress, whether they leave office doors open or closed, whether their desks are clean or cluttered, and whether women are welcomed or not accepted at men's informal gatherings. Josefowitz also points out that the same norms may not apply to men and women: a family picture on a man's desk may suggest to others that he is a solid, responsible family man, but on a woman's desk it may give the impression that she will put her family before her career. At this moving-in stage, women must also learn to understand the informal power structure and take risks in order to prove that they are competent.

The third phase for women, according to Josefowitz, who teaches at the University of New Hampshire, is settling down. This is where women start to think of moving up. They must master new skills, use office politics, and become assertive. After these three steps, a woman is ready for her climb—to supervisor, middle manager, top executive. At the middle-management level, a woman must pay particular attention to her boss, who holds power over her, as well as to her colleagues and subordinates. To get to the very top, she will need determination, confidence, energy, and the support of family, friends, co-workers, sponsors, professional associations, and whomever else she can find.

Following are profiles of four women, each of whom has displayed determination, confidence, and energy in entirely different ways. Not only are they of different ages and in different fields—corporate life, nursing, politics, and banking—but each came to a realization of her own ambitions at a different point in her life. Thus, each one took a different path to power, and at least two made a couple of false starts. Only one, the corporate executive who at thirty-four is the youngest of this group, took the kind of straight career path that one would expect of a man, aiming for a position of authority from college on.

At thirty-four, Carolyn H. Smithson is a good example of a woman who is climbing the corporate ladder in a very orderly way. She is assistant treasurer of The Coca-Cola Company and manager of its Latin American treasury services. Based in Atlanta, she handles such items as foreign exchange, bank relations, and cash management, and oversees the finance managers who work on location in Latin America.

Smithson is one of the new breed of women in business who pursue their careers in much the same way that men do. She majored in economics and business administration at Fisk University in Nashville, got her M.B.A. in finance at the University of Chicago, worked at Citibank in New York City for five years, and then moved to Coca-Cola five years ago, where she started as a financial analyst and worked her way up. Smithson has done all this despite being both a woman and black. "I think most women and minorities have to be willing to work hard. I do work harder than most men." She works from fifty to sixty hours a week, and in addition must do some after-hours entertaining of bankers and field managers.

Despite the machismo of Latin American men, she says, they have accepted her in her professional role very easily; they allow her to pay for dinner, and they take her advice. "We have developed a good rapport, probably better than with other men here. They understand that I can help them if they are to achieve what they want to achieve. They have to deal with me, and we have a mutual goal. We have to work together." The goal is not just more soft-drink sales but protecting the company's assets through periods of hyperinflation and currency devaluation, so that, for example, during Mexico's recent devaluation, the company owed more than it was owed by others, and could pay back its debts later with inflated currency, or cheaper pesos, thus turning devaluation to the company's advantage.

Smithson started out with day-to-day investing and banking for the company before entering the world of currency exchange and foreign regulations, which she finds challenging. "I have to exert authority. We have money moving around, and it's our responsibility to protect the company's policies. I'm often making decisions and conveying those decisions to our field finance managers. You get rebuttals, but the final decision rests here." For example, she says, if she anticipates a devaluation, she would want the company's money in dollars. The local manager, however, is likely to get a very high interest rate on investments if he keeps his money in the local currency, and his net income looks better. "So you can understand how he feels," says Smithson. She tries to persuade him to change his view, "just the way I'm talking to you now, with a smile. It's nothing personal."

She has read that some female managers tend to be harsh in dealing with their peers and subordinates and has conducted her own private poll asking friends outside the company how they feel about female managers. "Some said women carry around a lot of baggage, that they felt they had paid too much for being where they are, that it was more difficult to deal with them than with their male counterparts." It was mostly peers who felt women were more difficult to deal with, Smithson says, while superiors of female managers were pleased with their accomplishments. Men working for women were often pleasantly surprised, while female managers themselves often felt they were not given the same kind of respect as male managers, that their remarks were received differently.

"I guess you have to be very careful. I try to be me. I feel if you have a sense of humor, and you know your job—most women know their jobs better than men—you have to get respect for it. In general, I can understand some of the men's comments, but I understand the women's point of view, too. Many have had to work hard and are very protective and territorial, particularly those who have been in corporations longer. They were pioneers. I'm sure they had a more difficult time."

Smithson, one of very few women working toward a business degree when she was an undergraduate, was nevertheless able to develop a "working kind of sharing relationship, a mutual respect" with her male classmates. She never had any problems relating with them, which probably eased her transition to the working world. "When I started working in a male-dominated environment, I didn't see my subordinates, peers, or supervisors as men or women. I just saw them as people. It probably made me stronger, being black and a woman."

Her mother was a nurse, her father an aviation machinist. "All they wanted was that I get a college education, that I do something worthwhile." She is the oldest of five children and "assumed the role of leader" as she was growing up. She considered becoming a doctor before deciding that business suited her personality better. "This is more conceptual, with less memorization." She and her husband grew up together and married while they were in graduate school, twelve years ago. They were both bankers at first—he is a stock-broker now—and for a while they commuted between Chicago, where his job was, and New York. "We would meet on weekends, in one place or the other. I guess I am independent. I do things for myself. I make decisions regarding investments. I bought my own car, in my name. We're atypical. We are two independent decision makers, though we try to discuss things." They have a six-year-old son, who is lucky enough to have a "surrogate mother," Smithson's seventy-seven-year-old grandmother, who lives with them and "takes care of everything." That situation also makes it easier for her to travel for the company.

While moving up the corporate ladder, Smithson says she has tried to learn from both her good bosses and her bad ones. "When I first came out of school, women were not well accepted. At that time, men, both superiors and co-workers, were unaccustomed to dealing with women, and some thought all women were bimbos."

One experience in that first job helped her to understand how she would have to behave in order to survive. Her superior, a man, thought she was being "too demanding, too intolerant" as a supervi-sor. She was learning from him, however, how to treat subordinates and was using the same methods he used. He criticized her in a written evaluation. Her response was to write a very formal rebuttal, which went to her boss's superior. Her boss's boss said he "could not support what this fellow was saying," and she ended up with a good review of her performance. Smithson believes that her super-visor had the notion that women were not supposed to be strong or demanding supervisors, though men could be. She also learned that "basically, women have to stand up for themselves....I think I'm flexible and get along with everyone. I learned from that how to deal with superiors as well as subordinates."

She has had no female role models because she has worked mostly with men, including a few who have acted as mentors. "Per-haps the reason I've been able to move quickly here [at Coca-Cola] is the fact that I've had good mentors, who don't just give advice but can do something to help you." Some people, she thinks, may have resented her quick rise, and she does not know how much of that resentment is exacerbated by her being a woman or being black or both. "I've had to work for everything, probably harder than most people. But that way, you can be proud of your achievements. There are people who are riding the crests [getting advantages simply because they are women or black rather than because they are talented], but in general, I think, the majority of women who work for corporations do have to work to prove themselves more than their male counterparts." There is also a particular struggle for minorities, she says, to prove to themselves that they were given a position because of merit and not because of their minority status.

"My background is probably different from the average white woman's, because I worked the greater part of my life. I feel much more of a responsibility to succeed than, I would think, a woman from a middle-class-or-above family, which is what I perceive of most white people. They didn't have the same struggle I did."

Although her family is middle-class black, that is not the same, she says, as middle-class white. "I worked in the Neighborhood Youth Corps. I did secretarial work in the evenings there, and was a teacher's aide in the summer. I started around fifteen." She also did some babysitting, but the Youth Corps work was "real working." She had a scholarship, without which she probably could not have gone to college, and started out at Dade Junior College in her native Miami. She stayed in the work-study program there one year before transferring to Fisk, where a scholarship covered all her costs.

Smithson is a member of both Atlanta Women in Securities and the Coca-Cola Forum, which started as a women's network but now includes men. "I think it's very important for women to network with women on the outside and inside the company. It's an important part of success on the job. . . . Men can go into the restroom and talk about what's going on. Women don't have that opportunity to do that with them. The old-boy network still exists. They talk on the golf course. Even if women learn golf, it would be difficult to establish that kind of relationship with men. In addition, men have not yet learned how to deal with women on a professional basis. Some feel intimidated, and it's hard to say who's to blame."

Part of Smithson's method for getting ahead has been to make a special effort to reach out to the men she works with, both superiors and peers. "I invite them out to lunch, either individually or in groups, so we can have a laugh. Lunch is a good time for that. I just use the cafeteria here." If she did not invite them, it would probably not occur to them to invite her. "After a while, though, they begin to invite me. I like to be one of the guys, too. They will continue to go out with each other if you let them. You have to be assertive. I hate to eat alone. Even some of the older fellows—you'd be surprised—after you've invited them, will invite you, too." She lets the men pay for themselves, and they chat and tell a joke or two. "Plus, I feel there's a lot that I can learn from them. And I think they can learn something from me. We talk about what happened during the day, maybe something in their territories and how it can relate to mine. Sometimes it's funny, sometimes it's gossip. Basically, it's sharing information."

At Citibank, she says, her peer group was more well defined. Every Friday, they would go out for cocktails. In Atlanta, however, most people go home to their families. "I'm generally included in most things, parties and so forth. I smile a lot. Maybe that's it." Maybe, but it is her savvy and her careful planning that keep her moving on the career track she wants.

While Patricia Woods was visiting her father after he had a cataract operation, she had to excuse herself. It was a working day.

"I'm going to a meeting to work on new construction and budgets," she told her parents.

"Construction? Budgets?" her mother exclaimed. "But you're a nurse!"

Patricia Woods is indeed a nurse, by training and title. But *nurse* is only part of her title. She is acting director of nurses at Long Island Jewish-Hillside Medical Center, a large, prestigious hospital in Queens. She is in charge of fifteen hundred nurses, orderlies, aides, technicians, clerks, and receptionists and is responsible for budgets totaling more than $17 million a year.

"I've got a big job," she concedes. "I have the largest budget and the largest working force in the hospital." The "acting" in her title is by her choice, because she is still considering which course her career should take. She had not intended to go into management when she got her nursing diploma in 1954, but once she took her first job as a head nurse, she decided that she would work her way up with the best tools possible.

To gain those tools, Woods took management courses and closely observed the ways of power in the hospital's bureaucratic structure. She is a firm believer in management training and offers courses to her head nurses and other unit heads. She is an example of a woman who has followed a rational career course to one of its highest peaks while discovering on her own some innovative ways to master the mostly male hierarchy of a hospital. Through it all, she has remained well-liked by co-workers.

Although she is in a female-dominated field, it is one that can be recommended to other women who want to excel as leaders. Pearl M. Kamer, chief economist for the Long Island Regional Planning Board, analyzed national statistics for the *New York Statistician* and found that job outlooks are dim for people with degrees in any of the so-called female-dominated fields except nursing. In general, she suggests that women consider shifting to mathematics, economics, business, and physical sciences. However, she says, "between 1976 and 1985, it was estimated that some 83,000 registered nurses will compete annually for a like number of jobs." And nursing, Woods points out, is a much more sophisticated profession than is sometimes thought. The nurse is often involved in patient assessment, planning of care, and management of psychosocial problems.

Though Woods supervises many women, she has found that the higher she has moved, the more she has become involved in the male-dominated hospital hierarchy. Her experience has been similar to working in a major corporation. As one hears about her job, one is tempted to echo her mother: "But you're a *nurse!*" She still spends an hour every day visiting with different nurses, talking to them about their problems ("otherwise they see you sitting in an ivory tower"), but she has come a long way from the patient's bedside.

For our interview, she suggests we sit at a low, round table in her office rather than at opposite sides of her desk. Woods's face looks stern when knotted in concentration, but her eyes—magnified by thick glasses in large frames and set off by short-cropped blond hair—sparkle when she smiles. She often leans forward to answer questions, and one can easily imagine the kind, understanding bedside manner she must once have had. These days, however, her mild manner is mixed with assertiveness. Woods has been acting director for a year. Before that, she was associate director for two years and assistant director for thirteen years, following her stint as head nurse in an operating room.

Patricia Woods married in 1955, soon after her graduation from nursing school. "I intended to work until I had a family," she says, "though I thought I might continue part-time, because I love nursing.

But then, we wanted to get a house, then things for the house.... I got caught up in the economics."

Woods worked part-time only a few years, following the birth of her first child, now aged twenty-three. She was already working as head nurse full-time when she had her second boy, now aged fifteen. Her husband, a superintendent in the New York City sanitation department, always managed to work a shift opposite hers, so they needed little child care. "You really need a supportive husband and a supportive family," she says. Her husband, who came from a more liberal background than hers, helped her to break out of the rigid mold of her Irish-Catholic background. Her father, a New York City policeman, and her mother, a department-store saleswoman, had always insisted on a strict, parochial upbringing. Now, she says, her father is proud of her, her mother a little stunned.

Recently, she considered leaving LIJ for a less demanding part-time job, so she would have more time to finish her master's degree. But her children objected. "They got upset," she says. "They're proud that I work at what they see as a prestigious hospital."

When Woods was first offered the head nurse position, she talked it over with her husband, who urged her to take it. It meant working full-time and entailed much greater responsibilities than those of a staff nurse. She became responsible for staffing the operating room twenty-four hours a day, and if a nurse called in sick or went on vacation, she had to find a replacement. Another part of the job was evaluating the performance of the forty other people on her staff. Her original motivation for taking the job, she says, had much to do with her altruistic nursing background. "I wanted to help more people."

It was not until she went a step higher that she got involved in planning, budgeting, and other administrative chores. "I had been assistant director only a few months when the hospital started to expand, and they started throwing blueprints at me. I was told to order new equipment for new operating rooms. I was given a budget." Once she learned necessary administrative skills, she began to enjoy those chores and found as much satisfaction in doing them as she had in nursing. "I decided, if this is the way I'm going, then I'll make the best of it and do the best job." Administration is still one of her strong points, she says, along with maintaining good communication with her staff and being able to solve personnel problems.

"I had a lot of difficulties at first as a supervisor," she says. "You want everybody to like you." The transition may be even harder for a nurse, she explains, because of the intrinsic helping nature of the profession. "I procrastinated in writing evaluations on poor performances. I let people drift, which I shouldn't have done, because after a year I would blow up and tell them what a poor job they were doing. It's better to tell them they're doing a bad job and let them develop."

The transition was particularly hard for her. "I'm not an authoritarian-type person. I'm a more democratic-type leader." Her socialization as a parochial-school girl and as a nurse did not help her become a leader. "Twenty-five years ago, nursing was a very subservient role. At nursing school, you learned to step back at an elevator to let the doctors go first. You only got in if there was room for everyone else first. You leaped to your feet when a doctor came in, and you followed the doctor around with the chart. Nursing wasn't recognized as it is today as a profession."

Woods solved her initial problems with supervising largely with the help of a colleague, who taught her how to make fair and objective decisions. "She showed me you could do the job and also have a good working relationship with the people who work for you. I think personality has a lot to do with it, and self-confidence and good self-image. Some supervisors feel they must be tyrants, and some are afraid to develop their own staff for fear they'll take over [the supervisor's] job. I see [staff development] as making my job easier." In fact, one of the first things she did as acting director was to hire and train an assistant.

Her own sense of self-confidence has been closely tied to her education. She felt she needed more training to be a good supervisor. Earlier in her career, after becoming assistant director, she set out to get administrative training. In her first encounters with budgets, she says, "I didn't know the difference between a capital and a payroll budget. I was learning by trial and error. Finally, it hit me that I needed a management course."

Until that time, Woods was equipped with only a two-year nursing diploma. She took a succession of courses—in nursing management, administration, and budget—and got her B.A. at age thirty-eight. "Your self-image improves," she says. "The courses made me more self-confident. I needed that, because I was working with hundreds of physicians. Self-confidence is very important, and

I'm a firm believer that it comes from education." Woods learned about organizational skills, planning, communication up and down the corporate ladder, her responsibility to her staff, and their accountability to her. "Now I'm giving a management course to my new nursing coordinators [the current term for head nurses]. I feel it's important not to promote someone without the proper guidance."

LIJ, she says, is now one of the most democratic hospitals for nurses in the country and often serves as a model for study by other hospitals. But it was not always that way. Woods cites a case in which her male co-workers were being overly "helpful" to her by accompanying her when the state sent investigators to do routine surveys of her staff to see if regulations were being followed. The surveys required the ability to read, understand, and retain many regulations. "It took them [other hospital administrators] a while to realize I could read like everyone else." In fact, she had taken a speed-reading course so that she would be able to flip through reports and regulations more quickly and with better retention—an innovative action, and a good career-plotting step. (Women do seem to be more willing to admit their shortcomings and find creative ways to overcome them, I have observed. One female journalist I know took a shorthand course just before accepting a daily reporting job after a long hiatus. Few reporters ever do that, but it turned out to be an invaluable tool for her.)

For the first two state surveys, Woods allowed the male administrators to follow her and the state team around. "I had to build up my self-confidence, too. If I made a mistake, they could say, 'She wouldn't accept help.' It was very political."

By the third survey, though, Woods found a diplomatic way to indicate her independence. She asked one administrator, "Would you like me to invite you?" When he answered, "Do you need me?" she responded, "No, I was just asking as a courtesy." That way, she says, she let him know that she was handling it and that, if he came along, it would be at her invitation.

Career plotting, then, does not only mean creating a dream or earning the right college degrees. It also means learning the subtler forms of holding authority, and using them to win respect from those who will help decide one's next career move.

One reason Woods says she has not applied to be director is that the job entails more public speaking and public relations than administration. The associate director handles the organizational matters, such as staff problem-solving and budgeting, and she enjoys that. "I'm not comfortable with public speaking," she says. "I also feel it would be better for me to go to another institution as director, where I could offer a new approach. I've been here too long to bring in a fresh approach." She also would like to finish her master's degree before moving to another institution, and she would like to spend more time enjoying her family.

Few men would refuse to grab the next rung of power when it was offered. Few would cite as considerations an evaluation of their own perceived shortcomings or a desire to spend more time with their families. It is nice to meet a professional whose ego is not entwined in her job. Woods proves that there is still room at the top, and on the way up, for human values.

Assembly member May Newburger had no difficulty calling the meeting to order. She had only to lean toward the microphone and say, "We're ready to begin." Her voice was firm and calm. Television lights flashed on, reporters' pens were poised, and the scheduled speakers grasped their written testimony firmly, ready to stride to the podium. The hearing on a proposed bill to curb sexual harassment in the workplace proceeded.

May Newburger of Great Neck, Long Island, one of a handful of women in the New York State legislature, came to her position of authority by a long and winding path. Some of her sidetracks and false starts have to do with the fickle fortunes that all politicians endure, but a great many of her route's twists and turns reflect the fate of women in politics—or any traditionally male field—until fairly recently.

Newburger, for a variety of reasons, could not plot her career path in the way that today's young women can. Instead, she laid the groundwork for her career by improving skills in such areas as public speaking, by forming political alliances, and by understanding the legislative process. Thus, when the tide for women in politics changed, she was ready. Many women today still suffer from a lack of direction, at least in their youthful years, or are in fields still largely closed to women. Newburger, in her fifties now, can serve as an inspiration to those women who cannot or will not rigidly plot out the march of their careers. She has shown how flexibility and resilience can also lead to success.

A strong feminist who has used her position to further women's causes, Newburger nevertheless has ambivalent thoughts about mixing career and family—a factor that most women plotting a career must take into account.

For this interview, we meet at her comfortable home in Great Neck on a Sunday morning, sitting around a sunny kitchen table and drinking coffee. Our conversation is punctuated by the ringing of her phone and short conversations in which she gives directions to her staff or trades political gossip with the callers. Later, a staff member comes by to pick up an envelope of official papers.

May Newburger is one of the few women I have ever met who uses the same tone whether addressing men or women. She is subdued but firm in her manner of speaking, and she does not flirt with or sweet-talk men, nor does she handle women carelessly. Her character was forged out of disappointments mixed with insights and strengths.

Newburger's father was a British architect who left her mother when Newburger was eight, and she never saw him again. "He was unreliable," she observes dryly. Her mother had tuberculosis and could not take care of her daughter when the condition got worse, so Newburger was raised by a succession of aunts. "They were wonderful to me," she says, but she always felt dependent and she always felt frightened. "Other people tell me I was a happy child. But I felt, What if somebody doesn't want to keep me?" She was always on her best behavior. The experience of feeling so dependent, she says, may have helped her to identify with the downtrodden, which has led her to activities in various social justice causes, particularly civil rights and fair housing.

Although shuttled around to seven different elementary schools, Newburger entered college at age fifteen and was elected to Phi Beta Kappa. After graduating, she decided she wanted to write, but instead took a job an aunt had arranged for her with a dress manufacturer, a first step in the fashion career that the aunt wanted for her. She held several other jobs thereafter in the fashion field, until she met her husband, a stockbroker. Listening to the conventional wisdom of the time, she quit her job when they had trouble conceiving a baby. "People suggested that I stop working and relax," she says. It did not help, and eventually they adopted a son, who is now a musician.

But Newburger had become involved in politics during her college years—driven by her interest in social justice causes—and she continued her activities in suburban Great Neck, where the couple had moved to raise their child. Her first campaign was Adlai Stevenson's, in 1956. Slowly she started learning the ropes and paying her political dues in the Democratic party.

When her son was nine, Newburger returned to college to get a master's degree in counseling. She had inquired about going to law school, but the teacher of her "family law" class (now the dean of a respected law school) told her, she recalls, " 'Lady lawyers are terrible. If you're aggressive, no one will like you. If you're nice, they'll stick you at the end of the hall, doing leases.' " That was a long time ago, and May Newburger quietly accepted his advice. "I'll never forgive myself," she says. "I retreated." But for a woman a dozen years out of college to have entered law school in the 1950s would have been a mighty step indeed. Today, getting a law degree is as casually considered advisable for a woman with political ambitions as it is for a man.

In 1961 May Newburger helped found a human rights committee for fair housing in her community. Fair housing became her mission for many years, bringing her local prominence and membership on regional committees, taking her to Washington conferences and introducing her to the public podium.

"When I was in high school, I couldn't speak before an audience," she says. "I would choke, my face would turn red, my mouth would be dry." In 1962 she was scheduled to speak before two thousand people at a rally for Martin Luther King. "I thought I would die," she says. She recalls that she may have sipped a glass of sherry or two to get her through. But she made it, and has been improving as a public speaker ever since. "I got over it by doing," she explains, her motto in many areas. Getting practical experience is an important element in career plotting.

Because of her age, Newburger has lived through some blatant sex discrimination that women today rarely face. She says she was aware of it at the time, although without today's labels. In 1965, for example, she was asked to run for the state assembly by a powerful labor leader, the kind of man whose support can mean victory. "But I couldn't get the support of the people in my own [Democratic] club," she says. "That was before women ran." Instead, she started running the campaigns of male candidates, including the local campaigns of presidential candidates. "I had roles that were further advanced than those of most women. Of course, most campaign workers were women, but they stuffed envelopes and licked stamps." Even with her lofty-sounding titles, though, she still had problems. In one campaign, the male candidate's best friend told people he was the candidate's campaign manager—even though she held the title. The candidate, she relates, said nothing to contradict his friend in public, although he would reassure her in private.

"I had a recurring experience in politics and on the human rights committee," she says. "I would come up with a suggestion or an idea, and people would look at me but say nothing. A few minutes later, a man would come up with the same idea, and everyone would say, 'Good idea.' I don't think it was stealing. People were not listening to women. They didn't hear when a woman said it. It was very frustrating."

Newburger had to wait for perceptions of women to change, although she did not wait quietly. She learned how to make people listen by becoming a more effective speaker and by gaining positions of greater authority. Although Newburger says she and other women she knows have a gentler attitude toward gaining power than many men do—not lusting after it for its own sake, she believes—she has indeed achieved the trappings of power. Even in her freshman term, she headed her own commission—on water quality. She frequently introduces legislation, gets a fair amount of it passed, and gets on the right committees.

Until she won her position in 1978 (and reelections since), she often found her way blocked. For example, when a local candidate whose campaign she managed became an assembly member, he asked her to head the staff of the education committee he chaired. But the job was divided in two before she got there, and she received $7,000 a year, while a younger man (with a family to support, the assembly member pointed out) received $8,000.

To make matters worse, the caption of a *New York Times* photograph in which she appeared identified her as the legislative secretary of the education committee. Her title was legislative director. A female *Times* reporter, enraged by the error, called her editors and insisted on a correction before Newburger herself could call.

The incident was emblematic to her of men's assumptions, as well as of the strengths of informal women's networks, which are another important element in many women's career paths. All along the way, she has helped women and has been helped by women, she says—starting with her aunts. "I feel that good women should be supported wherever possible."

After one more disappointment, defeat in a 1976 state senate race, Newburger was ready to give up on active politics. She tried to develop a women's political center at Hunter College with a female professor, but the would-be program encountered financial problems. Then she decided, finally, to attend law school. She was doing well when, suddenly, her husband died. Her life was greatly disrupted emotionally, of course, and she needed an income. Just then, in 1978, the assembly seat opened in her own district, in which she had outpolled her Republican state senate opponent. Her chances looked good—and they were. She won the race, and has since won re-election, finally putting her in a position to help other women directly through legislation.

Newburger, who sponsored numerous women's issue bills, among them a bill to give incentives to companies to provide on-site day care for children, thinks women younger than she have advantages as well as disadvantages.

"I think younger women have defined their personal roles earlier and more clearly, and they go into marriage with those roles already begun or in mind. I think that's a better way," she says. "But a problem I see emerging is that as they develop professionally, they want to have a family. They feel they have to be the world's greatest psychologist or social worker or whatever, and the world's best wife and mother. We've put a terrible burden on ourselves."

Through her legislation, Newburger is trying to make life easier for younger women. But she also makes it easier through her example of determination and doggedness. Despite numerous career blocks, she has effectively carved out a career in treacherous terrain.

At forty-two, Susan E. Davis is a vice president at the Harris Bank in Chicago, which sounds like a job that requires a staid and steady background. Yet her own career path, like that of so many other women, is a study in zigzags, dead ends, and daring forays forward. Her courage in trying new projects and in bouncing back after disappointments makes her a good example of a woman who has forged a career where others might have found failure.

Davis graduated from Pembroke College of Brown University in 1963, with a B.A. in Russian and American literature, a major she designed herself. Because her father was building his own business while she was growing up in Rhode Island—he had bought Bancroft Racket Company, which makes sports rackets, when she was five—she developed an interest in business. "I learned a lot about it. We discussed it at the dinner table." Her mother, a "professional volunteer," inspired a strong interest in social issues.

Davis wanted to attend Harvard Business School but did not have the money—besides, the school was allowing very few women to enroll the year she graduated from college. Instead, she got a job as an editorial assistant at the Harvard Business School's magazine, *The Executive.* Seven months later, the magazine stopped publication and Davis, picking up her mother's social service interests, moved to the Nigerian Project, which was directed by the Harvard Graduate School of Education. The project designed curricula for a model school in Nigeria. She was hired as a secretary—the only type of job anyone discussed with her during her employment search—but the director of the project "recognized that I was not a secretary, and took me under his wing. I used to tell him what I thought about things. I was somewhat shy, but I cared so much that I did speak up."

The director encouraged Davis to take anthropology courses, and she was set to go for a master's degree in the field, until she spent the summer before she was to enroll at Harvard working as a volunteer in Roxbury, a ghetto area of Boston. There, she met a group of people who were starting the *Bay State Banner,* a black weekly. She joined the staff as advertising manager.

Working at the newspaper, she says, allowed her to combine her interests in business, publishing, and social issues. "I decided a newspaper was more relevant to the real world than a degree." In the course of selling ads to large companies in Boston, she found herself in a field that few women had entered at that time. "I got invaluable experience," she says. "I was raised fairly traditionally as a woman, and I don't think I would have had the guts to be a salesperson unless I was working for something bigger than I was. That gave me the courage to take more risks." She was meeting with top-level executives when she made her sales pitches.

Three years later, when she felt it was time to leave the newspaper, Davis tried to get a job as an outside sales representative, a lucrative position, selling a company's wares or services to other firms, which usually requires travel. No one—not even placement firms—would interview her. It was still not considered a job for a woman. She gave up after six months. What she was able to get was a position as an administrative assistant to a university president. She was selected from among twelve hundred candidates for the job, which paid a low $8,000 a year and was considered a "women's ghetto" position. She accepted but, while visiting Chicago before beginning her new job, met a man who was starting a national urban-affairs publishing company. John Naisbitt, now famous for his best seller, *Megatrends,* offered her a job at his Urban Research Corporation. She asked for $12,000, and when she got it, she started there instead of at the university. At the publishing company, Davis became editor of a newsletter for minority businessmen. "I researched it, wrote it, edited it, produced it, and sold it. I had no staff. It was very profitable from the beginning." As at her previous job, she worked long hours and very hard.

As she traveled to cover minority business conferences, she found herself "treated strictly as a woman, with some very offensive remarks. . . . I got angry, and I wanted to channel it." So in 1969, just as the women's movement was blossoming, she started a national newsletter for working women, *The Spokeswoman,* which she believes was the first national publication marketed to career women. Davis had already been active in the movement for some time. For a year or so, she had been meeting informally for lunch with a few other women, mostly high-powered professionals who held support-level jobs. They had discussed their frustrations and, although not all had children, organized a day-care center.

Despite her growing feminist consciousness and self-confidence, Davis still approached the newsletter in a typically female way: she offered to do it around her regular job until it became successful, and she suggested pricing it at seven dollars, compared to fifty dollars for the black businessmen's publication. "Women were invisible, don't you remember? There was no known market. Plus, the women's movement was sensitive about money. I was attacked by one women's liberation newsletter for trying to 'rip off' women. It hurt at the time, though some part of me knew I should ignore it."

Working on it "around" her other job, she says, was definitely something a man would not have done. "I wouldn't do the same thing now. I'm older and wiser." Back then, however, she put her "heart and soul" into *The Spokeswoman*—while running affirmative-action conferences around the country for her company.

After a year, Davis realized the newsletter would not make money; it was having trouble gaining subscribers because of its connection to the larger, mainstream firm. She asked Naisbitt if she could buy the magazine for one dollar, and requested cutting back to working only half-time at the firm. Naisbitt agreed, and she started to publish out of her bedroom. "I had nearly four thousand subscribers. I wrote, researched, typed, did subscription mailings, billings, everything. I worked night and day. I was very happy doing this, and *The Spokeswoman* grew to be successful. I finally hired someone to help me. . . . I was proud I had made a financial success of the newsletter."

Davis let someone else take it over, however, when she got interested in an even bigger project—a national news magazine aimed at working women. It was designed to be similar to *Newsweek,* covering women's advances in all areas. "I pulled together seven other women in Chicago, and we incorporated and raised $100,000 from a woman investor." They put together a prototype for *Woman News,* sold ads, and did a $55,000 direct-mail test. Then she approached venture-capital companies. She traveled all over the country and came close—but not close enough—to raising the money needed.

Three reasons prevented her success, she feels. First, she was looking for $1.5 million in 1973, a year that was full of reverses for venture capitalists. Second, there was skepticism about whether an all-female corporation was viable. And third, the women naively insisted on retaining 51 percent control—so that women would remain in charge—without putting in any more capital. Her youth and lack of experience in a large-scale publishing enterprise were also factors. "Even so, we came awfully close." She stopped after two years, when one company withdrew from a deal that would have raised enough money.

"I gave up, went to bed for two days, and put the covers over my head. I was in a state of shock. I had felt it couldn't fail if I refused to say no. But it had failed." Instead of brooding longer, she took a succession of jobs that relied on her organizational skills and on contacts she had made through her previous work experiences. Although Davis never plotted a career in the way Carolyn Smithson did —she did not expect to become a banker—she held to her course of working for causes she could believe in, and she steadily built a

collection of accomplishments, competencies, and contacts. Immediately after the demise of the magazine venture, she was hired by
some friends who had just bought a bank. They wanted her to build
up a neighborhood development portfolio, and she eventually built
one of $26 million. It was the first neighborhood development cor-
poration in the country, she says. She stayed at the small bank for
seven years and became a vice president.

During that time, Davis began another type of organizing that
led to her present position with the much larger Harris Bank. She
combined her interest in feminism with her business skills by organizing women's network groups. In 1978 she helped start a group of
the top one hundred businesswomen in Chicago called the Chicago
Network, Inc. Later she helped found the Chicago Finance Exchange,
for seventy-five top women in finance.

In 1981 Davis conceived the idea of forming a group of the top
200 female business owners in the country. They would be asked, in
formation, to provide working capital for a group of smaller entrepreneurs, called the National Association of Business Owners. Davis
then took the job of reaching this goal. Out of that assignment grew
a powerful organization called the Committee of 200, which hopes to
have an impact on public policy. It garnered a great deal of media
attention, largely because of the caliber of women that Davis was
able to attract. Many had never before joined a women's group. Each
member of the committee either owns a business with an annual
volume of at least $5 million or heads a corporation or corporate
division with sales of at least $20 million annually. Among the mem-
bers are Katherine Graham, chairman of the board of the *Washington
Post;* Sherry Lansing, former president of 20th Century Fox; and—
among the women interviewed for this book—Diane Johnson and
Mary Farrar.

Davis's work in organizing the committee impressed a prominent female officer at the Harris Bank who also had been a cofounder
of the Finance Exchange, and led to her present job. "Networking
was really working," says Davis. At Harris, she is in charge of the
personal trust development division, a sales area. So her early work
in selling ads has paid off by providing a building block that has led
to later career development. Davis had assembled many such blocks
to build her career—experience, good professional contacts,
achievements in visible areas. The blocks fit together felicitously to
bring her to her present peak.

Davis's life is different now from when she ran the newsletter and tried to start the magazine. She married in 1974 and has two children. "I have three to-do lists—one at work, one at home, and one for the children. It's nerve-racking." Her only regret is that she could not afford to attend business school right after college. That building block, she believes, would have made her career climb easier.

Although every career path is different, and although the plotting of it—if a woman has the opportunity to plan ahead—depends on the individual, the profession, and the specific workplace, some general principles can be derived:

• Being late starters should not discourage women; people who have blossomed later in life have succeeded. But once awakened to the possibility of a career, women should think ahead to where they want to go and begin acquiring the necessary training and contacts.

• Networking with other women is important, both to learn specific information about jobs and to share and overcome some of the obstacles to women's success.

• Making contacts with men and building easy working and networking relationships with them are also essential.

• Women will often find it worthwhile to take courses to learn management skills quickly and to accumulate credentials.

• Women with ambition should be alert to slights—being left out of meetings or being given unfair performance reviews—and should react assertively. Asking for added responsibilities can expand their importance in an organization.

• Women must learn to say no or at least "Let me think about it" to job offers that conflict with their career plans or their family plans. They should, however, be flexible enough to change course if a really good opportunity comes along.

• Women already in the work force, or older women returning to work. should consider getting advanced degrees, because they will be competing with many well-qualified young men and women.

• Disappointment and failure should not stop determined career women, who forge ahead with new plans—such as going for another degree, another job, or another career—if they cannot realize their original goals, or if their aspirations change.

━━━ **9** ━━━
Juggling Family and Career

Brenda Ruello is one of life's great jugglers. Many women trying to balance family and career know just what that word means, and what a feat it implies.

Ruello is an executive not just in the office but in the home: she employs a housekeeper and a personal shopper; she lives by lists, for business appointments and for household groceries; she masterminds a weekly retreat to a country house; and she constantly makes decisions in the evenings on such important matters as whether to finish her own report for next morning's meeting or help one of her children with homework. Hers is not an uncommon existence for today's woman of authority, although she has an economic advantage over many. But her busy schedule, built with consciousness and control, points to an area in which women must be particularly thoughtful and especially resourceful.

Decisions on social, family, and personal priorities are essential for a female manager. If she is not thinking clearly in these areas, she will never exude the self-confidence she needs at work.

Women often follow different career patterns from those of men, usually because they put their personal and family lives first—or at least give them more consideration than most men do. The two most crucial points on which career and family life are likely to clash are the issues of having children and relocating—moving to advance one's career, one's husband's career, or merely to get a job for oneself or one's husband. Both considerations, relocation and children, are important when a woman chooses a career, a company, and a career goal. Ideally, these choices should follow an assessment by the woman of what her personal priorities are. Small companies and nonprofit organizations, for instance, may offer greater time flexibility and less pressure to relocate for career advancement than a large corporation might. Academia is often a good place for women having children because of the elastic work schedule.

"You can be more flexible in academic work. Maybe that's why many women are drawn to it," says Carol Schwartz, forty-three, an economist and professor at Adelphi University School of Business, explaining one reason why she never went into private industry or government work, where her salary would be higher. "I have three children, fourteen, sixteen, and eighteen. When they were younger, I could adjust my schedule. I could take a lighter or a heavier teaching load. "My first son was born during summer session, just after I got my Ph.D. It was a race to see which I would get first. My next two were born at intersession, so I took no time off. I tried to plan it that way. When I was in the hospital with my second child, I had to grade a set of papers."

Her husband, a lawyer, sometimes stayed with the children while she taught at night. If she had an article to write, she was likely to do it from the children's bedtime at 10:00 P.M. until 4:00 A.M. "But at least I could sit at a desk at home. I didn't have to be at a desk on Wall Street."

Relocation is still a tricky issue for many women, and some women, unwisely, avoid thinking about it until confronted with an actual job offer. Carrie Ives Lincoln, now director of executive search for Abbott Smith Associates, a search firm in Millbrook, New York, says that often when she calls women with a relocation offer, they are taken completely by surprise. In fact, she says, they frequently do not understand her message at first. She usually says to an executive, "Your name has been given to me as a resource. Can you suggest some names?" Men, she says, always understand right away that she is asking them if they want the job, but doing it in such a way that they will not be embarrassed if others in the firm learn of the call. Women usually start trying to think of names.

"When I finally say to the woman, 'I don't suppose you'd be interested,' there's a lot of hesitation. There are women out there who would relocate at the drop of a hat, but they're in the minority." Lincoln thinks those who will not move are damaging their careers.

"Women do a lot of things to hurt themselves, and that's one of the biggest. Women don't take risks. Ultimately they would earn more money." If a husband and wife are both pursuing careers, she says, they should talk about possible relocation, "not just put it on a back burner." Many companies are now amenable to finding work for a spouse at the new location, either in the same firm or in another. Women approached by their own firms or by an outside firm with job offers in new locations should definitely ask about that possibility.

Deciding on whether to relocate is often difficult and may depend on the particular time in one's life, says Massachusetts career development consultant Ellen J. Wallach. "You have to look at the balance between work and family. Women traditionally have focused their energies on the family, but in this generation, the focus is on balance. If the kids are in the tenth or eleventh grades, the family probably would not want to move." The decision not to move for family reasons is being made more frequently by men these days, too, she says. There is still a stigma attached, however, to the man who follows his wife to a new location. "People in general don't find it acceptable, or they wonder about it." The same stigma does not attach to a woman. Wallach compares attitudes about relocation to attitudes about women who travel for their jobs. "The husband will be asked, 'What do you think of it?' Or he'll be asked to dinner. When my husband travels, no one asks me to dinner, but when I'm gone five days, people say, 'Oh, that must be tough on your husband.' "

The issue of balance between career and family, whether applied to relocation or to having children, is still a women's issue, Wallach says. When she keynoted a 1983 conference at the Boston University School of Medicine on the "Myth of the Superparent," she found that of 150 people attending, only 14 were men—and 6 of those had come with their wives. Younger people may be changing, she says, but women in their thirties and older are still feeling guilt when they make choices for career instead of family. "As the women's movement started, we were told we had options, but our heads believed one thing and our guts believed another. The gut is saying we should be home making brownies." Though Wallach believes that women can have perfectly fine careers without relocating, she thinks a woman in a mostly male bastion, such as law, medicine, or business, must question how much of her career she is sacrificing if she takes off more than a few months to have children.

But having children—as any parent knows—entails more than

taking a few weeks or months off from work. Finding babysitters, being called for emergencies, and just plain wanting to spend more time at home are all part of the job of parenting—and much of the work, liberation or no, still falls to the mother.

Of thirty-four female Harvard M.B.A.s interviewed by *Fortune* in 1978, all said that, if they did have children, they would expect to earn less or move forward less rapidly in their fields. Still, those who had opted for motherhood were not at all sorry that they did. In fact, not all working mothers feel their parenthood has been detrimental to their careers.

It is probably impossible to measure, in any meaningful way, the effects of parenthood and time off on women's careers, says sociologist Cynthia Fuchs Epstein, a professor at Queens College and Graduate Center, City University of New York, and resident scholar at the Russell Sage Foundation in New York.

Although women were once able to take time off and return to work with their careers intact, Epstein says, they may not be able to anymore. More women are in the work force now, so companies may be loath to set precedents, and unemployment is high, making it difficult for anyone to find a job.

Epstein addresses the problem of having a career and children in her 1981 book, *Women in Law*. She finds that many of the young female lawyers she interviewed are either deferring children or deciding not to have them at all. Of those who want children, many are trying to decide on the best time to do so. The answers vary, from early (before or during law school) to late (after becoming a partner in a firm). Moreover, many female lawyers are choosing specialties that will allow them to work shorter, fixed hours or get more time off. One has deliberately chosen to prepare briefs and do research and to avoid trial work, because she would not be able to leave a courtroom if her child were sick.

Most law firms do not want a woman to work part time, says Epstein in an interview. "Women still have to prove themselves, prove that they're committed." In general, she says, it is probably better for a woman in any field to establish herself in a career before having children. "The more career investment she's made, the better off she is." An added benefit of waiting, she says, is that a woman is more likely to have defined herself and her role in life and is less likely to feel ambivalent about her choices.

Epstein's feeling in talking to young college women today is that many of them have "no sense of the history of discrimination. Without that perspective, they feel they can do anything they want, that the system will bend to them, that they can take time off. They have a clearer sense [than older women] that they would like careers, but they're not too practical about the continuing discrimination out there."

A woman who takes time off or curtails her hours usually does slow her rise up the career ladder, although the harm is often not irreparable, as some of the following stories will show. On the other hand, a woman who, like Brenda Ruello, tries to do it all is likely to have everything but time to herself. Not everyone can stand such a pressured life. The following stories concern women who have made different decisions about how to mesh family and career.

Betsy Adams has chosen, for the time being, not to do everything at once. She has tried all the variations since having her two children: working part time, working full time, and not working at a regular job at all. A holder of an M.B.A. in her mid thirties, she has worked for General Foods and for Fotomat. Currently, she does not work for a firm, but is doing some consulting work.

Although she is looking for a full-time job, Adams expects that her career may stay on hold for a while. Because of her children, she is unwilling to commute more than a half-hour from her Stamford, Connecticut, home, nor will she be willing to work the twelve-hour days or weekends that are necessary for an executive in strategic planning or financial marketing analysis—two of the fields in which she specializes—to move up in most corporations.

"I always assumed I would be working full time, regardless of children," says Adams. When pregnant with her first child, she worked until the day before she gave birth. "I was as big as a house, of course," she says. She expected to go back to work full time three months later, but a fortuitous congruence of her husband's wishes that she stay home and a company offer of part-time work changed her path. She is as surprised as anyone that she has had a change of heart about pursuing a career single-mindedly.

Actually, when Adams grew up in Rochester, New York, the daughter of a homemaker and an instrument maker for Kodak, she never thought she would work, at least not at a career. "I thought I would get married and be relieved." In college, she took marketing courses, though, instead of the usual straight liberal arts, because she wanted to live in New York City and wanted skills that would get her a job there.

She did get jobs as an assistant buyer, first at Bloomingdale's and later at Montgomery Ward. But they were just jobs, and she soon left to go to California, during the hipppie era of the early 1970s. "I floated around without direction. I just decided to move to San Francisco, where I had some friends, and took silly jobs to live on. I dropped out."

Then she met Bob, the man she was to marry. When they decided to "be serious," she says, they "decided to look for what we called real jobs." He encouraged her to get her M.B.A., which she did in San Diego, and then they both moved to Stamford, where Bob is now a product manager for a large industrial firm. She got a job with General Foods as a senior financial analyst.

"I got disenchanted with corporate life in a big corporation," she says. She found herself getting very competitive, which she did not mind, but she did not like the repetitiveness of her work. She wanted to work for a smaller, younger company, preferably one where she could work on a project basis so that she could be doing something new periodically. She found such a job with Fotomat in nearby Wilton, Connecticut. There, she worked on projects in corporate development, marketing, and financial analysis.

Then she got pregnant.

"Bob felt, after the baby came, that he wanted me to stay home. I didn't want to." It became a point of contention between them, and their compromise solution was that she would ask the company if she could work part time. "Six weeks after my leave started, I had lunch with my boss. He asked what I wanted to do, and I said I wanted to work three days a week. He said that three days a week was what he was about to suggest. It was ironic, totally surprising."

It turned out that her boss's boss, the vice president of marketing, had made the suggestion. "I don't know what I would have done if they hadn't let me work part time," she says. She was surprised that the marketing VP, a Harvard M.B.A. in his mid thirties whose own wife stayed home with their only child, would be so sympathetic. "I guess he was just open, though by rights he shouldn't have been."

She worked part time, at 60 percent pay, until her son was ten months old. Then she went back full time because—another surprise —she got a promotion. "There was a reorganization of the company, and I became manager of marketing analysis." She was pregnant again at the time, although she did not tell her employers that when she took the promotion.

A larger company probably would not have promoted a part-time worker, Adams says. "There were only 150 people at the corporate headquarters, because many of their people were still in California, where they had moved from. So the company was small and flexible. My impression is that General Foods or American Can would not have allowed a part-time worker at all."

When she told them she was pregnant again, they were very supportive, she says. Again, she worked right up until her delivery in May.

But this time, an announcement came that the company would be moving to Florida at the end of the year. She could have returned three months later and worked until the end of the year, or she could have moved to Florida. Moving, she determined quickly, was not an option. She decided which way she wanted to balance her life at that point, as career counselor Ellen Wallach would say. Adams also concluded she did not want to go back for just a few months, since the company offered her severance pay in May. After taking the summer off, she started looking for a full-time job.

"I'm ready now to work full time. I have everything set up." Before the move was announced, she had already arranged for a full-time live-in person to care for her children. Her son is enrolled in an excellent child development program at the local YWCA, and her young daughter goes there three times a week, too.

"I expect I will find a good job, although probably I won't progress as fast in my career as I would if I didn't have the children. But I'm willing to sacrifice for them. Maybe my career will stay on a plateau for five or ten years. Careerwise, I'll be losing. But it's a sacrifice I'm willing to make." Her husband, she says, is supportive, although he has not made the kinds of career sacrifices she has. "How do I justify putting my career on hold? He makes more than I do. I don't put a lot of thought into it, because I could get angry. So I just sublimate."

Adams received two job offers in New York City before she decided that the three hours of commuting each day would be too much. "I'd just be a wreck. Life is too short."

What she has been doing in the interim is working for Barbara Keck, a New York City mother who founded an innovative consulting firm that employs mothers who want to quit the corporate life but would like to continue working on a part-time basis. Like Adams, the mothers can work from their own homes. Keck's story follows, as a good example of how a woman with strong feelings against leaving her children for a full-time career can solve her dilemma.

While I interview Barbara Keck on a weekday during business hours, her 3½-year-old boy punctuates our conversation with various demands and distractions, from showing off his crayon drawings to getting into his mother's briefcase. His mother patiently takes the interruptions in stride. The full-time babysitter is out on a walk with Keck's sixteen-month-old son, but after all, being there with her children was the main reason for founding Keck & Co. Business Consultants three years before. The office is a former bedroom in her Manhattan apartment, now jam-packed with two desks, a typewriter, a personal computer, and a printer.

"Martin, don't put your toys into your tape recorder. It will ruin your tape recorder," Keck says calmly at one point. Later: "Martin, why are you looking in Mommy's briefcase?" Martin and Mommy seem to have a very good working relationship.

"Being at home works fine in most cases, but you've got to have child care, unless you have a catatonic child. The tough thing is—Don't slam the door, Martin—putting one hat on and taking the other off. You have to be a quick-change artist."

Keck, now thirty-six, was a marketing manager at Continental Can in Stamford, Connecticut, when she became pregnant. A graduate of the Harvard Business School, she was on the fast track, working sixty to eighty hours a week, "the standard management work week." She now works what she calls part time: thirty-five hours a week.

She had already founded a group called Women in Management, for female professionals in Connecticut and New York. During her first pregnancy, she organized a program on combining motherhood and career, which was attended by sixty women. This was her first confirmation that she was not alone in her dilemma about what to do.

Keck grew up in a small Indiana farm town. Her father owned a hamburger place, her mother stayed at home as a housewife. She went to Douglass College, the women's college of Rutgers University, and got jobs as a science writer for the United States Department of Agriculture, in public relations, and in advertising, before returning for her M.B.A. at age twenty-eight. She was in a middle management position with Continental Can when she left.

"I suppose I was thinking of corporate management, working my way up to executive vice president-type work." She is not sure just when she decided to leave that world.

"I would not say I was ecstatically happy in corporate America. I think politics got in the way of good performance at all levels. I'm not a player. I don't like it and I don't do it well. I don't know when I decided to think about doing my own thing." She does not know if she would have gone through with it—doing her own thing—if she had not had a child.

After a six-week maternity leave, she asked if she could work part time or on a flexible schedule at Continental Can. She was turned down. She knew that, if she went back, she would be working long hours and spending about 40 percent of her time in Chicago. She did not go back.

"I believe part-time work is not consistent with corporate America as it's now structured. Once in a great while, a corporation will make an exception, as a bridge to full-time work, kind of as a favor. My company [Continental Can] wouldn't do that for me, and I guess I can understand why. If you set a precedent like that, and you offer it to a woman, then you have to offer it to men. And when you have 63,000 employees worldwide, you don't want to set a precedent. I think they're wasting a great resource. We're proving it can be done."

Keck now has fourteen associates, more than half of whom are mothers who want to work a flexible schedule and who would not be working at all if they were not working for her. All of them have management or computer skills—backgrounds that make them good management consultants—but do not want to sell their services themselves or are not good at selling.

Keck specializes in helping young companies, such as those that have just gone public, with interim management. Her associates do not mind working full time for a limited period of time, or part time over an extended period. For example, she says, she might provide someone to set up a new company's financial reporting system for two months while the company looks for the right person to fill a controller's position permanently. But she also has a few associates without children who can pick up at a moment's notice, fly to Los Angeles for eleven days—as a recent project for General Electric required—and have a report ready a few days later. "Mommies can't live that fast," she says.

Keck is providing an alternative, she says, for "professional women who have built management acumen, then in their thirties realize that time is running out for having children, and when they're faced with a decision between a corporation and a family, choose family first. But that doesn't mean the choice has to be exclusive."

In her first year as a consultant, says Keck, her income matched what her salary had been at Continental Can. Now she is taking in less, only because she has invested in office equipment in a bid to expand her business. She feels, though, that in the long run she will be better off as an independent businesswoman than she would have been staying in the corporate world, and she learned more about business in one year having to find her own clients, make contacts, organize her company, and sell herself, she says, than she did during her four years at the large corporation.

She never tells her clients about her home office, her children, or the part-time status of her associates. "There's definitely a resistance to that. I don't want to transfer to clients information that would feed their prejudices I don't want to press the hot button that corporation managers have been conditioned to when they hear 'young mothers' or 'part time.' They ring: 'Not for us, not for us.' I want to prove it can be done by doing it. There's no sense in my acing myself or my colleagues out of work—Martin, that's a wonderful lion. Why don't you draw your name on it? That's right, up in the air, down to the ground. . . . You get used to shifting gears. But, as the quote goes, 'It is a far, far better thing that I do than I have ever done.' If I had a kid today with an asthma attack or a broken finger, I have the flexibility to take care of it, to administer physical and psychological care."

Barbara Robinson, a lawyer, faced the same dilemma as Adams and Keck when she had her first child fifteen years ago. Unlike most of the women interviewed by sociologist Epstein, she was able to persuade her firm to allow her to work part time. She still faced difficult choices, however.

"When my first child was born, I had worked here two years. In those days, there weren't many women in law firms. I had not given a lot of thought to children. I did want them, but I hadn't wrestled with the issue.

"When I was pregnant, I went to the firm and asked for a leave of absence. There was no paid maternity leave then. They gave me six months. To my absolute astonishment, when the child arrived, I thought this was terrific. I wanted to stay home more," says Robinson, now forty-one. "I didn't like babies in the abstract, but when mine came, I thought it was the biggest miracle that ever happened. I was flabbergasted. I tell people now that until the moment of birth, you can't anticipate how you will feel. You can't map it out."

Instead of returning full time, as she had planned, she asked if she could work on a regular schedule from 9:00 A.M. to 6:00 P.M. four or five days a week. This represented a condensed schedule, compared to the marathon hours she and the other corporate lawyers in the firm, now called Debevoise and Plimpton, usually worked.

There had been three other female lawyers in the firm before her, and all had quit when they had had children. Robinson did not want to do that. "I spent a lot of time and energy developing my skills, and I didn't want to waste it. Also, staying home [full time] didn't appeal to me." Part of the reason she felt this way was that her own mother had a career. She had returned to school after Robinson was born, gotten a degree in education, and become first an elementary school principal and then an administrator. Her father was a pharmacist with his own business. Furthermore, Robinson attended Bryn Mawr College in Pennsylvania, where "it was assumed that the women students went and did things. It was very Ph.D. oriented. It was just expected that you would be a serious scholar."

The firm allowed her to work a regular schedule, but suggested that she specialize in trusts and estates instead of broader corporate work or litigation. Trusts and estates—dealing with wills and tax problems—has traditionally been a woman's field. Robinson thinks it was a "mistake" to be forced to choose a particular field simply because she wanted to work a regular or part-time schedule, even though she feels it worked out well in her case. "It was just a tiny period of time in the course of a professional career that I worked part time." First she worked five days, then four, and finally three days a week for the two years after her second child—now aged twelve—was born. Her short schedule lasted five years. Instead of being made a partner seven years after joining the firm, as is common in the field, she was made a partner ten years later, but that was a delay she did not mind. "When I was part time, I was just out of the whole running. I wasn't worried. It just wasn't an overriding role for me. I had different priorities."

Robinson did, however, have qualms. "It's hard for everyone. It's hard for the person doing part-time work, and it's hard for the firm to find the right kind of work for the person to do. It's not a panacea. I felt I was doing nothing wonderfully, at home or at work. I had mixed feelings all the time. I always felt I was never doing enough, no matter where I was. When I went back to a full-time schedule, it was a terribly hard decision. Sometimes I would feel, 'Why am I neglecting my family?' I would meet with a few other mothers I knew who worked, and we would share our collective guilt."

Though it is difficult, she believes in giving women some years off from full-time work. "If women want to do it, then it's important to allow them to try."

Several women in her firm are now following the same path she took, although they no longer have to limit their choice of specialization, which she thinks is better. One senior woman in corporate law gets calls at home from clients, which is fine with both lawyer and client. "It can work out. It's short-sighted for firms not to do this more. It's a finite period of time." A couple of men have been allowed to go part time, too, one because he wanted to try teaching and another because he wanted to get into politics.

Robinson finds it sad that many students she has talked to—including, recently, some women at Columbia Law School—"have stopped themselves before they tried. I see them fail to try to do certain kinds of jobs because they think the firms won't accommodate them, so they switch out of firms and into government or nonprofit work. Government and nonprofits are fine if that's what you want to do, of course, but not if you don't. Many are doing this even before they're married."

Her advice, unlike Epstein's, is not to wait until you are a partner before having children, because the demands on a partner are much greater than on other lawyers in the firm. (Her firm has 200 lawyers, 60 of whom are partners.) She has management responsibilities that include hiring and firing, training young lawyers, and running the office. "It would be very hard to be a part-time partner. You would stop being a partner for a while. The only differences are you're a little older, so you're ready, your self-identification is stronger, you're a little better organized, and you make more money."

Even now, she says, with her sons older, she still finds life crammed full. "If you like to do a perfect job, there's always more you can do to make it better. That's true for the law and for my life as a parent. One of the banes of my existence is socks. There are never any that match. While I'm working on law, I'll be thinking about socks, or about arranging a birthday party or calling the pediatrician. At home, I worry about a case, or I'm tired and feeling stretched.

"When you're part time, you can't have the full and final responsibility for things, so there are trade-offs professionally, and it's frustrating if you like what you're doing. I felt it at both ends. And then there were mothers who didn't work who made you feel inadequate. I hope that that has changed."

One aspect she thinks has not changed is that it is still the woman who takes primary responsibility for child care. Her husband, a banker and spare-time serious artist, is supportive, she says, but must work long hours and travel frequently for his job. "Once he was gone a month. That was hard." They have had a sleep-in housekeeper since the oldest child was one or two years old. "No matter what fathers say about making child rearing equal, there is only one child bearer. Just as there can be only one executive officer, there's only one person who's mentally on the line. There's only one who will call the other parent to delegate responsibility, and only one who worries when the housekeeper doesn't show up. It tends to be the mother." She thinks it important to her marriage that her husband does not feel "competitive or threatened" by her success.

Looking back, Robinson says, she might think, "I worked too hard. But mothers who don't work think that too. That's just the nature of raising a young family, speaking in broken sentences for a few years. Delegation is a job, too. If you have a housekeeper, you are a manager. So everyone feels terribly tired and terribly stretched.

"I tried to get one day to myself, but mostly I just did errands and spent time with the children. You have to understand that things won't run the superb way you'd like. You can't cook or have a magnificent house or have the children always clean and looking terrific. I wanted all those things to be perfect, and I worked hard at it. Maybe I should have been more relaxed about some of those standards. But it was a challenge.

"I made up my mind that my personal time in a sense was my work. That's what I wanted to do. If I couldn't see my friends, or go to museums or have dinner parties, then I wouldn't. But we feel it was a reasonably good juggling job. The kids are pretty nice."

Robinson's feelings about juggling are similar to those of Brenda Ruello, who also is pleased, on the whole, with the decisions she has made. They and other working mothers have found what some recent research confirms: that the combination of working and parenting, while bringing with it a "cost of success," can also be the best of both worlds.

Ruello is the only female senior vice president at the executive search firm of Heidrick and Struggles and the mother of two children. "My own observation is that there are trade-offs. There is definitely a trade-off. . . . But, I feel, if you can do it all, why not?"

Ruello's trade-off, like Robinson's, has been a lack of personal time. It is a complaint often cited by working mothers. She has handled the problem, though, in a very in-charge way. She uses a personal shopper for her clothes so that she never has to waste time in department stores. She phones in all her grocery orders. She has a housekeeper four days a week. She schedules breakfast, lunch, and dinner meetings, but she never, never schedules a weekend work or social engagement. Weekends are reserved for the family's country home. She changed her hobby from painting, which she found too time-consuming, to photography, mostly confined to picture taking during the one big vacation that she and her husband, Sam, a high-level executive in management consulting for Coopers and Lybrand, take every year.

Ruello, whose children are from a previous marriage, often takes work home, where she and her husband share the dining-room table after dinner for their after-hours labors. She is obviously a success. "I'm extremely motivated. I feel a drive to be a success. If I have a proposal to write, for instance, I never deliberate between that and something else, such as if someone calls with theater tickets."

But it is harder for her, as a woman in the high-pressure "head-hunting" field, than it would be for a man. "It's more difficult as a woman to be a success. You don't have the benefit of mentors. You have to prove you are good, distinguish yourself. There's always a feeling of 'show me' from the clients, until you've worked for them several times."

To be the high-powered success she is—what she describes as a superwoman—takes high energy, "a mind like a computer," and, very often, self-abnegation. When there are conflicts between her wishes and the demands of her teenage children, their demands win. "I'm constantly torn. I often give up the thing I want to do when someone else wants me. I'll put off a bath or reading a magazine because someone wants help on homework. But having someone always want or need me for something is a nice feeling."

Although her husband is as committed as she to their two-career family life and is very supportive, Ruello says, she would never ask him to do some of the planning chores—such as making house-keeper arrangements or calling for groceries—that take up much of her mental energy. Her reasoning is an echo of the feelings of the other women interviewed: "It's usually the woman who does the planning. I think that's just a tradition," at least among women of her generation, now in their forties. She sees different arrangements, she says, among some couples in their twenties.

Brenda Ruello's problem with time is a common one for successful career women, whether they have families or not. A 1982 survey of 107 top women executives from 64 of America's largest corporations, taken by the firm of Kane, Parsons and Associates, reveals that the majority felt they had given up something to get where they are. More than 60 percent of that majority cited relationships with other people as among the sacrifices they had made. This category included family plans, social life, time with friends, and personal pleasures such as dancing, reading, or hobbies. Of this group of 107, only 46 women were married and only 29 had children. Of course, men must give up family and social time, too, but probably not to the same extent as women—who must prove themselves more in their jobs and to whom the burdens of planning family life still largely fall.

"Women often do an injustice to themselves," says Judy Machanik, a New York-area management consultant. "They don't allow enough time for solitude, for their own renewal, a walk down the street or to a pond or getting together with friends. We're not as kind to ourselves as we could be." Men, she says, have usually not been taught to feel "those different magnets pulling at women" such as demands from children or the feeling that it is one's duty to prepare meals and keep house or at least find someone else to do these chores for you.

A report, featuring coast-to-coast in-depth interviews, issued in 1982 by the research firm of Judith Langer Associates found that many women, especially those who had been full-time homemakers for a period of their lives, saw their homes as a refuge rather than a trap. "Home to me means comfort, escape, tranquility, serenity," said one woman. "My home is a little cocoon to get away from the hard world out there. It's really a joy to me." Many of the women enjoyed decorating their homes. Feelings about housework, however, were mixed.

Several ex-homemakers felt "resentment and contempt for housework," according to the Langer report, entitled *Working Women: A Matter of Priorities.* Some women tried to do it as quickly and efficiently as possible. Others, interestingly, found it a good release for pent-up energy and a psychologically satisfying activity. Others lowered their housekeeping standards, and many wished they could afford a cleaning person. Some of those who could afford that service, however, had difficulty spending money on "something I should do myself."

The variety of attitudes toward housework expressed in this survey reveals the huge ambivalence that women still feel about their traditional duties at home. It is an area that is bound to hold women back from a true sense of authority at work and at home. If nothing else, doing the work or being the sole person in her household (no matter how supportive the husband) who arranges for the work to get done is a drain on a woman's energy. But the implications are even more serious. First, if a woman takes on the chores and the planning herself, she is implicitly admitting that she does not feel these lowly activities are worth bothering a husband about. She is admitting that she does not value her time—or herself—enough. Second, if she can afford household help but does not get it, she may be saying that the salary she gets at work is not a true measure of the value of her time. Typically, a single man making $30,000 a year would not hesitate to spend $30 or more a week for household help, if he wanted it. But I know several women in that salary range who would not, and do not. They do spend hours themselves vacuuming and dusting. Ironically, men who do not hire help also do not dust as much. Society (or their perception of what society wants) does not expect them to have as neat or clean a house as a woman's. In marriages, it is still very common to find situations in which the wife has tried to share work with her husband, found that he botches the

job or does not take as much care as she, and has returned to doing
it herself.

It is crucial that women aspiring to management careers set
realistic housekeeping standards, says Marge Rossman, author of
When the Headhunter Calls: A Guide for Women in Management
(1981). "I don't think you have to give up the family, but you have to
manage it in a different way. You can't be the only one taking care of
the children when they're sick. Maybe we'll have to give up some
perfectionism about the household. Maybe it's okay if the children
make their own dinner sometimes," she said at a recent seminar for
women in management positions. No one, she said, should try to be
a superwoman: "If you come home and put on your Superwoman
cape, you'll make yourself crazy."

Even Ruello, who has her life pretty much in control, did not
come to her present state easily. Born and raised in Florence, South
Carolina, she was the daughter of a store owner and a housewife,
neither of whom expected her to pursue a career. She went to Dana
Hall School in Wellesley, Massachusetts, and to Syracuse University,
where she majored in art. "I was just brought up to go to college and
get married," which is what she did five years after graduating.
She had her children and stayed home for four years. But she had
discovered early on that she enjoyed working, first at her job in
merchandising at Bloomingdale's and later in in-house recruiting at the consulting firm of Booz-Allen and Hamilton. However,
she did not think of work as a career until she got divorced.
"That," she says, "turned it around"—at first purely for economic
reasons.

By the time she came to Heidrick and Struggles, her present
firm, she had made up her mind to succeed. Meanwhile, her children
were turning into independent, bright, and active teenagers, which
pleased her. At work, each new client, each newly completed search,
built up her confidence, and now she feels proud of all aspects of her
life. "My family knows my work is important to me and they support
me. I also make a commitment to them, so it's mutual. I give to them,
and they're giving to me."

Ruello's feeling about balance in her life is one of the positive
aspects of having both career and family. It is confirmed by the 1982
Kane, Parsons and Associates study of executive women mentioned
earlier in this chapter. Though the majority of those women felt

success had led to many sacrifices in their private lives, three-quarters of them said that, even if they could maintain the same life-style without working, they would continue to work. Obviously, the "psychological benefits" (along with the monetary benefits) of being women in top executive positions outweigh the costs to home and family life.

Relocation is the other big family problem for women, whether it is for the benefit of their own or their husband's career. Single women usually feel much less restricted about relocating for a new job than do married women, and it can make a difference in their careers. A 1980 study showed that married academic women who lost their jobs as a result of mass layoffs had a much more difficult time finding a new job than did their single sisters. The study was conducted by Robert E. Kapsis of Queens College and James M. Murtha of Columbia University and the Office of Institutional Research and Analysis at the City University of New York. The explanation, they found, was that dual-career marriages limited the married women's employment options. Although their study applied to New York, the researchers felt that "the plight of married women dismissed from an institution in a college town would be much worse. Only a few would be able to accept work outside the area, while the vast majority, especially those with school-age children, would be left in the community to join the ranks of the unemployed and underemployed."

Felice Schwartz, president of Catalyst, a national nonprofit organization that has conducted extensive studies on two-income families, gives an explanation that is simple but true: "We have not outgrown sex-role stereotyping. The idea that a man's job is more important than a woman's still lingers."

The flip side of a married woman being more reluctant to move when she loses a job or is offered a promotion is that she may be forced to move when her husband's job requires it. Luckily some women, at least, have found innovative answers to this dilemma. It is not always a happy situation, of course, but sometimes relocation can jar a woman into finding a better job.

One woman who has coped successfully—several times—with such a situation is Elaine Hendrie, who has made five moves between Washington and New York during the past ten years. "I feel like a Ping-Pong ball," says this public relations specialist whose husband, a scientist, was chairman of the Nuclear Regulatory Commission under President Carter.

Hendrie started out in New York with various jobs that helped her gain employment when they moved to Washington. She was an assistant account executive with a public relations firm and then did some free-lance consulting of her own, particularly with school districts seeking to pass budget proposals or to build new schools. Rather than ask the government to help her find a job—which many employment counselors now suggest for two-income families asked to relocate, though it works better with private firms—she set out on her own. She did some unpaid work for the Smithsonian Institution until she found a position as public relations director for Religious Heritage of America, Inc., a nonprofit group.

"My advice to women relocating is to do something, anything, while waiting for your contacts to help in your job search, your resumés to bear fruit. Do volunteer work in the area you hope to get into professionally, if possible. It maintains contact." That is what happened for her, and she was able to use her Smithsonian colleagues as local references.

When Hendrie returned to New York, she landed a job as director of Women in New Directions and also had her own radio show called "Woman to Woman." She had to give that up when she and her husband moved to Washington again, three years later. This time she held jobs first in a trade association, for about a year, and later with the United States Navy, for another year.

Because her job changes were the results of relocation instead of unsatisfactory performance, and because in Washington, at least, her employers knew beforehand of her limited tenure (such is the nature of political Washington anyway), she had no problems with potential employers questioning her job stability. In fact, her resumé looks very reasonable, with only five major jobs listed, and two of those simultaneous.

"I looked on both moves to Washington as an adventure." Her husband would have remained on Long Island had she wanted it, she says, but the reasons for moving were much more compelling. "I always got a better job than the one I previously had, and I might not have 'reached out' to a new position if it hadn't been for the relocation. Also, I saw each move to Washington as a time when I could take chances. I always had the feeling that if I did something new and fell on my face the folks back home wouldn't know about it. And that freed me to widen my scope and areas of action. Interestingly enough, I never did fall on my face, so now I am a confirmed risk taker and think women ought to make themselves take risks." Risk taking involves one of those neglected muscles that women in charge must learn to flex more frequently.

Hendrie's talisman in making a move, she says, is to work out a "worst-thing scenario": What is the worst thing that could happen to me when I apply for a new job? "It's always worked. Many women are afraid to seem brassy about asking for a job, going in and saying, 'I'm qualified.' But my worst-thing scenario [such as being laughed at or thrown out] has taken care of everything. The worst thing has never happened to me."

Although Hendrie started out a "traditional" woman, believing her career secondary to her husband's ("I came from Ohio. I got married very young. I wore a hat and gloves."), both have had their consciousness raised. And if one's children are any barometer of one's success as a role model, then Hendrie has done pretty well: one daughter is a mechanical engineer who does research in solar energy at MIT, and the other is a TV producer. "I feel good about myself, my husband feels good about me, my children feel good about me, and that makes a big difference."

Her solution, she admits, is not the one for everyone. She knows of another colleague of her husband's whose wife remained at Cornell University when he got a job at Brookhaven National Laboratory on Long Island. They see each other on weekends. "Every marriage is different. You have to work out what's best."

Every marriage changes, too, and what works at one time may not work at another. For example, Linda Keller Brown, thirty-nine, author of *The Woman Manager in the United States* (1981), was apart from her husband for six months in the 1970s, working on a Fulbright scholarship to help reorganize colleges in Japan after the student riots there. Later, from 1976 to 1978, she was a resident scholar with the United States Information Agency (USIA) in Washington, while her husband remained at his New Jersey law firm and lived at their New Jersey house. "It was kind of neat. We spent weekends in my apartment in Washington or in the house in New Jersey, every weekend unless there was a crisis." Also, she traveled sometimes, but it did not damage their marriage. "Work has been central to our lives," she says.

Toward the end of that Washington job, which ended in 1978, Brown experienced one of those epiphanies that often move people to action: she slipped down the back stairs of her house, had a vision of her own mortality, and decided to have a child. She had been married twelve years. She finished her work by staying on through her ninth month of pregnancy, then wrote her book and started a new job at Columbia University, as director of the Cross National Project on Women as Corporate Managers at the Center for the Social Sciences.

In 1981 she was called back to Washington for a political appointment, as deputy director of the Educational and Cultural Division of the USIA. Her husband—by "happy circumstance," as she calls it, since the Reagan administration did not orchestrate such things—was also given a presidential appointment. She is not sure that they could have commuted again. "I don't know if you could do that with a child. Getting us all out of here at once in the morning is a huge task." With good household help, she could perhaps have lived alone with her child, but she does not think her husband could cope with their daughter. "If a career is central to your life, having a child or children means you've got to shift priorities in ways some people can't do after age thirty-five."

Both of them have found it difficult to shift gears to relate to a very young child. "We muddle through, though I wouldn't say we're dynamite parents. If you're always career oriented, you don't see many children, and we often don't catch things as early as we would if we were around full time." For example, she says, her daughter had an eye problem that required surgery to prevent blindness, but she did not notice it until her sister pointed it out. Then it was promptly corrected. It was a very subtle thing, and even her housekeeper, who had raised ten children of her own, had not noticed.

Brown says that her own research and that of others whose work she has surveyed indicate that being married or having children makes no difference to a woman's power at work—as long as the woman is still working full time. But, she adds, companies must still make many structural changes to allow women longer maternity leaves or temporary part-time work, because there are also indications that many women with children have left the work force altogether. Moreover, she says, "In a hard job market, some people may end up choosing having a job over having children, and that would be unfortunate."

Her advice to women who do not want to risk falling behind in their careers would be to establish themselves first and to try to find the right moment for having children—as she did—so that they lose a minimal amount of time from their careers. Those who are willing to shift priorities—Barbara Robinson, for example—would disagree.

Women face difficult choices when they want to combine families and careers, and even those who have found a resolution for themselves still may not feel entirely satisfied. Having children means shifting one's life around so that one can enjoy them and still make a contribution in the professional arena. Being faced with a relocation decision—one's own or one's spouse's—means taking a hard look at each partner's priorities and at the balance in their relationship. Although one woman's decisions will not always work for another, a look at the considerations that other women have explored, the soul-searching they have gone through, and the practical advice that they have amassed can help each woman make her own clearheaded choices:

• Women must decide whether to pursue careers full-blast while their children are growing up, or whether to take some time to slow down. It is usually easier to make this decision after having worked for a while, but it is never easy. Some women find that they change their minds after a first child arrives, so trying to keep options open as long as possible is a good idea.

• Once having decided to devote more time to their families for a while, women should try first for the cooperation of their employers; failing that, they should try to find some other approach, such as consulting or working free-lance. They may encounter more difficulties at a larger firm than at a smaller one.

• Women planning to work at home should make sure they have adequate day care or a full-time babysitter, just as though they were going to an office. Many women find working at home more pleasant, and in this way can spend time with the children during breaks. But they do not get very much work done if they must also keep an eye on a young child.

• If relocation is imminent, remember that there are several options: one partner can commute, or the partners can trade visits to each other's cities. This option becomes less viable when children are involved, however, since neither partner is likely to want to spend weekdays away from them. Most important, do not neglect asking the relocating firm to help find work for the other spouse in the new location.

• Women trying to find work on their own because their husbands have relocated must be exceptionally brave, innovative, and flexible. Doing professional volunteer work in a new city is one way to establish new contacts and references there.

• Though juggling a career and family is difficult and has drawbacks, it can be done, one way or another, and many women who have done it look back with more satisfaction than regret.

10

Age and Authority

Whether a woman is young, old, or somewhere in between, her age is a significant factor in how she is perceived in the workplace and in how she perceives herself. Usually, both the response of others to her age and her own feelings about it differ from those of men of the same age—sometimes positively and sometimes negatively.

Maturity is a double-edged sword for women who aspire to managerial positions, concluded researchers Anne Harlan and Carol L. Weiss. They conducted a three-year study for the Wellesley College Center for Research on Women, where Harlan, a Wellesley professor, is a project director. Their 1981 report, *Moving Up: Women in Managerial Careers,* examined a hundred male and female managers in two large retail corporations. They found that supervisors tend to look favorably upon older women—more so than upon older men— and to give them high performance ratings. On the other hand, although middle management preferred these women, who tended to be less aggressive, senior management wanted young, dynamic women for the top executive positions. "Older women are seen by their supervisors as highly competent, but the women may get stuck because senior management relate youth to high promotability," the researchers wrote. The other side of this phenomenon is that the younger women are not getting a good chance at top positions either, because their supervisors are not promoting them to middle-management positions.

Sometimes, the myth and reality of the effects of age are widely divergent. In a 1980 study by Working Women, a national association

173

of female office workers, entitled *Vanished Dreams: Age Discrimination and the Older Woman Worker,* it was found that, although older workers are perceived as less stable than younger workers, in fact their turnover rate is one-sixth that of younger women, and their absentee rate is lower, too.

On the management level, age may have some subtle effects on relationships between women, says New York clinical social worker Deborah Karnbad, vice president of Help-Line for Working Women, a group that offers counseling and workshops to career women. "Older women who have worked long and hard to get where they are often see the bright, younger women with degrees as a threat," says Karnbad. "Sometimes they view them with resentment and anger. They feel, 'I worked longer and harder to get here than you.' This is most likely in fields that have been male dominated for many years, where it is hard for a woman to even get a foot in the door, and where men already hold most of the managerial jobs."

Ellen J. Wallach, a career development consultant based in Lexington, Massachusetts, says that age discrimination is closely linked to the kind of field a woman—or a man—is in. "With the high-tech companies," Wallach says, "even men over forty have problems, because everyone who works for them seems to be twenty-two." However, in fields where an individual must give advice—such as management consulting—youth can be a disadvantage, more so for women than for men. "Men have traditionally been the ones seen as experts, as the ones who have knowledge. Men do more talking, more interrupting, and they're listened to more at meetings."

Discrimination is one aspect of the effects of age, but women's own feelings about themselves as a result of age are an equally powerful force in how well a woman will do in her career, say three women interviewed at Grumman Aerospace. They conclude that what they call "psychological age," rather than chronological age, is the factor that distinguishes a woman who actively seeks a management career—and who usually is then perceived by management as capable—from one who takes a passive, ineffective approach to seeking power. That is, a woman of forty may see herself as a young, dynamic rising star, with plenty of years and opportunity left. Another woman of thirty-five may be bound by a more traditional and stereotypically feminine view of herself and feel confined to her job instead of seeking advancement.

Their conclusion that chronological age is not as important as it might seem is upheld by a study conducted by Rosalind C. Barnett and Grace K. Baruch, *On the Psychological Well-Being of Women in the Mid-Years,* published in 1982 by the Wellesley College Center for Research on Women. Barnett and Baruch interviewed women aged thirty-five to fifty-five, with a mean age of just over forty-three and a half. They found "no evidence of age-linked crises. We conclude that for a woman in the middle years, to know her age is to know only that. Age is not a marker and contributes little to our understanding of psychological well-being." Among the factors that do relate positively to a woman's sense of well-being, they found, are having multiple roles—wife, mother, and worker—and having high-prestige occupations.

In 1979 Grumman Aerospace held a management training seminar for women, the first of what was to become an extensive program of training courses for women. Most of those who attended were in their late thirties or in their forties, and they agreed that they faced problems quite different from those of the aggressive younger women—many of them holding M.B.A.s and other advanced degrees —who had entered the company more recently. Some of the older women felt the burden of having for years only taken orders instead of giving them, of never having dared to dream of the opportunities now being offered to women.

"As a woman, I had to hold back; I had to think twice about challenging a man," said Fran Mills, who was forty-three when the seminar was held, and who at that time had worked her way up from a clerical position to an audio-visual specialist. "And," she added, "there was no other woman to go to for support."

"There is a difference in the attitudes of younger women," said Joelyn Iannone, then forty-one, after that seminar. "They're not tied to the company [by years of service], not afraid to speak their minds, to present ideas." Although she did not count herself among the "younger" women, her attitudes and experiences in the aerospace company appeared to be about a generation apart from those of Mills, although their ages vary by only two years.

Fran Mills can remember having to train a man to be her boss. She was a clerk-typist at the time and had developed a new job. "I was doing the job very well, and then they brought a man in. I hadn't asked for the job, but I felt confident they would approach me. Once they didn't, I made a comment, but it was too late."

Now she is much more sophisticated about how to go about getting a management job. In fact, for the past two years, she has worked as a management development instructor, teaching other women how to get ahead. She thinks, however, that even if she had been better educated in the 1960s, when the boss-training incident happened, she still would not have gotten the job. She feels that her company was not ready then to accept a woman in a leadership position. "The attitudes have changed. The environment has changed. That's made the difference. Even if I had been educated then, I still don't think I would have approached them. They would have had reasons why I couldn't do it."

There have also been changes in the attitude of Fran Mills toward her job in the intervening years. In some ways, she has become psychologically younger. When she first came to Grumman in 1957 as a clerk, a twenty-one-year-old with a high school diploma, "My ambition was to have five children—really. I wanted to be home with five kids." She came from a large family herself. She never knew her father, but her mother had worked hard as a domestic worker to be able to raise her children.

Mills's dream of staying home ended with her divorce, after having one daughter. She had to work, but she did not want a career, with its added responsibility. "I had to devote myself to being a one-parent family. I felt I couldn't do both things at once, so I took my role as a mother very seriously. Now that my daughter is grown [she is twenty-seven], I'm doing things for me. I changed my thinking when she was in high school, when she was a little more independent. I started going to school. It took me ten years to get my bachelor's degree." Mills is now halfway through her studies for an M.B.A.

Even before Mills decided to pursue a career, however, she had sought administrative jobs. In one case, she applied for a position as an administrator while working as an executive secretary in that department. "I felt I knew the job, but the man insisted that I wouldn't know the company, that I couldn't learn. So I felt I couldn't learn, even though as an executive secretary, you can learn an awful lot about management. I really felt I wasn't promoted because I was a woman." She did not feel the discrimination had anything to do with her being black. "At that time, I don't think that women in general were viewed as people who were taken seriously. I'm not talking about Grumman, but the whole industry. And then, in the sixties, it was really minorities, and that meant minority men. So it wasn't until the seventies that they started considering women. And then by the seventies, I was more mature. So it could have passed me by, but it didn't."

Mills still thinks that she would not mix young motherhood with a high-powered career if she were starting out now, during an era when many younger women are attempting to blend the two. For her, the shift in attitude is related to the shift in her circumstances as a mother. She says, however, that other women her own age have gotten stuck in secretarial jobs because they have been unable to make the leap to new thinking, while she feels she has a whole new life ahead of her. That is one reason she thinks chronological age does not matter as much as psychological age—her attitude toward her own potential.

"I'm still young, and I feel now that I still have another whole career to go, that I can do anything. I feel very positive." She worked her way up in stages: executive secretary, then administrative assistant, then audio-visual specialist, before her present job teaching management courses. Mills's age, or more particularly her background as linked to her age, does put some limitations on her career. She will never move into the top management of the company, because she does not have the requisite technical degrees that would be required in a company such as Grumman. A forty-seven-year-old female engineer with management experience would probably find her age an advantage for a top position. However, very few women in America fit that description.

In her current job, Mills sees many younger women with old, or at least old-fashioned, attitudes. "It depends on where a woman is at in her position and her training. I had one class with twenty-four men and one woman, and the woman said, 'I'm just a secretary, and I don't know why I'm here, but I'll try and learn things.' And she said it in a meek, timid voice. So during the break, I went over to her and I said, 'Please do me a favor and never, ever say you're just a secretary. Say loud and clear, I am a secretary.' It's a very important position in the company. She may have more power than twenty of the twenty-four men in that room. They may have the title, but she has the power. I said, 'Don't apologize for learning.' She said she realized herself how she sounded after she said it. Women often feel, I don't know why I'm here."

Daniel Knowles, Grumman's vice president for personnel and administration, says that age discrimination, for men and women, often starts at around age forty-five. "The problem is old wives' tales, that there's no sense training people over fifty, that they're not adaptable, that you can't teach an old dog new tricks, or that older people are sick more often. That's not true." It usually is not possible to tell if a woman has been discriminated against because of her age or her sex, he says. But he has noticed that "the expectations of younger women in general are greater than those of older women. . . . I guess overall the younger women are more interested in careers and see themselves as working for a longer period of time." The women in their twenties do not yet have a sophisticated awareness of the company's subculture, but the ones in their thirties and forties, he says, are as sophisticated as any of the men.

Those in their fifties, however, often come from a different cultural background. He cites the case of one woman in his employ, now in her mid fifties, whom he promoted to head a department about ten years ago. "She wanted the job of manager, but she didn't want to supervise people. I'm sure the reason was cultural. She didn't perceive herself as bossing men around. She hadn't thought it out. She wanted the title and the money. But there was another woman in the department she was afraid of; she didn't have the confidence that she could stand a confrontation with her. Now she's the best manager I've ever had in that job, in terms of her energy level and innovativeness." She got over her fear after attending a management training program and with the help of supportive bosses, including Knowles, who told her she had to be accountable for such matters as making performance appraisals, giving merit raises, and explaining to people why they did or did not get merit raises. Knowles stuck with her, he says, because "she was the most qualified person. She had the knowledge and the ability. She had the empathy, the best ability to deal with people, but not the confidence. She's now one of the top twenty-five women in the company."

Miriam Reid, the company's assistant manager of media relations, says that about 10 percent of all the managerial and professional positions at Grumman Aerospace are held by women, but that a large concentration of those are in the personnel and public relations departments, the "velvet ghettos" where women are often concentrated in any industry. Of the entire work force of 18,000 at Grumman Aerospace on Long Island, 16 percent are women. About 46 percent of all female employees hold secretarial and clerical positions. About half of the women in management, she says, are under the age of forty-five, especially in the technical areas of the company. "Female engineers over fifty are hard to come by." Most high-tech companies have similar breakdowns, she says. "There are more women in managerial positions in banking, but then, they also get less pay there in general."

In addition to the department head described above, Knowles had praise for Joelyn Iannone, forty-five, whom he sees as a striking contrast, even though the difference between their ages is only about ten years. Iannone came into the company in 1974, after a career as a school administrator. She had a bachelor's and two master's degrees, in contrast to the other department head, who had no college degree at all. "She trained for a year to familiarize herself with the industry, and then she became manager of personnel development. That was a short period of time. She handles promotions, upgradings, job postings, and counseling with no problem. After she was there about four years, she took on added responsibilities in employee training. I would rank her as the outstanding woman in the company. She is one of the top paid. She's a real honest-to goodness professional, and she's been in supervision from an early age. . . . She's an outstanding role model. She came out of a different era. She's better educated."

Knowles mentions that the first woman he described in this interview "is a housewife first, though she doesn't have children. She picks up her husband at the train station every night. Her orientation is different. Joelyn is very much a career woman." His praise for Iannone extends to her "good attitude about women's liberation. She doesn't see the necessity for antagonism, for tension between men and women." This comment is particularly interesting, since Iannone, who in fact does avoid antagonism, is extremely aware of the tension that women suffer because they must deal with sex discrimination that is practiced in very subtle ways, of which men are usually unaware. She was the one who had the experience, described in chapter 1, of being in a meeting at which male architects who were contracted to design a new building for her department directed questions to her male assistant rather than to her. She struggled for a low-key, nonthreatening way to insert herself into the conversation without embarrassing her co-worker or offending the architects. The solution she found was effective and worthy of her professional "career-woman" image. She spoke up quietly with her ideas, then stayed after the meeting to discuss a few points with the architects, mainly to make sure they understood her position in the firm.

The way she handles such situations now has less to do with her age, she says, than with "the responsibility you have on the job. The more responsibility you have, the less fearful you are." Soon after she first arrived at Grumman, she would find herself the only woman in a meeting and would not say a word. Her boss later pointed this out to her. "I said, 'Wait a minute. Some of the men didn't say anything, but you only noticed me because I was the only O among all those X's.' He didn't have an answer, but he realized what I said was true. The reason I hadn't spoken was for that reason: everyone would have looked at me. You were really on display. I think now it's changed. Now I can be in a meeting with all men and feel comfortable, because I have a track record. I have credibility. If you make a mistake, you have a background, and they won't judge you on that one issue. So it depends on where you are in your career, and what you've been doing, and how comfortable you are."

Iannone makes an encouraging point here, that the positive results of age—experience, credibility, a track record—can be among a female manager's most valuable assets.

Iannone had the advantage of growing up in an environment in which women were dominant. "I never realized that women didn't have power. I was educated by the Sisters of Saint Joseph, who are dynamic ladies. They never told us there was a world out there that doesn't respect women. I went to a college [Saint Joseph's, then all female] where all the women professors had Ph.D.s from places like Yale and Columbia. They were on boards; they went to Washington. They told us, 'There's a world out there, go out and conquer it.' There was never a question in my mind that women could not effect change. I must say, it was a shock when I came here."

So Iannone—like many younger women today—sought a career from the very beginning, though at first she thought it would be in teaching. She taught in a religious high school run by nuns and had become an assistant principal when she decided it was time to leave the field. "One of the things I learned about myself over the years is that I'm competitive. That's frowned upon in education. You're not allowed to compete with your fellow teacher. And if you're competitive, you're almost looked down upon. I found it harder and harder to work in that environment." The father of some of her pupils told her that Grumman was looking for women and arranged an interview. That is when she got her first view of the real world.

"Even during the interview, I picked up the signals," she says, signals she attributes to the general attitude of any technical company toward women in 1974. "They didn't say it, but the message was, 'How will you handle yourself in a predominantly male environment that has never experienced the educated woman, the woman who has had a leadership position?' What they were trying to get was my philosophy, what role I would have, what I was looking for. I would love to say that I had thought it through, but my reaction was intuitive, and I'm thankful for that. I think that if I had come on strong, if I had walked through that door with an M.B.A. and said, 'I WANT TO BE A WOMAN MANAGER, AND I'M LOOKING FOR MANAGEMENT TRAINING, AND I SEE MYSELF AS HEADING A DEPARTMENT IN ONE YEAR,' I would never be here today. For some strange reason, I knew enough to shut my mouth. I said I was looking for a professional job in which the experience and talents I have would be used. I never said I wanted to be a manager, and thank God for that."

Young women today do not have to be quite so circumspect, she says, but she would still advise that they "watch where they're being interviewed. They should look at the company, at how many women are in the company and how many have been promoted, and what has happened to women. Some companies are way behind us. It does pay for a woman to research a company [by talking to contacts in the firm or in the same field, and by reading professional journals, the company's annual report, and perhaps its in-house newsletter]. I only researched what they make. I did research, but not like that." Iannone thinks it is also important to find out, once there, what the "subculture" of a company is: what are the prevailing rules on what to wear, which country club to belong to, how much socializing with co-workers is expected, how long you should stay at night to demonstrate your ambition, how much competitiveness you are allowed to show. Women, particularly older ones, she says, often do not understand that, when they attend company social affairs, they are working. Iannone, who is single, attends by herself those that she thinks are important. She does not bother with an escort because she knows she is not at a social occasion.

Iannone was hesitant about attending an all-woman management seminar when they were first started by Grumman four years ago. Now she is in charge of the program. "I felt, this is the very thing you don't want, to segregate the women and the men; if you want women to function, you should throw them into an environment where they have to compete with men. They dragged me kicking and screaming into that class. The class itself did not give me any information I was not aware of. But I was tremendously grateful to find out where women were at. And I found that women needed it. It was the first time they could articulate many things, such as the stress they felt on the job, or things they didn't understand but were afraid to ask. They felt secure in that environment, and they found that other women were having the same problems. . . . And I became aware that maybe I was a little blind about the problems that other women were having, and I had to readjust." Having been fortunate in entering the company at a time when they were promoting women, and in having bosses who encouraged her, Iannone realizes that this has not been true for women in all parts of the company. "There are people in other departments who have not had that. Not that people were out to get them, but they were certainly not making it easier for them. And that opened up my eyes."

When Iannone entered the company, she encountered her biggest problems not with men but with "women who had been here a long time. They feared the 'new wave,' who seemed to be moving up faster and getting spotlighted more quickly. I remember giving a talk and calling it, 'I Have Met the Enemy, and She Is Us.' That's definitely what I was feeling." Some of those problems have been smoothed out now, partly because of the three leadership training programs for women that now exist in the company, and that she oversees. From her vantage point midway between the "older" female worker and the young woman fresh out of college, Iannone can look both ways now and provide concrete help and a role model for both age groups.

One slightly younger woman who had worked for Iannone and is an admirer is Joyce Sparling, forty. Sparling is now assistant to the benefits manager for Grumman Aerospace, a subsidiary of Grumman Corporation. She joined the company five years ago as a management instructor, the position Mills now holds. Like Iannone, she entered from teaching. "I had been a teacher for several years, and it came to the point where I knew I had to leave. . . . I had thought of going into school administration, but I decided to leave."

Unlike Iannone, she did not always want a career. "When I started teaching, I wanted the typical Cinderella story, that I would meet someone and get married. I wasn't thinking in terms of a total career then." She is single now.

When she arrived at Grumman, she was more concerned about making the transition to industry than about joining management. Her first job, though, included coordinating the management development courses. She took some courses in management theory at a nearby college to help train herself. She said that many people helped to train her in those early days, both formally and informally, and that she had a tremendous desire to educate herself in her new field. She does not classify herself among the younger women who come straight into industry from college, well armed with all the credentials. If she were younger, her career outlook now would probably be brighter. "I think the younger women do see things differently. Many of those of us who are older are pathfinders. We've made the way for them, so this world will be a little bit easier for them, though it's not perfect, because industry is still a man's world. They're still going to have their problems, but the road will be smoother. They'll be able to set their goals a little more clearly than we did. And many of them are looking for a career, while we kind of fell into one."

It does not bother her that some young women do not seem to realize the problems that older women have gone through. "Youth doesn't sense the struggle. It's true for anyone who is young, not just women. They only sense the now. They'll go through their own history, get hurt and realize the struggle. They're fun to work with. I get annoyed with them sometimes, but then I remember how I was, how I was going to change the world and change the system. So they kind of give you a spark, too. I don't get angry."

About women older than herself, she cannot make generalizations, she says. "Some have helped me along and shared their experiences. Others who have struggled up the line haven't been helpful."

Even if she had gotten married, Sparling believes she would have worked, "given my energy level. But I don't know if I would have looked to a career." Her mother worked as a clerk from the time she was seven, and her father, a carpenter in his spare time, often took her and her younger sister along when he did maintenance jobs for others. "We went with him on his truck. I was handing out screwdrivers, mixing paint, and counting out money from the time I can remember. It was his joy to take us with him." That experience had a profound influence on how she felt about herself as a competent, able person. "You were expected to get out on your own and compete. He never thought of us as people who would be taken care of."

Part of what all three women have tried to get across in the courses that all have been involved with is that women must learn how to plan a career and move around in a company, and that they must train themselves, with outside courses and degrees, if necessary, for the jobs they want. They must also learn how to handle themselves in business situations, including meetings and travel, and learn how to dress appropriately. The three training programs open to women at Grumman include one on professional awareness, in which they are taught how to go about building a career, if they want one, and of the trade-offs in their personal lives they may have to make if they are serious about a career. The second one, a year long, gives them exposure twice a week to an area of the company other than the one in which they currently work, although they are not guaranteed a job at the end of the program. The third is on leadership strategy, for women who are already on the management track.

"There should be an equivalent training for men," says Iannone. "A lot of men get lost in the subculture, but there are so many men here that people don't notice." The women's training programs started, she says, only because women lobbied for them.

All three of these women, interviewed in Iannone's nicely appointed corner office, were wearing conservative business suits with feminine touches, such as a ruffled blouse or a piece of jewelry. Each —perhaps because they were the product of the same training courses—exuded an air of calm self-confidence and spoke assertively and, occasionally, with animated humor. Each in her own way has transcended the strictures of her chronological age to emerge at a psychological age that seems to combine the enthusiasm of youth with the considered wisdom of maturity.

Now that women are entering management in greater numbers, different problems are emerging, said Grumman Data Systems Corporation president John O'Brien, who at the time we spoke was executive vice president at Grumman Aerospace and in charge of its original training programs for women. At Grumman, he said, some women had asked for these programs. "They felt that we don't promote enough women. But when we offered some women jobs, they turned them down." In addition, many women do not have the technical backgrounds that are required for managerial positions in most areas of the company. "The younger woman, twenty to thirty, probably played with computers or used them in school. The older woman might feel, My career will be over before I'll need to use one."

But now that women are in management, he said, "All the same things that men have been complaining about for years, and still are, are showing up among the women." These complaints include feelings that someone else was promoted because she looks better or is a little older or a little younger or knows how to "bat the bull with the customers better." Men, he said, often complain of age discrimination. "They often say, 'You didn't promote me because he's five years younger.'" So, if it can be any consolation to women, age is a sensitive subject for the other sex, too.

A woman's age has an impact on how she is treated at work. It also is a factor in how she perceives herself. Older women, because their backgrounds are likely to be traditional, sometimes lack the confidence that younger women have. On the other hand, a younger woman's self-confidence may work against her if her male superiors perceive her as a threat. The women at Grumman have found that age is more than a chronological condition and that behavior is just as important. If one is mature in one's judgment but youthful in one's energy and enthusiasm, chronological age may not matter much. The lessons that these women and the experts who have studied the impact of age on working women have drawn can help to guide women, young or old, who are concerned about the ways that age will affect the course of their careers:

• Young women should try not to appear too cocky. It is fine to be assertive and enthusiastic, but youth should remember that there are still barriers to women and that older women have smoothed the way for them.

• Women are never too old to get the training necessary to move ahead and to learn some management skills. It is important to take courses that will prepare them directly for the jobs they want, instead of just those courses they enjoy.

• It is crucial to learn how to dress and behave appropriately. Older women, particularly, who may decide late in their careers that they want to move ahead, must pay special attention to developing a new and polished image.

• Having a track record is an important asset and one of the benefits of greater age and experience. Some of the pressures of being a lone woman among men—feeling on display, feeling that it is dangerous to make a mistake—are eased considerably once a woman has demonstrated that she can make good decisions and bad decisions, just like men.

• Women, especially older ones, often do not understand that, when they are attending company social affairs, they are still at work. They do not need an escort, and they should relate to their colleagues in the same way as they would during office hours.

• Women in their forties and fifties have many working years ahead of them, and it pays to start planning a career, even at that point, in their own field or in another.

• Whether young or old, women should strive for a calm, mature approach in dealing with unconscious sex discrimination from more traditional men. That is one area where the wisdom of age and experience will serve a woman better than the impetuosity of youth.

11

Styles of Authority

Successful women do not have to copy men slavishly in their management styles. They do need to develop a range of techniques, but they can also adapt them to their own very "womanly" styles. They do not have to abandon the warmth, compassion, and different sense of values and time that women learn in order to be effective women in charge. They can benefit both sexes if they bring a more human measure to the workplace. The important criteria are whether they feel comfortable and self-assured and are able to function effectively. Some women find it easier to fit into traditional models of authority, whereas others find that they must adjust the mold slightly to fit their different social conditioning. As long as they do their job, women have found, both ways can work.

In traditional business-school terminology, *management style* has a specific meaning. It refers to the way a manager behaves toward subordinates, and, sometimes, peers and supervisors. There are various models, or theories, which divide management styles into three or four different groups.

One theory divides managers into three types: the authoritarian, or task-oriented manager; the democratic, or relations-oriented manager; and the manager who has combined a high concern for people with a high concern for production into a "team" approach. Often a fourth, laissez-faire style is included. This manager lets workers do what they want, more or less, an approach that can be appropriate if the workers are highly skilled and motivated and would resent active management. Many books also conclude that the best manager is

187

one who can switch styles like an actor with a repertoire of performing styles to fit the particular script. In discussing these styles, most management books do not differentiate between men and women.

One would think that, given most women's family and "people" background, female managers would gravitate toward the democratic style. At best, a woman might combine that style with the production-oriented one and emerge with the highly prized "team" approach. Sadly, this is not always the case. Research has shown that women are *often very narrow* in their view of what their position of authority is and end up with an authoritarian style. Women often concentrate on getting perfect work from their subordinates, even doing it or correcting it themselves. They are afraid to allow a measure of freedom or independence to those working under them; they are afraid to share with them. Although the authoritarian management style is appropriate in some situations, such as supervising unskilled workers or managing a person who responds well to close supervision, it is not a good style when supervising other managers or highly skilled workers. Certainly, it should not be the only style that a manager can use.

Yale University sociology and management consultant Rosabeth Moss Kanter argues in her 1977 book, *Men and Women of the Corporation,* that women often take such a rigid view of their positions of power because they are, in fact, powerless. The way women behave is the way all powerless people, male or female, tend to behave, she says. Conditioned for secondary roles, women try to produce measurable results in production, which they hope will be recognized by higher-ups and will lead to promotion. But becoming indispensable in one job is not the way to be promoted. Those considered promotable, Kanter says, are those who delegate authority, share information, train a replacement, and in general prepare their office for change so that, when they are promoted, their departure will cause little disruption. Powerless people typically protect their territory, establish themselves as indispensable, and become rigid and authoritarian. Women are trapped into powerlessness in two ways: first, they are usually perceived as powerless by both men and other women, and therefore stay that way; second, they gravitate toward certain types of jobs, such as in personnel, research, and public relations ("good-with-people" positions) that are not powerful in most organizations. Kanter also mentions that women tend to work in highly structured professions—such as teaching, nursing, and government bureaucracies—and that, when women are singled out for leadership positions, they are often watched closely, which makes them more cautious and rigid.

Once women actually get real power, Kanter says, they behave just as capably as men, and their styles of leadership cover the same range, with no sex differentiation.

I would like to expand on Kanter's conclusions in two areas. First, among those women with real power who have mastered the same range of management styles as men, many lean toward the team approach, also known as the collaborative approach. "Because of their life experience, women tend a bit more toward the collaborative style than do men," says Julie O'Mara, a consultant in human resources development and president of the American Society for Training and Development. Relying more on a team is the management style of the future, O'Mara believes. "No one knows all you need to know any more. A manager is someone who by definition makes things happen through people, and women in general have better ways of dealing with people."

Second, even when a woman's behavior is the same as a man's, her actions are not always perceived the same way by those who work with her. Thus, a woman who considers herself to be highly democratic may be seen as authoritarian by a worker who does not like to take any orders from a woman. This means that a woman must have an acute awareness of how each action or gesture is perceived by those around her as she builds her management style. She must also be aware of how feminine conditioning inhibits or aids her. And she must decide how many of her feminine-conditioned responses she wishes to—or is able to—discard.

Some characteristics definitely have to go: passivity and timidity, for example. A woman who assumes a position of power should ask herself how she will handle certain situations, such as asking for a raise, correcting an employee, or making a presentation. What will her manner be, and how can she change it if she is not pleased with it?

"A lot of women have what I call a 'little-girl style,'" says Sharon Bermon, a career counselor with a private practice in Manhattan. She believes firmly that women can discard many of the behavior patterns that hold them back in the workplace. "They say, 'Will you

please do this, if you don't mind?' in a high and girlish voice."
Through assertion training exercises, which Bermon has taught to
thousands of women, women can be taught to "stand up for their
own rights without treading on the rights of others"; that is, to be
assertive without being aggressive. Women, she says, often apologize
as they ask subordinates or superiors to do something for them, such
as type a letter or give them a raise. Instead, they should state what
they want, simply and concisely. In another variation, women will
often be too timid, for instance, to ask for a raise, she says. Instead,
they will complain about not getting one and allow their anger to
build up until they are aggressive rather than assertive when they do
finally ask.

Sharon Bermon says that one reason she has lost her aggressive
edge when she asserts herself is that she has rid herself of some of
her anger. As Rosabeth Moss Kanter might have predicted, this transformation came with power and success. "Ten years ago, I was rest-
less and unhappy. Like other women at the time, I was desperate to
be somebody," says Bermon. "It liberated me when I admitted I
wanted power and when I got enough to stop being hungry. I think
it's not true that people always want more power. Now the pressure
is in my own control." Having more control over herself, she can be
much more aware of her styles of authority.

Sharon Bermon is an effective career trainer for women partly
because she has struggled herself with many of the same problems
that women in her workshops face. At home, she has worked hard to
come to an understanding with her husband of twenty-three years
about sharing the household work. At work, she has developed her
managerial skills by applying her own formulas. The biggest problem
for most women, she says, is in the area of personnel management:
hiring, firing, and telling someone else how to do something, or correcting that person if he or she does it wrong. Although women may
through their upbringing be more people-oriented, their high level of
caring and compassion for others often gets in the way of effective
production-oriented management.

Only in the past year or so has Bermon managed to master that
problem herself. She took a certain pride, on the day I interviewed
her, in being able to turn to a temporary clerical worker and correct
the way the woman was placing information on an index card. "I felt
strange, telling this well-educated woman to print and to put the first

name first on the top line, not on the second line of the card," says Bermon. But she did it gently and well, explaining why she needed uniform files, and explaining it as soon as she noticed that the woman was not following the original directions precisely enough. She did not allow her frustration to build up.

Bermon's approach is not really different from the team approach that management theorists advocate. With an eye toward good production, she used a human approach by explaining to the woman the reasons for precise files. But there was one added note that a male manager might not have struck with a temporary worker. Bermon had chatted earlier with the woman, had found out that she was college educated and was returning to work after several years at home. Having set up that rapport, that personal interest, and having the knowledge that the woman was an intelligent and educated person, she was able to temper the way she presented the correction. The woman immediately began filling in the cards correctly, and their relationship ran smoothly and efficiently for the rest of the day.

Although many women, like Sharon Bermon, work hard to unburden themselves of that feminine duo, passivity and timidity, others feel that they can achieve effective styles of authority by keeping the best of the female strengths. An example of this follows, with a woman who is not at all ashamed of her feminine qualities and feels it is more important to be true to herself than to someone else's image of what a woman in charge should be. After hers comes a profile of another woman who, while keeping her individuality intact, has developed a sterner managerial style.

Sally Ann Slacke strikes one immediately as a woman of warmth. On the telephone, counseling her daughter on how best to get to work while her car is in the shop—whom to call and whom to call next if that person does not work out, and if those should fail, not to hesitate to call back her mother, who would find a way to get her there—her conversation exudes calm and maturity.

For this interview, Slacke wears a black suit accented by gold jewelry. Her curly hair is loose and modern but too neat for an ultrafashionable frizz. Her movements are bold and self-assured. This is, after all, a woman who owns her own business in a field traditionally associated with men. Sally Ann Slacke is president of the Slacke

Test Boring Company of Smithtown, New York. She is also the only woman on the executive board of the Long Island Association, the most powerful business group in a suburban area of 2.7 million inhabitants. Yet she brings us coffee herself, from across the hall in the small office building she shares with a dozen other firms.

Madeleine Gardner, a business professor who knew Slacke, once told me that she considered her a "transitional" woman, similar to the twenty-five women in Margaret Hennig's 1970 study who had stayed with the same firms for their entire careers and moved up gradually and somewhat deferentially. These women, as described in Hennig and Anne Jardim's 1977 book, *The Managerial Woman,* eventually became top achievers but initially aspired only to middle-management positions. Low-keyed about their ambitions, they were closely tied to a male boss who gave them their start, always as a secretary or administrative assistant. For their time, they played their cards right, but they are different from women starting in business today.

"The new breed of women is going to do it the way men do it. They will credentialize and move around in a company. We need that in management," said Gardner, who headed a program to train women for management at Adelphi University until her death in 1983. "The new breed of woman is not going to stand for some of the things Sally accepts," such as what Gardner saw as the "implied paternal attitude" of some of the men Slacke works with.

But Slacke need not be perceived as a woman willing to compromise. As she says, "I feel comfortable being a woman. I don't have a chip on my shoulder.... I'm not a touchy person." Slacke, at forty-five, has made her peace with the man's world she travels in, and does not let small condescensions bother her. But she has also brought to that world a sense of caring and a personal touch often found wanting in the male business arena. She has developed what may be described as a "feminine" style of authority, and it works for her. Her management style is definitely people-oriented, with a heavy reliance on the team approach, but carried off with a warmth and heartiness that few men would attempt. "I am always me, and that's very important. I think of myself as me, not as a woman in business."

Sally Ann and her husband, Felix, started their test-boring business more than twenty years ago, when both were in their mid twenties. Sally Ann's family, although traditional Italians, did not disapprove of her role, which they saw as "helping her husband." She had the inside job of bookkeeping, answering the telephone, and otherwise holding down the office. Felix worked with the crews who drilled into the earth before construction was to begin at sites all over the New York metropolitan area. They hauled out samples at various levels, letting the engineers and architects know what kind of structure each plot could support. Felix made the business contacts with the contractors, engineers, and architects who hire test borers. Felix decided whom to hire and whom to fire. Felix made decisions on when to buy new equipment or refurbish the old. In 1975, Felix Slacke died suddenly of a heart attack. Sally Ann took over.

"My children were worried that I wouldn't make it," she says, on the personal and business level. Felix and Sally Ann had been very close. In fact, she says, it came as a shock to her to find out after Felix's death that other people's marriages were not just as happy. "I felt I had been living under a rock. It was the biggest adjustment I had to make. When Felix died, there was never any question that I would keep the business. My husband was always positive. He said I could run it. He said I was intelligent enough. I didn't really believe it. I thought, Okay, he loves me. I would always have him to fall back on."

But then she no longer did have him, and had to rely instead on herself. "I went through a lot of misgivings. I felt that when decisions had to be made, I just wouldn't be as good. I had never gotten into bids. That was the biggest job." But she soon learned how to estimate and prepare bids—and more. She had taken over the business in the middle of a recession, when new construction was nearly coming to a standstill and all the related trades were scrambling for work. "I had to hunt, do everything to get a job," she says. "I would go see general contractors, architects, everyone. I told them I really wanted the job. It became almost an obsession. Fighting became a method. It became a salvation for me."

Slacke still handles her business in a very personal way, often delivering samples and analyses herself rather than by mail or messenger. She also answers the phone herself when her secretary is away from the desk or busy with another task. All the workers have stayed, and the foreman has taken on extra on-site technical duties. As she shows off her bottled samples and explains a chart, one can see why workers and clients remained loyal: here is a woman who loves her work, understands it thoroughly, and can make test boring sound interesting even to a lay person.

People told her, after her difficult period of adjustment as head of the business, that she did not appear to be as nervous as she felt. "I have a lot of energy and enthusiasm, and I guess that was the part that came through." She was also influenced by a position she had held ten years ago as Smithtown's coordinator for senior citizens. "I saw that those who were spunky had been spunky all their lives. Those who were down had been down all their lives. . . . I saw people who still had pride, and I felt, 'You can do anything you please.' It's the desire that counts. I'm younger at forty-five than I was at twenty. At twenty, I worried about everything."

Slacke had all the prerequisites that researchers, such as Hennig and Jardim, and Elizabeth Douvan and Joseph Adelson in their 1966 book, *The Adolescent Experience,* have found that successful managerial women usually have. She was the oldest child and was treated —particularly by her father—more as a boy would have been. These characteristics, the researchers found, lead to a higher level of self-confidence in girls, as well as other behaviorial patterns, such as risk taking, usually reserved for boys. Such characteristics prepare women better for competition in the marketplace.

Patrick Magdalen, Slacke's father, was also in the test-boring business, as were his brothers. They did not have their own business but worked for others. "I went out on jobs when I was young," says Slacke. "I had a good relationship with my father. He treated me maturely. I would type reports for him."

Although Slacke comes from a background where all the women in the family stayed at home, she has turned out differently. "When women and men get together, I stay with the men. I find business talk very stimulating." Her identification with her father, her preference for male company, and her choice of a male-oriented career similar to that of her father (in her case, her choice of husband preordained the career choice) are characteristics that Hennig and Jardim and other researchers have found to be the common marks of successful women in charge. She agrees that early training and treatment were important. So was the support of her husband, she adds. "Nearly all the successful women I know have supportive husbands or are single. Of course, some of them are divorced because their husbands felt threatened by their success."

When Slacke was appointed a delegate to a White House conference on small business, she met many young New York City women, whom she found to be different from some of the noncity women she usually sees. She had an argument with a city woman over how to react when a man referred to them as ladies. The other woman became angry. "I said, 'I'm a lady.' She said, 'People like you are stopping the women's movement.' I said, 'People like you are killing the women's movement.'"

She meets young female engineers, she says, who "tell men what to do—but the men would be equally offended if a young male engineer told them what to do, and he would be just as ostracized. You have to be a person first."

People often ask Slacke if her position on the Long Island Association's executive board is not just a token spot. She does not see it that way. "They seek out my opinion, and I'm given many responsibilities because I do a job." The men have been very careful and respectful in their treatment of her, she says, and it was she who started the custom of kissing them when she arrived at a meeting, instead of shaking hands. It is not a habit that the young women of New York City she meets would ever tolerate—but it is part of the naturalness and sense of her own identity that Slacke and women like her who choose not to or cannot break out of their traditional womanly roles have turned into a strength. It is an effective style, because it has brought her success and power, as well as personal happiness; she has not had to create an artificial style that would be foreign to her sense of self.

Perhaps the greatest testimonial to Sally Ann Slacke as a woman of authority—or as a "transitional" leader into a new world of women in charge—is the career orientation of her three daughters. The oldest, twenty-two, works in a hospital but plans to become a police officer soon. Her middle daughter, twenty-one, is a private secretary, and her youngest, nineteen, left data processing to take a job on one of her mother's rigs. "She's in the Bronx right now, working as a driller's helper. I told her, 'That's really hard work.' But she said, 'That's how you learned the business!' She rides horses. She's a daredevil. She's perfect for this."

Slacke is cheered by many of the younger women she meets in business. The "chip on the shoulder" belongs to their slightly older sisters, she thinks. The women in their twenties are more easygoing, more likely to take criticism well and to understand that young men are just as threatening to their older male bosses as young women are.

"Many women say we have to reeducate men, that we have to make an impact," says Slacke, whose positions may not always be in sync with those of her female colleagues in management, but whose integrity is unquestionable. "I think there will be evolution, not a revolution. It won't come overnight, no matter how many conferences and panels we have on the subject. I think it will take another generation, and then it will come as easily as breathing."

It probably will not come that easily, that quickly. Slacke had her way smoothed, after all, by a doting father, a supportive husband, and a set of circumstances that do not fall every woman's way, and that has no doubt rosied her vision. The labyrinthine politics of a large corporation, institution, or other bureaucracy usually forces women (and men) into a fighting stance.

But when the day comes when women are in authority with all the naturalness of breathing, maybe a few—and a few men as well—will bring the coffee to their guests instead of making a secretary do it, take time out from work to talk to their children, and communicate with warmth as well as efficiency.

Nearly everyone who meets Norma Rollins assumes she is a lawyer. She is not, even though she supervises some lawyers and makes important decisions requiring legal knowledge.

Rollins is executive director of Youth Advocates of Long Island, a New York Civil Liberties Union project that protects the rights of students. In that capacity she has testified before legislative hearings, lectured before groups of teachers, administrators, and school counselors, and confronted school superintendents when her agency entered a case. She directs a staff of fourteen, including three attorneys, and makes the final decisions about which cases her agency will and will not accept and which ones it will take to court. During her scant two years in the job, the agency has grown from a mere three people in one office to fourteen people in two offices, expansion that has been largely the result of her leadership.

She also has a lawyer's air of calm and self-confidence, projected by her wry smile and defiantly off-beat clothing. Here, it seems, is a woman who has trained long and hard to become a successful professional leader, who has studied the ways of power and mastered them, tailoring them to her own particular style. She does not bow to the present-day convention of tweed suit and silk blouse that has become the professional woman's uniform.

All of this is the more extraordinary because Rollins, at thirty-four, is neither a lawyer nor a person who has arrived at her position through ordinary means. While Sally Ann Slacke represents a woman who has worked steadily in a man's world and steadfastly preserved her own set of feminine values, Norma Rollins represents a woman who has made sharp breaks with her past but has arrived at a style of authority that management books would attribute to a tough, production-oriented boss.

Rollins's management style makes quite a striking contrast to Slacke's ruffle-trimmed team approach; it is marked mainly by a quirky individuality, neither masculine nor feminine, that is part of her personal style. She chats easily with her staff about such casual subjects as ending a smoking habit, and she often sits at a free desk among them rather than in her own office. But instead of cooperative planning with fellow workers, Rollins is extremely "directive," as she terms it herself. She makes office rules. She makes all final decisions. There are discussions and interaction with her staff, but no illusion that she runs a "democracy." Rollins's settlement on a harder-line, production-oriented management style stems from two unusual sources: a purple, red, and yellow camping van, and a disillusionment with what she now calls the "manipulation" of therapy, in which the counselor makes it appear that the client came by himself to the conclusion that the counselor had in mind for him all along. Rollins would rather give orders.

Rollins's story is unique, but it offers an important lesson about gaining a sense of authority: one must be willing to take risks. Once one has made that break with fear and the debilitating conservatism that holds back so many women, the world is open for exploration and conquest. Dr. Jean Baker Miller has addressed herself to this issue. "In the past," she says, "women entering work or 'public' life were made to feel that we had nothing special to bring. We felt as if we started from somewhere below par and had to catch on or catch up to the ways things were done. Then we had to get even better than men at doing it to hope for even a minimal admittance, and then feel grateful to be allowed to be there at all." Women have been confused and paralyzed by what they feel are their "weaknesses," Dr.

Miller believes. "Women were supposed to be the weak ones," she says. But being aware of weaknesses can be an asset. "Admitting to the weaknesses that do exist doesn't mean you have to stay in that spot. It is the first step in devising truly effective action toward greater strength."

Taking risks and working from strengths rather than weaknesses is foreign to most women's socialization. Norma Rollins has overcome this barrier. "I was brought up to be a Jewish American Princess," she says, sitting in her office, wearing black slacks and a turtleneck sweater covered by a flannel shirt worn as a jacket, with sleeves rolled up. One of her policies—for herself and everyone who works for her—allows for any form or manner of dress in the office, but calls for appropriate attire in public so as not to compromise their clients in any way. As a result, the three lawyers on her staff often come to work in jeans, but keep three-piece suits in the office closet.

"I left college after my sophomore year so I could put my husband through graduate school. I went to college to find a husband, and when I did, I didn't need college anymore." She dropped out of Queens College and held a series of secretarial jobs until her husband received his master's in social work. "Then I had a big house in the suburbs, two children, a pool, and a mother's helper. I had it all." But she also had a seething anger that she could not understand. "For the other women, it seemed, what they had was enough. For me, it wasn't enough. I envied them."

Her story to this point echoes what turned into the swan song of the seventies for many married women: vague stirrings, restlessness, growing expectations—and then departure. Films and novels have recorded these events.

Norma Rollins was married for seven years. By the time the marriage ended, she had gotten a volunteer job as telephone counselor and, later, research coordinator for Middle Earth Switchboard, a hotline and counseling agency with a counterculture flavor. "Counseling was the only thing I knew," she says, because of her husband's profession.

Rollins stayed in the ten-room suburban dream house with her two children for only six months after the divorce. Then, in 1972, she bought a converted van that once delivered Levy's bread, painted it yellow, red, and purple (with a huge Rolling Stones emblem of an open mouth with a tongue hanging out featured on one panel), and took off for the West with her children, aged three and one at the time. "I lived in national parks, I worked as a waitress, I was on welfare sometimes. . . . I had always lived either with my parents or my husband, and here I was with no neighbors, no friends, no one I could lean on. It was a discovery for me. I stayed away three years. I wanted to determine whether or not I could do it."

She was twenty-five when she started out. "I never experienced the sixties. This was my attempt to experience that freedom. I went to San Francisco." She lived on a farm for eight months and raised her own food. She found she could do almost anything, and above all take care of herself. It was her liberation. It was also a time when she confronted her parents as an adult. "They disapproved, and I told them that they had to accept me, even if they didn't approve of me, if they wanted to see me and their grandchildren again," she says. Her parents—her father a New York City cab driver, her mother a bookkeeper who returned to work only after her daughter reached junior high—accepted.

The event that brought Rollins back East was the divorce of a close friend who had been helpful when Rollins had gone through her own. "I felt I should be there for her," says Rollins, confirming a trait observed in many of the successful women interviewed for this book—a very strong personal allegiance to other women. Call it conscious networking or a natural interdependence, but women of power and authority seem to draw strength from other women. Dr. Jean Baker Miller believes that "women need a supportive community of other women," because they find that the ideas and feelings they talk about "are things that most women grasp immediately and that many men have great difficulty understanding." Witness the rapid growth of women's networks, where monthly meetings are eagerly awaited by female leaders who seek the support of their comrades in a man's world. They often talk of their difficulties in functioning at otherwise all-male business meetings, and they understand each other's nuances, angers, and unspoken emotions.

In Rollins's case, she had been able to weather the early months of her divorce because yet another woman, also recently divorced, had moved into her large suburban home-with-pool and helped her with child care and emotional support. So Rollins did the same for this woman when she returned from California.

The return, with her new sense of self-reliance, began what was to be the rise of Norma Rollins, a rise attributable, Rollins says, in part to her sense now that she can take risks. No matter what happens, she knows she will always be able to take care of herself. Her direct manner and her managerial style are results of her new machismo.

After coming back, she returned to Middle Earth Switchboard, where she took a low-paying job, but when a call came in from a YMCA outreach program looking for a counselor, Rollins left to work with troubled youth. She still did not have a B.A. After a few months, the head of the YMCA program took another job. With the encouragement of the outgoing director—a woman who was, in some ways, Rollins's mentor—Rollins became the new director. The job required an M.S.W., but Rollins worked out a deal. She would take the job and get her B.A. on her own time. The M.S.W. requirement would be waived.

Her very first interview with the county department that dispensed funds to her agency put her job on the line. The county was considering ending the program because of deficiencies under the previous director. Rollins had to defend the agency and convince the committee that it was worth continuing. "I was so nervous, my mouth was completely dry, and I couldn't speak at first." She had avoided nervousness beforehand, she says, by just putting thoughts of the meeting out of her mind, a trick she could pull off successfully. "I guess I smoked a lot of cigarettes." Using notes she had prepared the night before and reviewed that morning—still her modus operandi when delivering a speech of any kind—she got through the interview. Eventually, she was granted even more funds and was able to expand her staff. Her forthright, competent manner apparently helped to loosen the purse strings.

Rollins soon took her next step: the previous agency director, Rollins's mentor, who had left for a county job, needed a new director of youth employment planning and asked Rollins to fill the position. "I took the job because I wanted to learn how to write grant proposals, not because I thought I would want to stay long." In fact, she found the governmental-political world frustrating and left the job after six months to become director of Youth Advocates. But the grant-writing experience she gained in the county job is a major reason for the growth of Youth Advocates—so her plan had worked.

The greatest managerial lesson she learned from her mentor, she says now, was to avoid, above all, giving unclear directions. She learned this by being the victim of a manager whose instructions were less than clear. "She would always hand back letters that I wrote saying, 'That's not quite right.' I never knew what was wrong with the letter, but I would end up doing it over and over." Rollins finally did get the idea that the letter was supposed to have a certain tone of authority and "made it sound as though the person writing the letter had a right to say those things." When she arrived at the county job and handed in her first letter, the director said, "That's terrific. You've finally got it."

Rollins, who agrees that such a tone is needed in letters, takes a different managerial approach. "I'll tell people to rewrite letters, too, to get that certain sound, but I'm very careful to point out what I want." Because of the frustrations with her boss in the previous job —mainly over the letter writing—Rollins's present husband, who is very supportive, was surprised when she went to work for her again. Rollins explains, "She was the brightest, most articulate woman I ever met. I learned from her."

Rollins got an interview for the youth agency job, despite her lack of the required master's degree, by calling a New York Civil Liberties Union attorney she knew from a previous job. One of about twenty people interviewed for the position (from among hundreds of resumés sent in), she was able to convince the NYCLU that she had the best working credentials. At that time, the project was funded for only a few more months, but she was willing to take it anyway. "I'm not security oriented," she says. "I'm not afraid that I'll lose my job."

Rollins says that, when she first started working at Youth Advocates, she would ask prospective employees, "How do you feel about working for a woman?" But now, she says, she does not ask that anymore. "I feel more comfortable in the job." She has not had any problems with rebellious or petty attitudes from her male employees, but, she adds, men who work for an ACLU organization are more likely to be liberal in their views.

Her comfort in her new job has also extended to her feeling about clothing. "At first I thought, 'Should I cut my hair? Should I wear little gold earrings?' It was a big question in my mind. I am not the kind of woman most of these other women executives are," she says. "I had to step back and ask myself for what reason I didn't want to wear skirts." Part of it, she decided, was an "antiauthority thing" picked up during her van days, a rebellion in which she is no longer fully engaged. The result was her rule allowing jeans in the office—but not outside. And although she wears skirts outside, she has not cut her hair or bought little gold earrings. Her style is respectable, but still personal.

Another interesting rule in Rollins's office: when a school administrator calls an employee by his or her first name, that employee must respond by calling the administrator by his first name. "They try to set us up so we're not peers," she says. When the employee—usually a woman or a young man—responds with a first name, the administrators "are taken aback," but they get the message. Finding this innovative solution to a persistent problem is characteristic of the successful women in authority interviewed for this book, who are able to take a step back from a nagging daily problem and invent a clear solution to it.

At the Youth Advocates office, there is, in consonance with the employees' clothing, a decidedly casual air, which my personal "coffee litmus test" bears out: in contrast to Sally Ann Slacke's solicitous but rather formal act of bringing me coffee, I am referred here by Rollins to an ancient percolator, from which I am invited to pour my own.

Like nearly every other woman leader I have interviewed, Norma Rollins admits to an early reluctance to criticize employees who were not doing well. Like every successful leader, she has overcome it. At a previous job, she says, "there was a woman I had doubts about. I was not trusting my judgment much then. She had problems at home, in her marriage, and she brought them to work. I felt, Who was I to tell her what to do?" After delaying action, Rollins was forced finally to call the woman in and fire her. "I did it very blatantly. I said at the beginning, 'I'm going to have to fire you. Now I'll tell you why.' I was afraid I would never tell her if I didn't start out that way."

Nevertheless, procrastination in criticizing employees may be a problem endemic to all new bosses of either sex, Rollins believes. "I think the longer you're in a job, the easier that kind of thing is to do." She has not had to fire anyone recently, she says, "because I only hire if I'm convinced I'm right about a person. I have a good sense of people in an interview." At times, through the federally funded Comprehensive Employment and Training Act (CETA) program, she has had up to forty extra people working for her, and only three of those, she says, have had to be fired. In one case, she allowed her personal anger to show during the firing session, something she rarely does in any confrontation.

Usually, she says, it is the male school principals, with whom she negotiates on behalf of students, who get "off-the-wall crazy," sometimes pounding on tables and throwing things. "I don't take it personally. Men are so emotional," she laughs. "They really are. The calmer I get, it seems, the madder they get." Rollins lets them subside. Then, she says, she gets what she wants, which is usually the school records of a student her agency is representing. The cases (which she supervises) often involve students who have been suspended from school without the proper hearings, students who have been forced to leave school, and handicapped students who are not given the proper help. Occasionally, cases also involve brutality by teachers, and student newspaper freedom-of-the-press issues. Only a handful of the 400 cases a year end up in court.

These days, Norma Rollins is respected by her employees, by school administrators, and by the clients of her agency. "I would do anything for Norma," says one mother of a handicapped child who has been moved to a better school because of Rollins's efforts.

Slowly, Norma Rollins has changed her view of herself. "I used to think everyone else was dumb, that I was pulling the wool over their eyes," she says. She was slightly astounded, for instance, to find herself teaching a course to master's degree candidates at a local college, although she holds only a belated B.A. herself. Now she is proud, and bemused. "In the last year or so, I feel fully comfortable," says Rollins, leaning back at her desk with her hands behind her head and her legs stretched out before her. "I had set myself a standard of perfection. Now I feel that I'm competent. I'm capable. I'm good."

The stories of these two women demonstrate that widely contrasting styles of authority can be effective in different situations. The following guidelines, culled from their experiences and those of management experts, may aid the emerging female manager in developing the right style or styles for herself:

• Managers do best by building a repertoire of styles, from the authoritarian to the democratic, so they can use whichever is most appropriate for a given situation, or most effective for a particular employee.

• Women should avoid the trap that some inexperienced and insecure female managers fall into of becoming overly rigid and authoritarian in style, unable to delegate authority or to share information in a democratic manner when it is appropriate to do so.

• Women should watch out for another common pitfall—the "little girl" style. A woman in a management position should not be afraid to be assertive.

• Women most comfortable adhering to their own personal styles, however little they may conform to accepted management theory, should do so, as long as those styles get the desired results. Women do not have to follow slavishly the norms established by men; they are fortunate that some of their early training leads them to incline naturally to a collaborative, or team, approach, which many experts believe is a highly desirable style for a manager in this age of high technology.

• Managers who want to be informal in some areas and strict or production oriented in others should feel free to mix styles. Most important is to feel comfortable, which will in turn make others comfortable, and which can only help create successful managers.

At the Top

The typical woman at the top, at least in a corporate management position, is forty-six, currently unmarried, and has no children. She earns $92,159 a year and holds the title of vice president. That was the conclusion of a 1982 study cosponsored by the executive search firm of Korn/Ferry International and the UCLA Graduate School of Management. The study also found that of women earning more than $106,000 a year, 60 percent were between thirty-eight and fifty-two, but only 20 percent of those fifty-two and older—at the top—earned that much. The age distribution shows that, as with men, it takes a while for a woman really to make it in the corporate world, but that younger women are fast catching up on the salary scale. Most women who climb the ladder of business success, according to this survey, are either single or divorced and have not had time or inclination to have children. The "corporate wife," who takes care of domestic matters for a male vice president, has long been in existence. The "corporate husband" has yet to be born.

This chapter will profile two women who have made it to the top of their fields—or at least as far as women have yet climbed. In keeping with the scope of the book, the women we will look at do not necessarily conform to the "gray-flannel suit" image, and their achievements are a little unusual. One is a self-made millionaire who has also been a prominent public official; the other heads her own orchestra, as conductor and musical director.

Some of the women profiled in previous chapters are also at the top, and the women profiled here are hardly free of the same concerns that have been discussed elsewhere in this book. These two just present particularly good examples of women who have taken great risks, have been firm in their decision making, persevered, worked long hours—and succeeded. One additional attribute that distinguishes both is that they started their own enterprises. It will be a long time before a woman becomes the head of General Motors, but an entrepreneur will always be in charge of her own shop. When a Long Island magazine writer started looking in the late 1970s for women who earned more than $50,000 a year, the only ones she could find were those who owned their own businesses. Perhaps risk taking and decision making—two practices that many women find difficult in a large corporation—are easier for women who are in charge of their own operations. Moreover, women totally in control do not have to worry about sex discrimination, however subtle, from their bosses. Many women are discovering the advantages of business ownership; between 1977 and 1980, women became entrepreneurs at five times the rate of men, according to the Internal Revenue Service.

Both women profiled here have still higher aspirations. In this, they conform to the Korn/Ferry profile of top corporate achievers. The same spirit that brought them this far urges them always to look for new challenges. And women at the top, knowing they are blazing the trail for others, have an added incentive.

Muriel Siebert got her first job, at sixty-five dollars a week, in 1954. Thirteen years later, she had bought a seat on the New York Stock Exchange—the first woman to do so—for $445,000. By that time, she was already making a half-million dollars a year researching and trading stocks. Since then, she spent five years as New York State Superintendent of Banking, heading a department of more than 500 employees and supervising financial institutions with assets of more than $500 billion. That job placed her in the media spotlight, because she was deeply involved in the financial revolution of the late 1970s and early 1980s: the savings bank failures, the controversial takeover of commercial banks by foreign interests, and the battles between banks and money market funds. She often traveled to Albany and Washington to comment on new legislation and to handle negotiations that would merge banks to save them.

She left that job—after spending more time in it than a dozen predecessors had—to fight a long-shot campaign for a seat in the United States Senate. She lost, but is not unhappy that she tried. Now she is back with her discount brokerage firm, Muriel Siebert and Company, taking on a new challenge, getting it to grow again after her long absence, during which it was placed in a blind trust. She was a pioneer in the discount business, but during her tenure with the state, other firms outstripped hers. Now, she says, she must "play catch-up."

Siebert, known as Mickie to her friends, is blonde, vivacious, hard working, and luxury loving. No scrooge with her hard-earned money, she likes to live well both on and off the job. She requires a secretary who will do a wide variety of things for her, from keeping her schedule straight to picking up clothes from the dry cleaner. She does not have time to run her own errands and has no spouse to do them for her. She likes fur coats, fine restaurants, solo plane flying, tennis, and expensive holidays—she owns, in fact, a high-toned vacation condominium in posh East Hampton, complete with concierge and cleaning services. She is proud that she has enough money "on the side" so that she would never have to work again if she did not want to. For now, though, she wants to.

"I grew up in Cleveland, and my father was a dentist. We were comfortable until he got cancer. He died at a very early age, and this was before dentists made money." She was in college at the time, at Case Western Reserve. "I was going to class, and I was cutting class, and I was playing bridge." Just after he died, she left school, though she was only a few credits short of graduation.

The expectations her parents had for her were the same as those for most girls of the period: that she would return to Cleveland, marry, settle down, and have children. She did nothing of the sort, although it was not her plan at the time to deviate from the traditional pattern. "I didn't envision this. I didn't think." Instead, after leaving college, she came to New York thinking she would stay only four or five months and return home. She arrived with $500 and a beat-up Studebaker.

"I had been to New York once on vacation, which was the farthest away from Cleveland I'd ever been. My sister had come to New York, and I'd driven to New York with my mother to see her, and it looked exciting."

Siebert applied for a job at the United Nations, after visiting a cousin who worked there, and finding the place intriguing. But the UN would not accept her because she did not speak three languages. If she had been given that job, her life now might be completely different, she says. "I would have fallen arches, and I would have been the chief messenger girl by now."

Besides visiting her sister, Siebert had also stood on the balcony of the Stock Exchange on the first visit to New York. The view inspired her now to seek a job with Bache and Company. She had taken many accounting and business courses at college, often as the only woman in the class. She did not think she was doing anything unusual in taking these courses. Banking, money, finance, and corporations had interested her, and not much else did. "Actually, I am in some respects a very bad student. If something interests me, then I go charging into it. If something doesn't interest me, then I just couldn't care less. I found out that when I took those [finance] courses, I had to think. I felt that when I took the courses that they typically threw down to the women at Florence Mather College [the women's branch of Case Western Reserve], I was just memorizing. . . . They didn't challenge me. They didn't interest me." She especially liked courses taught by part-time professors who were full-time business people. So she was somewhat prepared for a life in the stock market.

"Bache offered me sixty-five dollars a week as a trainee in research, and seventy-five dollars a week in the accounting department. I took the sixty-five dollars a week. Research sounded like it could be more interesting." Unwittingly, perhaps, she had made a first risky business decision that turned out to be propitious.

Her salary was low even for 1954. "I remember Bache had a policy: When you were on the job six weeks, if you were good at it, they gave you a five-dollar-a-week raise. And I can tell you, when I got my three dollars and eighty cents more a week [after taxes] in my pocket, I could spend more on lunch. . . . I had to watch everything I did, but I lived on it. I shared an apartment. I pay more for a garage for my car now than I paid for an apartment for years." Now she lives in River House, a luxury cooperative generally filled with celebrities and millionaires.

When she began, women were just starting out in the brokerage business, usually in the research end. "When I applied for a couple of jobs, they said, 'You know you can never go out of town representing our firm.' So there was a lot of prejudice that existed at the time, and that existed for many, many years. In fact, there are still a lot of firms on Wall Street where I don't think you see a woman in the executive suite."

Being the only woman at most of the functions and meetings she attends—whether in her banking job or on Wall Street—has been fun, she says, but also a burden. "You know, it's a big responsibility when you're the only woman. Things are changing, but they're not changing fast. Some of them are cosmetic and some of them are real. They take time. They take effort."

Among the changes is the media's attitude toward her, which reflects to some extent that of the rest of society toward women. When she bought her stock exchange seat in 1967—a story that made the front page of the *New York Times*—she was referred to as a "petite blonde," and in a later story as "the girl from Cleveland." Another newspaper story characterized her as "the little woman on the Big Street." In contrast, news articles about her during her banking job, from 1977 to 1982, and her 1982 political campaign usually did not refer to her sex, size, or hair color.

Her transformation from researcher to broker, from working girl to career woman, came imperceptibly and without plan. There was no moment of revelation. "No. Look, I think at times things just happen. Now I will say that I had not planned to buy a seat on the New York Stock Exchange. That was not my original idea."

Instead, what happened is this: at Bache, she was assigned to research the airlines, an industry nobody else wanted. The more experienced analysts had railroads and shipping, and no one thought the airlines had much of a future. Of course, as it turned out, they did, and her knowledge of them put her in a good position when the aerospace and jet aviation boom started. By 1960 she knew nearly everything about some twenty-five airline, aircraft manufacturing, and air freight stocks. Soon she was getting orders from her institutional customers and by 1960 was making $150,000 a year as her share of the commissions on buying and selling the stocks. In the early 1960s, she moved to another firm, and then to a third, smaller firm, where she became a partner. She was earning $500,000 a year in commissions and considering moving to a large firm.

That was when she had an important conversation with a prominent money manager who had started with her at Bache. "Mickie," he said, "why don't you buy a seat on the exchange?" When she answered, "Don't be ridiculous," he replied: "There's no law against it."

The idea scared her. In all its 175 years, the exchange had been an all-male enclave. "No woman had ever done it. I had by that time made good money. I had found a couple of great stocks that I had put my money in. I was living well. I had moved into a one-bedroom apartment at 60 Sutton Place South. I had a nice guy, a good love affair. I was taking vacations, I was enjoying what I was doing." Why rock the boat?

"Then I started to think about it, and the idea fascinated me. It took me six months to make my decision. I wanted to do it, but it took me six months till I got up the nerve and did it. . . . I was scared. It meant I had to borrow money against my securities. I had made money by borrowing money—you always do when you start. But at the same time, paying $445,000 for a seat on the New York Stock Exchange was to me a big commitment. I ended up borrowing $300,000 and paying the difference."

She also wondered whether her clients would stick by her when they found out how much money she had. She worked with leading institutions around the country, including banks and mutual funds, but most of the portfolio managers she dealt with were making $25,000 or $30,000 a year. "I wondered how they would react when they found that they were paying me commissions in a year that [collectively] were maybe two or three times what they were earning." Siebert does not think a man would have had the same concerns. "I don't think a man would have thought that. I mean, I know a man wouldn't have thought that. When I started out, frankly, I would try not to dress better than the man's wife I was calling on, because I realized people can be under pressure on how they're supporting their families. And it was only after I bought my seat on the exchange and it came out on the front page of the *New York Times* that I earned a half-million dollars a year, that I decided that I'd better dress the part, that I would wear a fur coat."

The reaction was not what she had feared. "No, people were actually very proud."

She almost did not get the seat, however, because the stock exchange required a letter from the bank that first promised her a loan. It was a letter that the exchange had never required of men.

Worse, the bank did not want to write the extra letter. She mentioned her dilemma to a portfolio manager at Chase Manhattan, and he came through with a loan and the required letter.

"I've gotten very angry from time to time. When people ask, am I a feminist, I say, yes, I'm a feminist, because nobody should have to go through what I went through. It just isn't right. I mean, even after I joined the exchange, I purposely did not do any business on the floor [publicly do her own trading at the exchange] for two years because I knew that people were watching. . . . I wanted to prove to them that a woman would buy a seat not for the publicity, but for business reasons. This was all before the women's movement. On the day I got my seat, one of the governors of the exchange asked me, 'How many more are there behind you?' like I was leading a parade. And, you know, in the nine and a half years I was a member, I was the only woman for nine years of that time." When she assumed her state office, she transferred her membership to her firm's name.

The parade she actually led was not of women into the exchange but of brokerage firms into the discount trade. It turned out to be a good move, because many "research boutiques"—brokerage houses specializing in providing advice to elite accounts—floundered during the stock market slump of the late seventies, while discount houses, which buy and sell for commissions 40 to 50 percent less than other houses, have thrived. "I realized there would be opportunities for firms that could just handle orders at greatly reduced prices. There was no more research. When we started out, the Street hated me."

It is this sort of courage to buck the trend, to accept the occasional anger and envy of others, that makes for a successful entrepreneur of either sex. In Siebert's case, it may be that having been a victim of prejudice and distrust made it easier for her to stand up to the political system later on, when she entered public office. Both her ire and sense of justice had been raised, and perhaps that propelled her to take independent stands that others might have feared. Having as a safety net some money "on the side" did not hurt either.

When Governor Hugh Carey of New York was looking for a woman to fill the banking superintendent's job, hers was the name that repeatedly came up. Even though she is a Republican and he a Democrat, he appointed her. During her five years in the job, she gained the respect of the banking community.

During her term as banking superintendent, she often took unpopular stands as well and, at one point, even elicited anger from the governor who had appointed her. Knowing she had a job to go back to made it easier to take risks. Her securities firm, which she owns 100 percent, was always waiting for her.

"She's a gutsy gal, the most active bank superintendent in the country," says Frances Werner, director of the Albany office of the Savings Bank Association of New York, a woman of about Siebert's age. "Mickie will take your advice and suggestions, and if they don't work, she'll tell you it's a bummer. But she gives credit where it's due. She's not egotistical." John Torell III, current president of Manufacturers Hanover Trust and president of the New York State Bankers Association while Siebert was in office, said, "I think Mickie has done an excellent job. She has been creative, and she has been as vigorous a proponent of the industry as we've had in that office." At times, he said, two elements of the banking industry—the commercial banks and the savings institutions—were on opposite sides of issues, but she was able to be fair to both sides. Another banking person says of her, admiringly, "She's not a yes-man"—although refusal to become one has sometimes gotten her into trouble: she does not back down on decisions.

Her social life, during her time in office, suffered. "I go out a lot, but the last two years have really played havoc with my life," she said just before leaving office. "I work so hard, I find I'm tired at night. It's just too much. I'm not a workaholic. It hurts me when I have Philharmonic tickets and can't go. I love the Philharmonic, but I've only gone once or twice this year. I've given the tickets away. That hurts me. It hurts me when I feel so tired. . . . I like vacations. I like a good life."

She can see getting married at some point. "Sure. The one big drawback is that the more successful a woman gets [the more] a lot of men are scared by her. They are just plain outright scared. It's hard. I'm seeing two different people, but nothing is serious. It's hard."

Siebert lost her primary campaign for the United States Senate, but she is not letting that rest, either. She is suing the Conservative party, which backed the woman who won the primary (but not the seat, which Senator Daniel Patrick Moynihan kept), charging unfair campaign practices. She does not rule out running for office again, or accepting another high-level appointment.

After the campaign, she took six weeks off. "I just wandered a little bit." She visited California and a ninety-year-old uncle in Tucson, who still works every day at his firm, which manufactures plastic covers. "He's remarkable." He has always inspired her, she says.

A booming stock market and the desire to bolster her firm—Bank of America and Chase have recently bought discount firms, and she is eager to take on the new challenges—brought her back to New York. But, in keeping with her healthy outlook on life, some of her dreams lie outside the worlds of finance and politics. "If the stock market hadn't been booming, I would have packed one or two bags and gone to Europe or Japan. I've always had that desire, to pack just one bag, to go to the Pacific Coast and then Japan, stop when I feel like stopping, and go when I feel like going. I still plan to do that."

And that is part of what being on top is all about: to take charge of one's life, to enjoy luxuries in the little free time one has, to be proud of one's achievements, earned by hard work and perseverance.

When Eve Queler raises her baton to conduct the orchestra she founded and directs, she wears an elegant black dress designed for her by Stavropoulos and pins her long, dark hair up in a style she thinks looks authoritative to those behind her—the audience. All eyes are upon her. The musicians and singers follow her lead, as they must with any conductor. Here is a graphic image of a woman in charge: no violinist touches bow to string, no singer utters a sound, until this woman in the flowing dress motions them to do so, as an opera performance takes shape under her direction.

But those movements on stage are only "externals," Queler points out. They are the public display of a far deeper power, which includes selecting pieces and players and making musical and administrative decisions. They are graceful gestures concealing the long struggle of a woman to gain a podium that had been virtually the exclusive property of men.

Eve Queler is director of the Opera Orchestra of New York, a highly regarded group that performs rarely heard operas in a concert setting, without a full-blown stage production. She started the group in 1968, and by 1971 it had become fully professional and moved into Carnegie Hall. Stars such as Marilyn Horne, Montserrat Caballé, Shirley Verrett, and Placido Domingo have appeared in her concerts.

Queler is one of only four female conductors with national reputations and the only one, she says, who has combined a major career with marriage and motherhood. She has also been an outspoken foe of sex discrimination wherever she has encountered it—not among her fellow artists or her audiences, but in the ranks of the management of major symphony orchestras and opera companies. Starting her own orchestra was the only way she could find to head one, although she still hopes to direct one of the other important musical organizations someday.

Music critics persist in referring to her sometimes as "diminutive" or "petite," which she thinks means they are not taking her quite seriously. They rarely refer to the physical characteristics of male conductors in their reviews. She is short—five feet, three inches —and she is "pert," as another writer has called her. With dark bangs framing an animated, youthful-looking face, she is an attractive woman. She cares about her appearance and refuses to wear tails on the podium, as some female conductors do. She likes the Stavropoulos dress partly because it looks authoritative and partly because its chiffon panels hide from the audience any imperfections of her figure —imaginary, because she is fit and trim—she might be self-conscious about during a performance.

During the interview in her large, comfortable, but hardly luxurious apartment, she wears a soft, black exercise suit, ready to go a round on an exercise bicycle and to rearrange some furniture between phone calls on the administrative details of running an orchestra. Her day is precisely planned.

If some critics come to condescend, most stay to praise, and recognize her power on the stage. A *New York Times* critic, referring to a concert in which she "commanded a large orchestra, 15 soloists, a brass band and four choruses," said she "coordinated all those elements with the calm authority of a five-star general."

Her life began in the Bronx, where she was the younger daughter of a chemist who had somehow gotten into cheese importing—although he did not make much money at it—and a housewife who aspired to become a writer. It was a musical household. Her mother sang, her father played the piano, and a magnificent Mason & Hamlin concert grand was the focal point of the living room. Later, Queler's father would give her that piano as a wedding gift. It has been the centerpiece of her living room ever since—and at times a means of livelihood, when she coached singers while her children were young.

Queler—then Eve Rabin—was a child prodigy. She began piano lessons at age five, but had already begun to play two or three years before that. The fine piano notwithstanding, her family was poor, and this, she believes, may have contributed to her drive for success. Her older sister, now a school principal who has pioneered experimental programs for students, has a similar drive.

"I think it comes from where we came out of—a family where there was never any money," says Queler, referring to her sister and herself. "We couldn't afford anything. We lived in a small apartment in the Bronx, and we shared a room. There was a certain amount of relief when [my sister] moved out—and then she moved back in with her husband. And I slept in the living room for almost a year. But we always got along well.

"I think not having anything, only having yourself, your own devices, whatever you have, gives people more drive than we give our children today."

Queler's mother did not start writing seriously until her children were grown, and by that time it was too late to start a career. "She just missed out on the times, and she never went into it [writing] in a big enough way." Queler has been determined not to miss out on her time.

The family's lack of means had an impact on her career at an early stage. At the age of twelve she was accepted as a piano student at the Curtis Institute, a prestigious music school in Philadelphia. There she would have been totally immersed in music, with academic tutoring on the side, but her family could not afford the travel and other arrangements that would have to be made; instead, she attended the High School of Music and Art in New York. "So I became just an average high school student, and I took up roller skating as a very important sideline. I went constantly. The way I do anything is I bury myself in it, and I won't ever listen to what anyone says about whether it's productive or not. I'm one-dimensional about certain things. That's me. I'm a little stubborn."

This quality, which she believes is inborn, was a major influence in leading her into conducting—a path no woman had trod at the time. "That's where that streak has headed me, into this field that another person might not go into, that other people might have found discouraging, that when you start out you know you're not going to get in."

Her "stubborn streak"—which has led to her knowing exactly what she wants and adhering to her judgments, qualities that a conductor and music director must have—also caused her to make other career decisions. First, because of her dedication to the piano and her early ambition of becoming a piano soloist, she delayed going to college for a year. "I practiced seven hours a day. All my friends went to college, and I got all this pressure about going to school. It was impossible. One doesn't *not* go to school. After a year, I allowed myself to be persuaded. My schooling was really haphazard. I wouldn't listen to anyone."

She went concurrently to City College of New York for a traditional academic program and to Mannes School of Music, where, because of her previous training and because she has perfect pitch, she was able to skip many introductory courses and start at the third-year level. At City College, she met the man who was to become her husband, Stanley Queler. "I met my husband about the second week of school. . . . I had never planned to marry and have children. That's what I mean about being very headstrong and silly. I basically married the first person I fell in love with. We married as students." She is still married, happily, to the same man, who is a lawyer. They had their children within the first seven years of marriage. Her daughter, Liz, is now a successful pop singer, and her son, Andy, is still at college.

By the time she had her children she had already changed her career ambitions. While accompanying singers at the Mannes School —as a way of earning money to pay for school expenses—she "fell in love with the human voice" and decided to become an accompanist. This also was not a woman's field, although she did not know it at the time.

Meanwhile, "the dilemma of career and family began to hit. It's terribly important [for women]. There's no real role model really, so you can't make any order out of it. I did my best." When the children were young, she coached singers at home, which is one of the things that accompanists do. But it was different for her. "This space is open, and the children would be riding their tricycles into the room. . . . There was always interference. But it was a way to work at home."

She also had a job as a rehearsal accompanist for the New York City Opera just after her son was born. This was before musicians' unions became strong, and the pianists had to work long hours, seven days a week. "I just had no time. I never slept and I never practiced. I almost broke down. For instance, my baby was teething, and he was getting up at two o'clock, three o'clock, four o'clock, and I had to get up at eight o'clock and look at what was on my schedule, and ofttimes learn [a piece just] before I played it, because it was my first season, and then rush home to see him in a spare hour, when other people would just go down for coffee.

"I still remember a time when I rushed home to wash my hair, because the schedule said I had three hours. I was just coming out of the shower, with this towel wrapped around my head, and the phone rang. It was Julius Rudel [City Opera's musical director] saying, 'Where are you? I'm sitting here in this studio waiting for you, and why aren't you here?'" It turned out that an additional job had been penciled into her schedule after she had checked it at eight in the morning, and by the time of the phone call, she had already planned so much for those three hours that she was not able to make it back that day. "So he growled and grumbled, and I was not invited back the next season. And I don't blame them. It was really too much. I shouldn't have tried to do so much."

Throughout her career, she says, she has often "split" herself, because she has always tried to "be there" for her children, for the major emotional crises and for the minor emergencies a parent cannot avoid, such as taking home a sick child or bringing a pair of shoes to a child who has somehow lost one on the way to school.

During another season at City Opera, to which she returned in the mid 1960s, Queler asked for time off to prepare and give a seventh birthday party for her son. She got one day. "I didn't have time to bake the cake," which was a disappointment. "They grumbled, 'Why do we have these women here? If we have men, we don't have these problems.'" She does not blame them for that attitude, although now better scheduling has improved the situation for both men and women. She returned to City Opera later in her career.

Despite the conflicts, she needed to work to afford help with the children and to finance occasional lessons for herself. "I never had the luxury to stay home and practice. Once I got married, practice was stopped. There was no time for lessons. Later, I did it very spasmodically: I practiced when I could, and I took lessons when I could afford it." She was afraid to take any time off when her children were born, although she did take a month off from weekend jobs as organist for a temple and a church. It was just about when her children were born that she organized an opera workshop so that she could learn the opera repertoire. With herself as accompanist and music director, she and singer friends toured hospitals, old-age homes, and the like "for a pittance," long before such work was federally funded. Judith Raskin, who was to become a Metropolitan Opera star, was in this group.

Queler still had no ambition to conduct, only to accompany, and forming her own group was the only way to learn. "There were just a few opportunities, and I'm the type of person to create them if they're not there. I never allow myself to not do something because at the moment it doesn't exist. If something doesn't exist, you put it into existence. So I got together with a group of people I knew. Some went on to become famous, some not."

Queler soon realized that she had a problem as an accompanist: she was not getting any jobs. She was expecting a life of travel, accompanying singers on recital tour. "I discovered that I couldn't get concerts. Women wouldn't take me, because they wanted a man who would carry their suitcases. They thought ... it would look more professional to have a man accompany them. Men didn't want me because a lot of sponsors of these recitals are ladies' clubs, and they frowned on a woman and a man traveling together—though they didn't frown on the reverse, a man traveling with a woman singer as a semiservant, someone who came along to carry the bag, make the hotel reservations, and do things for her." With the male singers, their wives sometimes objected, too. In fact, Queler says, one French singer, for whom she played in his studio and who always complimented her playing highly, refused her request to accompany him on tours, saying, "But my dear, you are a woman. I could never do that. How could I do such a thing? What would my wife say?"

"I was a good pianist. That was not a problem. I got frustrated and started talking to people about it. That's when I first realized that there weren't any women accompanists. Then Marilyn Horne came to town with an elderly lady from California [as accompanist], and I thought this would be my big breakthrough [because a precedent had been set], but it wasn't.

People still refused to hire her. At about that time, one of the singers in the opera workshop she had organized suggested that, with her organizational talents, she should be conducting. She enrolled in a class.

"There was no precedent. I was the only girl in the class. I was always the only woman. . . . I went to my first conducting class in 1960. I didn't give up the piano until almost ten years later." It took her that long to establish herself in conducting.

Her being in the conducting class was "tolerated," she says, because many people take classes without actually becoming conductors. But she wanted to conduct. Five years after her first class ("Liz was five, Andy was eight," she says, marking years the way women often, and men rarely, do), she took a job as a pianist for the Metropolitan Opera National Company, which involved spending a summer rehearsing with them in Indianapolis. (Liz spent the summer with her.) As part of her duties, she completed some unfinished recitatives for a Rossini opera and played them on the harpsichord. The management then asked her to go along on the year-long tour to continue playing the parts she had written. It would be difficult, they said, to find someone else to fit in with the orchestra's tight schedule.

"I said I would go on the tour if I could be one of the assistant conductors and conduct. And they wouldn't consider that, which didn't surprise me." Although she knows she had had no experience, she notes that inexperienced men were often given a chance. "They had other assistants who had never conducted, who would conduct, say, the matinee in San Antonio." So Queler did not go on tour and instead returned to City Opera as an accompanist, where she stayed from 1965 to 1970.

"I was very careful where I asked [to conduct], because I didn't want to be turned down. I was always careful that I would be prepared before I announced myself as a conductor. You can't just suddenly say, 'I'm a conductor.' You can't just study it."

While still working at City Opera—and while working as an auditions accompanist for the Metropolitan Opera—she started her own group. At first it was to be an aid for young Met studio singers, to give them the opportunity to sing with a full orchestra instead of only a piano. "That was my justification for going to some of the people who supported the [Met] studio and saying, 'Can you give me a little money for this orchestra?' "

She got enough money to "get the janitor to open the door and turn on the lights." The group gave free concerts in a school. She would make tapes and play them to people in the music world, who soon became interested in her work. "I didn't realize I was fund raising, but I was." Voice teachers, other singers, ushers, and audition assistants attended the concerts and gave money. Finally, with the help of a small grant, the orchestra was able to rent space in Town Hall, which had much better acoustics. An advertisement offering free tickets drew a huge response, and that first audience still forms the basis of the orchestra's mailing list. The reviews were good, and she got another small grant. As an accompanist at auditions for musicians seeking foundation grants, she knew many of the officials and simply asked them for money. "I told them about my orchestra. I said I needed money. I didn't fill out forms or anything."

Next, the group was able to move into Alice Tully Hall at Lincoln Center. "We got a little more formal organization, a brochure printed for free, and people joined. They took out memberships for a certain amount of money.... I'm a very careful person. Opera Orchestra grew only as we had money to grow."

By now, financial need was no longer an impetus for her work, although it never had been the major one anyway. "I was determined to have a career. I just pushed myself to fit everything in," she says of her early days, before the conducting classes. "I never had any time. I don't think I missed anything. We had a social life. We had friends." Like the women profiled in chapter 9, the only thing she did not have was time to herself. "In those days [when her children were infants], I was still learning. I didn't know the repertoire, and I was caught in a web between my parents and my children and my husband and relatives and friends and everybody not understanding why you don't have any time for them, and having no time for my thinking. Time to yourself is just crucial. Now I'm conducting, and I have my own orchestra, for which I'm responsible. I no longer have the drain of small children, and my parents are gone and my in-laws are gone. The problems that people go through in later life are different. I mean, my children have problems, and I'm still the main person, or Stanley and I, and he has problems in his world, and Opera Orchestra is fraught with problems, which I'm always called upon to solve."

She is responsible for its budget—of about $400,000—for fund raising, for finding space to rehearse and play, and for the repertoire. Because the orchestra specializes in rare works, she often must do extensive research and arrange for rights, copies of the score, and other details. Often, she travels to Europe to do the research, trying to combine those trips with guest conducting jobs. "It's just endless.

I have to speak French, Italian, and German, and of late I've been conducting in Czechoslovakia and Hungary, and I'm studying those languages, too." The orchestra has a board of directors now to help it raise money. Most of the board members, of course, are men: "If you want to get corporate heads on your board, you have to get men. Very few women are in a position now to do for you what men can. The purpose of a board is to support the orchestra, not [to have] people who love or admire you."

Although her orchestra is doing well, she still has other aspirations. "A natural step would be to become a conductor of a large orchestra." Something on the order of the Chicago Symphony Orchestra, for instance, she says. But she does not know if she ever will, because of sex discrimination. She spent one good year, near the beginning of her conducting career, as an associate conductor with the Fort Wayne, Indiana, orchestra. "As a first job, it was fine." But discrimination still abounds "at the very top. When there's a position that involves good money—conductors are paid well, like any superstar—that's the position a woman won't get. If you want to look to where the discrimination is in my world, don't look to the musicians, don't look to the public, don't look to any of the people who aren't involved with the big money. Look to management, who wants to keep control. They're all men, and they want to keep control of the situation through other men.... Even the women on the boards will discriminate against other women." Why? "Why didn't ERA get passed? Why don't women want other women in charge? It's a psychology of not wanting another woman in charge of you. If you're going to have somebody take over your life as a woman, it's going to be a man. Women are competitive, they don't want another woman in charge, and particularly they don't want an attractive woman."

She made one choice herself at the beginning of her conducting career. She put family first in a way she does not think a man would have. She was offered a conducting job in Seattle, but the salary was too low, she thought, to justify relocating her family, since her husband was making more at the time than she was offered for the new job. She turned it down without even mentioning it to him. Later, he overheard her talking about it on the telephone. "He said, 'We could have talked about it. We might have worked something out. If there's something to do with your career, let's talk about it.' But by then it was too late."

Like many of the other successful women interviewed for this book, Queler has an extremely supportive spouse. She also has an innate sense of self-confidence. "I've never had any problem with power on the podium." Her management style is "persuasive, cajoling," rather than confrontational, she says. As a testament to her power as a peacemaker, she was chosen to conduct a concert coupling Shirley Verrett and Grace Bumbry, who have always been thought of as rivals, and she managed to have them sing beautifully together.

"I don't think I'll ever overcome my need to be loved by everyone. But I don't find a conflict between what I want as an artist and my need to be loved. I have to have total control, total authority. I know exactly what I want. I've always known exactly what I want. I don't fight with anybody. It's simply that if you want to play in my orchestra, you have to do what I want."

That is a powerful statement from a woman who has dared to stride onto a platform where few women had ever ventured before.

Women who make it to the very top usually have some special qualities—as do the men who make it to the summit of their fields. Like their male counterparts, women at the top must also struggle to get there and must be able to take advantage of fortuitous circumstances. Unlike most men, however, successful women often have to make more choices about their family and social lives, and must worry more about family concerns if they have children. They also must struggle with discrimination and with other blocks to their careers, blocks they face because they are women.

Very few women have reached the peaks that males define as the top: being chairman of the board of a Fortune 500 company, for instance, or president of the United States. But, as the stories of the two women in this chapter, and of the other women in this book, indicate, women often define top-level achievement differently from men, and leading a full, satisfied life is an important part of many women's definition of success. The lessons these women have learned can help to instruct other women who want to reach the highest pinnacles possible for them:

• Hard work and long hours are essential.
• Women on the top will have to give up much of their personal time, but may be able to salvage a family life, as Eve Queler did, or

the occasional enjoyment of special pleasures, as Muriel Siebert proves with her luxurious lifestyle.

• Aspiring women in charge must be persistent and take failures in stride.

• If opportunities do not present themselves, women can create them, even if it means opening one's own brokerage house or starting one's own orchestra.

• Women who want to make it to the top must take risks.

• Women can stick to their ideals or artistic dreams as long as they are also realistic about profits, overhead, and other aspects of the marketplace.

• Women can keep their traditionally "female" positive qualities, such as being nurturing, flexible, and sensitive to other people's feelings, though they must also develop good business sense and self-confidence.

• It is possible to be a woman in charge.

References

Ascher, Barbara Lazear. "Hers." *New York Times,* February 10, 1983.

Bardwick, Judith M., ed. *Readings on the Psychology of Women.* New York: Harper & Row, 1972.

Barnett, Rosalind C., and Grace K. Baruch. *On the Psychological Well-Being of Women in the Mid-Years.* Working Paper no. 85, Wellesley, Mass.: Wellesley College Center for Research on Women, 1982.

Bennetts, Leslie. "On Aggression in Politics: Are Women Judged by a Double Standard?" *New York Times,* February 12, 1979.

Broverman, Inge K., Donald M. Broverman, Frank E. Clarkson, Paul S. Rosen-krantz, and Susan R. Vogel. "Sex Role Stereotypes and Clinical Judgements of Mental Health." *Journal of Consulting and Clinical Psychology* 34, no. 1 (1970): 1–7. Reprinted in 1972 in Bardwick, ed., *Readings on the Psychology of Women.*

Brown, Linda Keller. *The Woman Manager in the United States.* Washington, D.C.: Business and Professional Women's Foundation, 1981.

Business Week, editors of. "What's Needed to Become a Company Superstar." *Business Week,* September 15, 1980.

Catalyst, staff of. *Upward Mobility.* New York: Holt, Rinehart and Winston, 1981.

Crosby, Faye J. *Relative Deprivation and Working Women.* New York: Oxford University Press, 1982.

Davis, Peter G. "Opera: *Khovanshchina.*" *New York Times,* March 3, 1981.

Douvan, Elizabeth, and Joseph Adelson. *The Adolescent Experience.* New York: John Wiley & Sons, 1966.

Drucker, Peter F. *The Changing World of the Executive.* New York: Truman Talley/Times Books, 1982.

Epstein, Cynthia Fuchs. *Women in Law.* New York: Anchor Press/Doubleday, 1981.

———. "Bringing Women into Management." In *Institutional Barriers: What*

Keeps Women Out of the Executive Suite, edited by Francine Gordon and Myra Strober. New York: McGraw-Hill, 1975.

Fleming, Jacqueline. "The Motivation to Avoid Success: Matina Horner's Theory 12 Years Later." *Radcliffe Quarterly* 68, no. 4 (December 1982).

Gilligan, Carol. *In a Different Voice.* Cambridge: Harvard University Press, 1982.

Goldberg, Susan, and Michael L. Lewis. "Play Behavior in the Year-Old Infant: Early Sex Differences." Research first presented 1969 and reprinted 1972 in Bardwick, ed., *Readings on the Psychology of Women.*

Harlan, Anne, and Carol Weiss. *Moving Up: Women in Managerial Careers.* Working Paper no. 86. Wellesley, Mass.: Wellesley College Center for Research on Women, 1981.

Hennig, Margaret, and Anne Jardim. *The Managerial Woman.* New York: Doubleday, 1977.

Holtzman, Elizabeth. "It's Better Being Boss." *Working Woman,* January 1983.

Horner, Matina. "Fail: Bright Women." *Psychology Today,* November 1969.

Josefowitz, Natasha. *Paths to Power: A Woman's Guide From First Job to Top Executive.* Reading, Mass.: Addison-Wesley, 1980.

———. "Management Men and Women: Closed vs. Open Doors." *Harvard Business Review,* September–October 1980.

———. "Women Executives: The Accessibility Factor." *Ms.,* February 1982.

Judith Langer Associates. *Working Women: A Matter of Priorities.* Langer Report 5. New York: Syndicated publication of Judith Langer Associates, Inc., 1982.

Kamer, Pearl. "College-Trained Women: Are They Preparing for Non-Traditional Careers?" *New York Statistician,* November–December 1979.

Kamorovsky, Mirra. "Cultural Contradictions and Sex Roles." *American Journal of Sociology* 52, no. 3 (November 1946).

Kane, Parsons and Associates. *A Survey of Women Officers of America's Largest Corporations.* New York: Kane, Parsons and Associates, Inc., 1982.

Kanter, Rosabeth Moss. *Men and Women of the Corporation.* New York: Basic Books, 1977.

Kapsis, Robert E., and James M. Murtha. "Adverse Impact of Retrenchment Upon Academic Women." Paper presented at the annual convention of the American Sociological Association, Toronto, August 28, 1981.

Korn/Ferry International. *Profile of Women Senior Executives.* New York: Korn/Ferry International, 1982.

Maccoby, Michael. *The Gamesman.* New York: Simon and Schuster, 1976.

———. *The Leader.* New York: Simon and Schuster, 1981.

Miller, Jean Baker. *Toward a New Psychology of Women.* Boston: Beacon Press, 1976.

———. *Women and Power.* Work in Progress Working Paper no. 1. Wellesley, Mass.: Stone Center for Developmental Services and Study, Wellesley College, 1982.

Robertson, Wyndham. "Women M.B.A.s, Harvard '73: How They're Doing." *Fortune,* August 28, 1978.

Rossman, Marge. *When the Headhunter Calls: A Guide for Women in Management.* Chicago: Contemporary Books, 1981.

Sargent, Alice G. *The Androgynous Manager.* New York: AMACOM, a division of American Management Associations, 1981.

Sayles, Leonard R., and George Strauss. *Human Behavior in Organizations.* Englewood Cliffs, N.J.: Prentice-Hall, 1966.

Sims, Naomi. *All About Success for the Black Woman.* New York: Doubleday, 1982.

Varro, Barbara. "Why Women Smile More." *Chicago Sun-Times,* June 22, 1982.

Working Women/National Association of Office Workers. *Vanished Dreams: Age Discrimination and the Older Woman Worker.* Cleveland: Working Women/National Association of Office Workers, 1980.

Permissions

Grateful acknowledgment is given for permission to reprint the following:

Chapter 1
p. 6: from Leslie Bennetts, "On Aggression in Politics: Are Women Judged by a Double Standard?" *New York Times,* February 12, 1979. © 1979 by The New York Times Company. Reprinted by permission. *p. 8:* from Michael Maccoby, *The Gamesman.* New York: Simon and Schuster, 1976. *p. 14:* from Mirra Kamorovsky, "Cultural Contradictions and Sex Roles." *American Journal of Sociology* 52, no. 3 (November 1946). Reprinted by permission of The University of Chicago Press. *p. 15:* from Cynthia Fuchs Epstein, "Bringing Women into Management." In *Institutional Barriers: What Keeps Women Out of the Executive Suite,* edited by Francine Gordon and Myra Strober. New York: McGraw-Hill, 1975. *p. 18:* from Matina Horner, "Fail: Bright Women." *Psychology Today,* November 1969. Excerpts reprinted by permission of Wadsworth Publishing Co. *p. 18:* from Jacqueline Fleming, "The Motivation to Avoid Success: Matina Horner's Theory 12 Years Later." *Radcliffe Quarterly* 68, no. 4 (December 1982). *p. 19:* from Susan Goldberg and Michael L. Lewis, "Play Behavior in the Year-Old Infant: Early Sex Differences." In *Readings on the Psychology of Women,* edited by Judith M. Bardwick. New York: Harper & Row, 1972. Reprinted by permission of Michael L. Lewis. *p. 20:* excerpt from Margaret Hennig and Anne Jardim, *The Managerial Women.* Copyright © 1977 by Margaret Hennig and Anne Jardim. Reprinted by permission of Doubleday & Company, Inc. *p. 21:* from Peter F. Drucker, *The Changing World of the Executive.* New York: A Truman Talley Book, Times Books, 1982. Reprinted by permission of the JCA Literary Agency, Inc.

Chapter 2
p. 25: from *Upward Mobility,* by the staff of Catalyst. © 1981 by Catalyst. New York: Holt, Rinehart and Winston, 1981. *p. 25:* from "What's Needed to Become a Company Superstar." *Business Week,* September 15, 1980.

227

Chapter 3
p. 41: from Barbara Varro, "Why Women Smile More." *Chicago Sun-Times,*
June 22, 1982. *p. 43:* from Barbara Lazear Ascher. "Hers," *New York Times.*
February 10, 1983. © 1983 by Barbara L. Ascher. Reprinted by special per-
mission of Rhoda Weyr Agency, New York. Excerpts from Naomi Sims, *All
About Success for the Black Woman.* Copyright © 1982 by Naomi Sims. Re-
printed by permission of Doubleday & Company, Inc., and by the author c/o
William Morris Agency, Inc.

Chapter 4
p. 64: from Jean Baker Miller, *Women and Power.* Work in Progress Working
Paper No. 1. Wellesley, Mass.: Stone Center for Developmental Services and
Studies, Wellesley College, 1982. *p. 71:* excerpt from Natasha Josefowitz,
"Management Men and Women: Closed vs. Open Doors." Harvard Business
Review (September–October 1980). Copyright © 1980 by the President and
Fellows of Harvard College; all rights reserved. Reprinted by permission of
the *Harvard Business Review. p. 130:* from Natasha Josefowitz, "Women
Executives: The Accessibility Factor." *Ms.,* February 1982.

Chapter 6
p. 101: from Carol Gilligan, *In a Different Voice.* Cambridge: Harvard University Press, 1982.

Chapter 7
p.118: excerpt from Natasha Josefowitz, "Management Men and Women:
Closed vs. Open Doors." Harvard Business Review (September–October
1980). Copyright © 1980 by the President and Fellows of Harvard College; all
rights reserved. Reprinted by permission of the *Harvard Business Review.
p.119:* from Elizabeth Holtzman, "It's Better Being Boss." *Working Woman,*
January 1983.

Chapter 9
p.165: from *Working Women: A Matter of Priorities.* Langer Report 5, syndicated publication of Judith Langer Associates, Inc. (market and social research firm, New York City), 1982. *p.167:* from Robert E. Kapsis and James M.
Murtha, "Adverse Impact of Retrenchment Upon Academic Women." Paper
presented at the annual convention of the American Sociological Association, Toronto, August 28, 1981.

Chapter 10
p.173: from Anne Harlan and Carol Weiss, *Moving Up: Women in Managerial
Careers.* Working Paper No. 86. Wellesley, Mass.: Wellesley College Center
for Research on Women, 1981. *p.175:* from Rosalind C. Barnett and Grace K.
Baruch, *On the Psychological Well-Being of Women in the Mid-Years.* Working Paper No. 85. Wellesley, Mass.: Wellesley College Center for Research on
Women, 1982.

Index